HENRY THE LION

HENRY THE LION

A BIOGRAPHY

KARL JORDAN

TRANSLATED BY
P. S. FALLA

CLARENDON PRESS · OXFORD
1986

Oxford University Press, Walton Street, Oxford OX2 6DP

Oxford New York Toronto
Delhi Bombay Calcutta Madras Karachi
Petaling Jaya Singapore Hong Kong Tokyo
Nairobi Dar es Salaam Cape Town
Melbourne Auckland

and associated companies in
Beirut Berlin Ibadan Nicosia

Oxford is a trade mark of Oxford University Press

Published in the United States
by Oxford University Press, New York

Originally published in German under the title
of Heinrich der Löwe: e. Biographie
© C. H. Beck'sche Verlagsbuchhandlung (Oskar Beck), München 1979
Henry the Lion text © Oxford Univeristy Press 1986

British Library Cataloguing in Publication Data
Jordan, Karl
Henry the Lion: a biography.
1. Henry, Duke of Saxony and Bavaria
2. Germany — Kings and rulers — Biography
I. Title   II. Heinrich der Löwe. English
943'.024'0924   DD801.S367/
ISBN 0-19-821969-5

Library of Congress Cataloging in Publication Data
Jordan, Karl.
Henry the Lion.
Translation of: Heinrich der Löwe.
Bibliography: p.
Includes index.
1. Henry, Duke of Saxony, 1129-1195.   2. Germany—
Princes and princesses—Biography.   3. Germany—History—
Frederick I, 1152-1190.   I. Title.
DD147.5.H5J6713 1986   943'.21024'0924 [B]   86-5165
ISBN 0-19-821969-5

Set by Wyvern Typesetting Limited, Bristol
Printed in Great Britain
at the University Printing House
by David Stanford
Printer to the University

Preface to the German Edition

THE plan for a biography of Henry the Lion has occupied me for several years. Unfortunately the completion of this book has been repeatedly delayed by other duties and especially the requirements of teaching. It also proved necessary to lighten the subject-matter by undertaking a number of preliminary studies, the results of which I have published in various articles.

The present work is intended to provide scholars with a monograph on the hero of the Welf dynasty, based on the research of recent decades. But it is also addressed to a wider circle of readers who are not satisfied with the 'literary' type of historical writing that has again become popular in recent times. The scope and arrangement of the book are dictated by these two purposes. It aims at describing Henry's activity as duke of Saxony and Bavaria, and also his part in the history of the German Empire in the twelfth century. Accordingly I have departed from a strictly chronological arrangement and laid more emphasis on a thematic treatment, even though in this way some overlapping is unavoidable. I have deliberately used the narrative form, which still seems to me the most suited to a biography.

I have to thank my friends and colleagues Erwin Assmann, Horst Fuhrmann, and Erich Hoffmann for valuable indications and advice. I am indebted to Mr Jens Ahlers, particularly for help in compiling the index and in proof-reading. My thanks go to the Deutsche Forschungsgemeinschaft for the provision of a grant.

KARL JORDAN

Kiel, December 1978

Contents

I

Henry's Inheritance and the Contemporary Scene

THE Welfs are one of the oldest noble families of Germany, and no other princely family in Europe can look back on a tradition covering a span of more than twelve centuries. As with many dynasties, legend has surrounded and embellished their origins, but a historical basis can be clearly discerned.

By the beginning of the twelfth century the Welfs had become the most powerful of the German nobles, and the imperial crown appeared within their grasp. Their claim to leadership at that time found expression in written accounts of their family history. The first genealogical records, compiled in the middle of the 1120s, first in Upper Germany and a decade later in Lüneburg, basically follow the sequence of generations. They were followed around 1170 by the *Historia Welforum*, the work of an anonymous Swabian cleric in the entourage of Duke Welf VI, in which the family's sense of its own importance is most clearly reflected.

The author proudly relates that according to an ancient history book the Welfs were descended from certain Franks who migrated from Troy and, after combats with the Romans, settled on the banks of the Rhine. The legend that the Franks were of Trojan origin occurs repeatedly in medieval chronicles by way of justifying the high prestige of the Frankish tribe. In this respect the *Historia* makes use of a popular literary motif, but it is quite right in claiming that the Welfs were of Frankish descent.

We may today regard the Welfic line as having begun with a certain Count Ruthard, a member of the high aristocracy of the Frankish realm under Pepin, the first Carolingian king, in the second half of the eighth century. He belonged to the eastern part of the monarchy, his estates being in Alsace and Lorraine. He became one of Pepin's principal helpers in the incorporation of Alemannia into the greater Frankish realm, and is once actually referred to as the governor of that territory. He acquired rich possessions in the subjected province and is mentioned in 769 as a count of the district of Argen, north of Lake Constance.

One of his descendants, probably a son or grandson, was a Count Welf, the first bearer of that name, which was not customarily used to denote the family as a whole until the twelfth century. Various legendary tales, invented to explain the name, are cited in the *Historia*, though not without caution. 'Welf', the older form of which is 'Hwelpo' or 'Hwelfo', is an abbreviation for the personal name Welfhard or Bernwelf. It signifies a puppy or the young of a wild animal, and is thus equivalent to the Latin *catulus* or its diminutive *catilina*. Hence the legend arose that an ancestor of the family had married the daughter of Catiline, a prominent Roman senator, and had given the latter's name to his son, who used it in the German form 'Welf'. According to another tale, a son was born to a member of the family who was at that time staying at the Emperor's court. When he showed anxiety to leave at once, the Emperor mockingly said: 'What a hurry you are in to be home, now that a "Welf" has been born to you.' Thereupon the father allegedly decided that 'Welf' should be his son's name.

The family's standing was considerably increased in the ninth century by a double marriage with the Carolingian dynasty. The then Welf's eldest daughter Judith, who was both beautiful and ambitious, played an important part as the second wife of the Emperor Louis the Pious. The claims she made on behalf of her son, the future King Charles the Bald of the West Franks, led to the settlement of a dispute between the Emperor and his elder sons which had been the cause of a severe crisis within the dynasty since 830. Judith's younger sister Emma married one of the princes, Louis the German, who was the first Carolingian to reign only over the East Franks, i.e. what was later the German kingdom.

Conrad, a son of Count Welf, was the ancestor of the two families which played a major part in the history of the ensuing centuries. His eldest son, also named Conrad, founded the Welf dynasty who soon became kings of Burgundy, which they continued to rule until the line died out in 1032. Conrad's younger son, who took his grandfather's name and is known as Welf I, founded the line of the South German Welfs.

In the struggle between Louis the German and Charles the Bald in 858–9 the Welfs took Charles's side, as a result of which they lost their leading role in the East Frankish realm; nor were they prominent politically in the earliest years of the German Empire. However, they gradually strengthened their position in south-west Germany; during this time they abandoned their Frankish links and put down roots in Swabia.

The power and prestige of a noble family in the Middle Ages depended to a large extent on its home base. The kernel of the Welfs' possessions lay in the Argen and Schussen districts north-east of Lake Constance, but by degrees they acquired estates in the more sparsely populated parts of Upper Swabia. Above all they began to clear land for cultivation in the direction of the Alpine foothills, and also extended their patrimony northwards along both sides of the Lech river. In this way a second power base was created on the borders of Swabia and Bavaria, particularly in the Ammer and Augst districts.

Later Welf historiography offers several different versions of the part played in this enlargement of the dynasty's possessions by Henry, the grandson (as it appears) of Welf I. According to one account, against the wish of his father Eticho he did homage to one of the Emperors, who in return promised him, as a fief, as much land as he could plough at noonday. Henry outwitted the Emperor by using a golden plough drawn by a relay of saddle-horses, which encircled a large area while the Emperor was asleep. Whether this fairy-tale motif has any basis of fact in this case is unknown; there is no record of a German ruler having bestowed a fief on this Henry, who on account of the story became known as 'Henry of the golden wain'.

In 935, in the middle of his large estate in the Schussen district, at the foot of his castle at Altdorf, Henry founded the family's first proprietary nunnery, which became the Welf burial-place. Altdorf was the family's chief residence, and frequently served to designate them from this time on. The Welfs also acquired a foothold in Bavaria proper through Henry's wife, a member of the nobility from the Weilheim area.

What Henry had begun was continued about a century later by his descendant Welf II, who married Imiza (Irmentrud) of the family of the counts of Luxemburg, which also had estates in Bavaria. By this marriage Welf enlarged his patrimony east of the Lech; he also acquired the county on both sides of the Brenner pass, but was later deprived of it by the Emperor Conrad II as a punishment for having supported the rebel Duke Ernest of Swabia. The Welfs also owned land at this time in the upper Inn valley, the Vintsch district, and the

Lower Engadine: this formed their third accumulation of territory, along with the possessions near Lake Constance and those on the borders of Swabia and Bavaria. Imiza's dowry also included estates in Lombardy, probably near Este, so that the Welfs for the first time acquired a foothold in Upper Italy. Near Altdorf, in the original Swabian lands, Welf II built the castle of Ravensburg, which became the family's principal seat and by which they were often designated thereafter.

With Welf III, the only son of Welf II and Imiza, the family again played a part in imperial affairs, as in 1047 Henry III conferred on him the escheated duchy of Carinthia. The Welfs did not possess it for long, however: Welf died unmarried in November 1055, and with him the race of South German Welfs died out in the male line. A few years earlier he had transferred the convent of Altdorf, which had suffered damage in a fire, to a site on the nearby Martinsberg and had renamed it Weingarten. Intending to be buried in the convent, he bequeathed all his property to it. The history of the Welfs in Germany seemed to be at an end.

In this situation Imiza, the energetic widow of Welf II, took the unusual step of contesting her son's will on the ground that she, his lawful heir, had not consented to it. During the reign of Conrad II her daughter Cuniza (Cunigund) had married the Margrave Albert-Azzo II of Este, of the Otbertine dynasty. The Otbertines were one of the most powerful and respected princely families of Upper Italy, possessing several countships and estates especially in eastern Lombardy, Emilia, Romagna, and northern Tuscany. Azzo and Cuniza had a son who, at the death of Welf III, was about twenty years old. Cuniza having also died, Imiza summoned her grandson to Germany to carry on the Welf tradition, and as Welf IV he became the founder of the junior line. A few months after his uncle's death he took over the whole Welf inheritance in Swabia and Bavaria. The convent at Weingarten was occupied by monks from Altomünster in Bavaria, and the Weingarten nuns were sent to Altomünster in exchange. Welf himself founded the congregation of Augustinian canons at Rottenbuch in the Ammer valley, which was to play an important part in the ecclesiastical reforms of the eleventh and twelfth centuries.

Welf IV's first marriage was to the descendant of an unknown Italian line; his second was to Ethelinde, daughter of Otto of Northeim, duke of Bavaria and one of the first dynasties in the Empire. In 1070 Otto was deprived of his duchy for alleged complicity in a plot against Henry IV, whereupon Welf repudiated his wife and took the side of the young king.

Thus began Welf's ambiguous role in the imperial politics of those decades. King Henry transferred the duchy of Bavaria to him, so that the family for the first time attained ducal rank. They continued to hold Bavaria, though with some interruptions, for more than a century, thus consolidating their power base in the Empire. Soon after 1070 Welf married his third wife, Judith of Flanders: two sons were born, Welf V and Henry, afterwards known as 'the Black'.

In their internal German quarrels of the 1070s Welf IV initially sided with Henry IV and gave him useful support against the Saxons. However, after the outbreak of the conflict between the king and Pope Gregory VII he soon joined Henry's princely opponents, playing a leading part in the election of Duke Rudolf of Swabia as anti-king in March 1077. For this he was deposed by the king, as were the dukes of Swabia and Carinthia.

Henry made new appointments to the two latter duchies. He bestowed the important duchy of Swabia on Count Frederick of Büren, who married Henry's daughter Agnes and thenceforth styled himself Frederick of Staufen, after his newly erected castle on the Staufenberg near Göppingen. Thus began, under the Salian dynasty, the historic career of that other Swabian family which was to become for a time the strongest rival of the Welfs. The king kept Bavaria in his own hands for the time being, but was unable to shake the position of the Welfs in their local stronghold.

Welf IV also aspired to create a power base for himself in Italy. His father Albert-Azzo had remarried after Cuniza's death and had two sons, Hugo and Fulco. After Welf's desertion of the royal party, Henry IV promised them the enjoyment of their father's rights and possessions in Italy. Welf IV sought to reassert his position by an alliance with the powerful house of Canossa in Upper and Central Italy. Through the intermediary of Pope Urban II, his son Welf V, then seventeen years of age, was married in 1089 to the Margravine Matilda of Tuscany, then aged forty-two or forty-three, who had been the most ardent champion of the papal cause in Upper and Central Italy since the time of Gregory VII. She had, probably in 1079, made a present to the Roman church of her extensive domains in Italy and Lorraine, but had received them back as a fief. Disappointed in his hope of inheriting these lands as a result of his marriage to Matilda, the young Welf cast her off a few years later, in 1095. This move was connected with a new change of front by Welf IV, who made his peace with Henry IV and was reinstated as duke of Bavaria.

When Azzo of Este died at an advanced age in 1097, his rich estate was the subject of a violent dispute between the sons of his two marriages. Welf IV put forward extensive claims against his step-brothers Hugo and Fulco, and was able largely to vindicate his demands as the result of an expedition to Italy. It was his last important success: a few years later he died in Cyprus, returning from a pilgrimage to the Holy Land.

Welf V succeeded to his father's inheritance in Bavaria, while Henry the Black upheld the dynasty's rights in Italy. Welf's govern-ment as duke of Bavaria (1101–20) was marked by a close under-standing between him and the royal house, especially Henry V, the last Salian Emperor. He is found accompanying the king on numerous occasions, including Henry's first expedition to Rome in 1110–11.

As Welf V left no direct heir, his brother Henry the Black succeeded him as duke of Bavaria. His rule lasted barely six years, but was of the greatest importance to the history of the Welfs. Henry, while his father was still alive, had married Wulfhild, the elder daughter of Duke Magnus of Saxony, of the noted family of the Billungs. On Magnus's death in 1106 the male line of the Billungs died out and their rich estates were inherited by Wulfhild and her younger sister Eilika, wife of the Ascanian Count Otto of Ballen-stedt. In particular Wulfhild received the extensive lands around the Billung family seat of Lüneburg and in the Bardengau. In this way the Welfs acquired a territorial foothold in Saxony also.

Henry and Wulfhild had three sons and four daughters. Conrad, probably the second son, became a Cistercian monk and died young, leaving his two brothers—Henry, subsequently known as 'the Proud', and Welf VI—as heads of the family. Their sister Judith married the young Frederick II of Swabia, who had succeeded his father Frederick of Staufen in the dukedom in 1105. The marriage of a Staufen to the daughter of the Welf princes seemed to guarantee a close alliance between the two great Swabian dynasties; but things took a different course as a result of Henry the Proud's action over the royal election of 1125 following the death of Henry V.

The direct male line of the Salians died out with Henry V, and by right of blood his nephew, Frederick II of Swabia, had the best claim to the throne. He was opposed, however, particularly by the ecclesiastical princes led by Adalbert of Mainz. Adalbert's candidate was his ally of many years' standing, Lothair of Supplinburg, duke of Saxony, who had been a powerful adversary of Henry V during the last years of his reign. Other aspirants to the crown were the Margrave Leopold III of Austria and Count Charles of Flanders.

At the election held under Adalbert's auspices at Mainz in August 1125 Lothair was proclaimed king by acclamation. The Bavarian magnates under their Duke Henry raised objection, but in the consultations of the next few days the Welfs were won over to Lothair's side. As a result he was elected king in due form on 30 August, the principle of free election thus triumphing over that of consanguinity.

The unexpected action of Henry the Black in supporting Lothair instead of his own son-in-law Frederick of Hohenstaufen was no doubt connected with the fact that during the Mainz negotiations it was agreed that his son Henry the Proud should marry Lothair's only daughter Gertrude, then ten years of age. As Lothair had no sons, she was sole heiress of the huge possessions amassed by her father over the years. Above all the proposed marriage gave Henry the expectation of inheriting Lothair's Saxon dukedom, and of the crown itself if Lothair should be elected king. Lothair, aged fifty, was elderly for those days and could not be expected to reign for long. If the dukedom of Saxony fell to the Welfs after his death they would be the most powerful princely house in Germany, and the throne thus seemed to be within their grasp.

Duke Frederick of Swabia saw himself deprived of his legitimate hopes of the crown by his father-in-law's decision. He thus became the bitter adversary not only of the new king but also of his Welf kinsfolk. In this way Lothair's election as king of Germany led to the enmity between Staufens and Welfs which had dire effects on German history for more than a century to come.

Next year Henry the Black died at Weingarten, where he had taken the monastic habit a short time before. Henry the Proud thus became duke of Bavaria, and married Gertrude a year later. The wedding was celebrated with great pomp on 29 May 1127 at the Gunzenlee, an old castle on a hill near Augsburg. One child, Henry the Lion, was born of this marriage to the Saxon princess.

The life and work of Henry the Lion, like that of any other historical personality, can only be properly judged by recalling, at least in broad lines, the nature of the world into which he was born. The Concordat of Worms, marking the end of what is commonly called the Investiture contest, was signed in 1122, a few years before Lothair's election as king of Germany. However, in the period between about 1075 and 1122 a great deal more was at stake than the question of control over church offices and dignities. In many fields of political, social, and spiritual life these years mark a turning-point in the medieval history of the Western world.

This is primarily true of the position of the two universal powers, the Empire and the Papacy. Up to the middle of the eleventh century the true ordering of the Christian world was held to consist in the harmonious cooperation of these two powers. The Emperor was regarded as the protector and champion of Western Christendom. This religious function gave a sacral character to his office and placed him as Christ's deputy (*vicarius*) on an equal footing with the Pope, the other head of Christendom. The sacrament of anointing raised the Emperor, like any consecrated monarch, from the status of a layman and gave him a priestly character. The duties peculiar to his office made him spiritually predominant over other Western rulers.

This concept had been shattered since the reign of Pope Gregory VII (1073–85). The Papacy, by laying exclusive claim to universal rule, had destroyed the traditional world-picture and called in question the spiritual basis of the Empire. As the new ecclesiastical doctrine disputed the spiritual character of the ruler's office, it was necessary to seek a new theoretical basis for imperial rule.

Though the Papacy had had to make various concessions to the kings of Germany and other rulers, it must on the whole be regarded as having emerged victorious from the great struggle. Rescued by the church reform movement from the depths to which it had sunk in the tenth and early eleventh century, the Papacy was once again a moral and spiritual force, asserting its authority, not only in church matters, as far as the remotest parts of Christendom. Admittedly this involved a danger that the Roman Curia might become too closely involved with political events and itself too strongly politicized.

The beginning of the twelfth century saw a change in the power relationships of West European states. Louis VI of France (1108–37) set about overcoming the feudal anarchy of the tenth and eleventh centuries, initially in the domains of the French crown, and thus created a basis for the gradual rise to power of the French monarchy. However, the royal authority suffered many setbacks under his son and successor Louis VII (1137–80), who was not without ability but lacked firmness of purpose.

King Henry I of England (1100–35) did much to consolidate the new Norman monarchy by creating a strong judicial and financial organization under royal control. After fighting for his inheritance for nearly twenty years, Henry II Plantagenet (1154–89) made the Anglo-Norman state the strongest power in Western Europe, embracing not only England and Normandy but also most of the remaining provinces of Western France. He held these, it is true, as a vassal of the French king, but in terms of power Henry was much stronger than his feudal lord, a fact which constantly led to grave tension between the two monarchies.

The most powerful Western ruler in the first half of the twelfth century was undoubtedly Roger II, the Norman king of Sicily (1101–54). Uniting in a single state the various territories conquered by the Normans in Sicily and southern Italy, he created a monarchy that stood far ahead of its time in terms of centralized power, making the Normans a major political force in the Mediterranean area. Not only were they dangerous adversaries of the Papacy and the German Empire in Italy, but their bold forays into the Eastern Mediterranean threatened the Byzantine realm. The power of Byzantium itself revived under the Comneni, thanks especially to the forceful policy of Manuel I (1143–80); this led to a second phase of the 'problem of two Emperors', the relations between East and West, which had existed since the assumption of the imperial dignity by Charlemagne.

The social changes of these decades also favoured the gradual evolution of national monarchies in Western Europe. Until the end of the eleventh century the relatively small class of the higher nobility had had the chief say in political and church matters in all European countries, but thereafter new social groups became prominent, in the first place the knightly class. The lesser nobility and the originally base-born *ministeriales* coalesced into a new class with rights and duties of its own, but also with a way of life and a code of ethics which for centuries had a decisive effect on European society. The development of this knightly class was much accelerated by the Crusades and contact with the Orient.

Next to the knights, though as yet of lesser importance, the bourgeoisie began to play an important part in the course of the twelfth century. The increasing change-over from barter to a money economy, and the enlargement of horizons as a result of the Crusades, gave a considerable impetus to long-distance trade. This economic expansion was of benefit above all to the merchant class, predominant in the cities. The bourgeoisie, conscious of its identity as expressed in guilds and similar associations, increasingly laid claim to a share in municipal government. In Italy, northern France, Flanders, the Meuse area, and some Rhenish episcopal cities in the last three decades of the eleventh century, we can perceive the growing emancipation of the bourgeoisie, which already at this time achieved important gains in several places.

A major factor was the rapid increase of population from the beginning of the twelfth century onwards. From that time on we hear more and more of a shortage of land in Flanders and on the lower Rhine. It was this large surplus population that made possible the settlement of territories beyond the border provinces of the Empire.

The changing times were notably reflected in intellectual life. In France, which stood in the forefront of European culture in the twelfth centry, there arose the new scholastic teaching which sought to make the truths of faith acceptable to the understanding and consonant with one another. Next to Anselm of Canterbury (1033–1109), one of the chief representatives of this new learning was Peter Abelard (1079–1142), who had much influence as a teacher in Paris. But the new dialectical method of question and answer was apt to lead beyond the teachings of the church, and Abelard found a bitter opponent in St Bernard, abbot of Clairvaux (1091–1153). Bernard was not an enemy to knowledge, but to him what mattered most was not intellectual understanding but the believer's contemplative experience of God. In this way he was a founder of medieval mysticism. The mystic vision of God spurred him to impart the gift of grace to others. He became one of the most effective preachers of his time, but also a political churchman not without a taste for power. For about a quarter of a century he was practically an uncrowned king in the West, scarcely any important event taking place without his knowledge.

The enhanced religious needs of the time led to the foundation of new monastic orders, especially the Cistercians and Premonstratensians. The former emphasized simplicity and asceticism in the religious life, while the latter regarded pastoral care as their chief duty. Both were of great importance in the colonization of Eastern Germany, especially the Cistercians, whose rule was that members of the order must live by the work of their own hands.

The new spirit also made itself felt in the arts and literature. In France, from the middle decades of the twelfth century onwards, the new Gothic style gradually took the place of Romanesque, which was at that time reaching its apogee in Germany. At the end of the eleventh and beginning of the twelfth century, in Germany especially, literature was still largely religious and didactic in character; but in the first half of the new century we also find a development of secular poetry and romance that is worldly in its inspiration. It arose in the new knightly class, and here again the Crusades and the encounter with the Orient had fruitful results, as vernacular literatures began to burgeon everywhere. Thus intellectual life in the early twelfth century presents an extremely varied picture and cannot be reduced to a simple formula.

The effects of this general transformation were felt even more strongly in Germany than in the rest of Europe. The Investiture contest led to the first great constitutional crisis of the medieval Empire. The balance of forces between the monarchy, the ducal powers, and the church had determined its internal structure since the tenth century. Since the time of Otto the Great the monarchy, confronted with the duchies and their independent sources of power, had increasingly drawn the church into its service, bringing into being the Ottonic–Salian ecclesiastical system which for a century and a half gave a special character to the medieval German state. This system was destroyed by the vicissitudes of the Investiture dispute. Although the Concordat of Worms enabled the monarchy to retain a large measure of influence over appointments to German bishoprics, the church became less and less subject to the royal power. In the turbulent decades at the end of the eleventh century and the beginning of the twelfth, the bishops were able to acquire many new rights and possessions and began to develop their various estates into territorial bases. Thus in twelfth-century Germany there came into being a class of spiritual princes of the Empire, such as did not exist in other Western states. The bishops developed from royal officials into vassals of the crown, no longer linked to the ruler by any bond other than feudal law. The German church, in fact, was becoming more and more feudalized.

The secular princes, like the spiritual ones, also emerged victorious from the struggles of those decades. In this way a change took place in the nature of the ducal system. In the tenth and eleventh centuries the basis of ducal power was as a rule the 'stem' or tribe. The duke was the tribal chieftain: he commanded the levy, summoned assemblies of the magnates, and maintained peace in the tribal area. But he was not the sole repository of public authority, which was largely exercised by the counts. Nor did the duchies comprise the whole kingdom: there were numerous districts subject to members of the higher nobility but not subject to any ducal authority.

From the end of the eleventh century this state of affairs began to change. Even earlier, we occasionally find dukes without territories of their own. The attempts of these titular dukes and other magnates to transform their family estates into duchies perforce led to a dissolution of the old system. Thus, as early as the end of the eleventh century the Welfs virtually exercised ducal authority over their Swabian possessions, independent of the suzerainty of the dukes of Swabia of the Staufen dynasty. From the beginning of the twelfth century the old type of duchy was replaced by a newer one based on territory rather than tribal identity. It became the chief aim of dukes and other hereditary rulers to knit together their possessions, which were originally only loosely connected, so as to form a self-contained territorial unit. The twelfth century in Germany witnessed the first important phase of this process, leading to the development of territorial sovereignty (*Landesherrschaft*).

At the same time, the extent of ducal authority from the outset varied greatly from one territory to another. This may be seen by comparing the two duchies later ruled by Henry the Lion, namely Bavaria and Saxony. In Bavaria, in spite of the repeated changes of dynasty, ducal authority was very strong. The dukes took over what had been important royal rights: the counties were generally at their disposal, and they frequently claimed reversionary rights in the estates of families that became extinct. In peace-keeping matters also the duke regularly figured as supreme arbiter.

The power of the Billungs, who were dukes of Saxony for about 150 years, was a great deal less than this. At the beginning of his reign Otto the Great had appointed Herman, the ancestral head of the Billungs, whose home was in the Lüneburg area, to be margrave of the important border district to the east of the lower Elbe; subsequently Herman was on many occasions empowered to represent the king as duke of Saxony. The ducal power of the Billungs developed out of these two functions in the time of Herman's descendants, who by degrees accumulated a large territory with its centre of gravity in north-eastern Saxony and on the middle Weser. In addition to extensive allodial lands they acquired numerous counties and church 'advocacies' (*Vogteien*). Their rule, however, did not extend over the whole area inhabited by the Saxon people. They had scarcely any power in the western part of Saxony: they were dukes in Saxony but not of it.

Next to the dukes came a large number of spiritual and temporal rulers, who derived their power from the king alone and saw it as the exercise of rights belonging to themselves. Among spiritual dignitaries we may mention first the archbishops of Bremen, who for a long time were the chief support of imperial power in Saxony. With the help of the kings these prelates were able to acquire the counties in their dioceses and thus rival the dukes in status. From the time of Henry IV onwards they were feudal lords of the important county of Stade. This led to severe tension between them and the Saxon dukes, a state of affairs which continued into the twelfth century.

Among temporal dynasties, some families of counts enjoyed exceptional power and played an important part in imperial history in the eleventh and early twelfth century: for instance the counts of Stade, known by their generic name of Udo. From the middle of the tenth century onwards this family created a domain for themselves between the lower Elbe and the Weser which was scarcely inferior to that of the Billungs. The acquisition of Dithmarschen (Ditmarsh) in the mid-eleventh century extended their power northwards across the Elbe, while at the same time they became margraves of the Nordmark (Northern march), later known as the Altmark. The counts of Nordheim similarly rose to prominence from the end of the tenth century onwards, building up a large domain on the Leine and the upper Weser including allodial lands, countships, and advocacies. The most important member of this family was undoubtedly Otto of Northeim, who was duke of Bavaria from 1061 till his deposition in 1070.

Among these and other Saxon dynasties the Billungs were in a sense only *primi inter pares*. Unlike the dukes of Bavaria they had no general right of summoning vassals to appear at court or in the field, though on royal campaigns they commanded their own tribal levy. Nor is there any evidence from the time of the Billungs that they exercised any special ducal rights of jurisdiction over and above those of a count. The three border provinces on the middle Elbe and Saale that came into existence towards the end of the tenth century—the Nordmark, Lausitz (Lusatia), and Meissen—were also fully independent of the Billungs and subject only to the king. The ducal rank of the Billungs was only a primacy of honour that they enjoyed in Saxony.

The male line of the Billungs came to an end in 1106 with the death of Duke Magnus. His two daughters were married to members of prominent families: Wulfhild, the elder, to the Welf Henry the Black, and Eilika, the younger, to Otto of Ballenstedt. However, neither of these sons-in-law obtained the ducal title: Henry V bestowed it on Count Lothair of Supplinburg, who till then had played little part in political affairs and possessed only a modest power base in Saxony.

The king's reasons for appointing Lothair are not certain. His object was probably to prevent too great a concentration of power in Saxony, where strong anti-royal forces had existed since the time of Henry IV. Lothair's elevation to the dukedom also meant the break-up of the extensive domains of the Billungs. Their estates went partly through Wulfhild to the Welfs, partly through Eilika to the Ballenstedter, henceforth generally known as Ascanians from their stronghold of Aschersleben. The border territory north-east of the lower Elbe, its countships and advocacies, fell to Lothair along with the duchy.

The Supplinburg patrimony was not large. Besides the countship comprising the Harzgau and the adjacent north-eastern foreland of the Harz mountains, Lothair possessed allodial domains of only moderate size around the ancestral castle near Königslutter. None the less he became the most powerful dynast in Saxony during the twenty years or so of his rule: this was partly due to the ducal office itself, but mainly to the fact that he was able to acquire extensive lands thanks to the extinction of several Saxon noble families.

His marriage to Richenza, a granddaughter of Otto of Northeim, brought him the prospect of only part of the Northeim lands, as Otto's heirs included not only Richenza's father Henry but the latter's six brothers and sisters. An important gain, on the other hand, was the complex of estates belonging to the Count of Haldensleben in the north-eastern foreland of the Harz, which Lothair inherited after the death of his grandmother Gertrude. Still more valuable was the estate of his mother-in-law Gertrude of Brunswick, with whom the important family of the Brunos died out in 1117. In addition to the Brunonians' rights in and around Brunswick this included the possessions of the counts of Katlenburg, whose ancestral castle lay to the east of Northeim. It was a great success for Lothair that by skilful negotiation after Gertrude's death he was able to secure the whole of her inheritance. He was now the most powerful lord in Saxony, far surpassing all his fellow-magnates in the extent of his domains.

It was Lothair's personal achievement that as duke he once again became the real head of the Saxon nation. This was shown, for instance, by his action in Nordalbingia, where he began systematically to include in the Saxon power sphere the frontier district which had existed since the tenth century. His chief helpers in this enterprise were the Schauenburgs, whose original home was on the middle Weser. Adolf I, the first member of this family whose name is known, was enfeoffed by Lothair in 1111 with the border county of Holstein-Stormarn, the nucleus of which lay in the area north and east of Hamburg. By establishing the Schauenburgs in his area Lothair ensured the successful beginning, in time to come, of German missions and settlement on the western shores of the Baltic.

The strong position that Lothair achieved in eastern Saxony also enabled him to extend his power in the western part of the duchy, especially Westphalia, where he had no direct authority but was able to assert peace-keeping rights and thus give further substance to the ducal office.

Above all he acted as the representative of his nation when, under Henry V, the conflict betwen the Salian dynasty and the Saxons broke out in all its violence. The Emperor's attempt to crush Saxon opposition by military force came to an inglorious end in 1115, when a Saxon army led by Lothair inflicted a severe defeat on him at the battle of the Welfesholz near Mansfeld. The royal power of the last Salian was thenceforth extinguished in Saxony. This was clearly seen in 1123 when Lusatia and Meissen—two of the three most important central German marches—fell to be reallotted. Ignoring the decision of Henry V, who had bestowed both fiefs on Count Wiprecht of Groitsch, Lothair installed Albert the Bear, son of Otto of Ballenstedt, in Lusatia and conferred Meissen on Conrad of Wettin. For the first time a Saxon duke had claimed the right to dispose of major imperial fiefs and thus clearly demonstrated the fullness of his power.

When Lothair became king of Germany in 1125 he retained the duchy of Saxony. Once again, as in the tenth century, Saxony became the chief nucleus of the kingdom. Naturally for the moment its internal affairs became less important to Lothair than imperial politics, where his chief concern was the contest with the Hohenstaufen dynasty. Duke Frederick II of Swabia refused to surrender the imperial lands he had been administering since the death of Henry V, as they were closely linked with the Salian estates on which he had hereditary claims. For this he fell under the ban of the Empire, but Lothair was unable to enforce the sentence. The position of the Hohenstaufens in southern Germany was for the present so strong that in December 1127 they were able to set up Frederick's younger brother Conrad as anti-king. Conrad, however, was unable to create a firm power base in the southern part of the Empire or Upper Italy, where he tried his fortunes in 1128. From the early 1130s onwards Lothair increasingly gained the upper hand throughout the Empire; the Staufen brothers had to yield, and in 1135 Conrad abdicated the kingship.

This gradual consolidation of the royal power enabled Lothair to turn his attention once more to Saxon affairs, more particularly on the northern and eastern borders of the Empire. In Nordalbingia he was the chief protector of the first Schauenburgs, who as strangers to the area were strongly opposed by the native nobility. Adolf II, who succeeded his father as count when the latter died in 1130, also had at first to cope with considerable local resistance. But the church too felt the benefit of the king's strong authority in furthering its missionary activity east of the Elbe.

No doubt owing to the intensified religious sense of the period, missions revived everywhere with fresh energy in the mid-1120s. In the archbishopric of Hamburg–Bremen, under Archbishop Adalbero, thoughts returned to the great missionary effort undertaken in Slav territory in the mid-eleventh century by the famous Archbishop Adalbert of Hamburg. The success he had achieved with the co-operation of Gottschalk, the Christian prince of the Obodrites, had been destroyed by a great Wendish uprising in 1066, when the pagan reaction destroyed the missionary bishoprics of Oldenburg in Wagria, Ratzeburg, and Mecklenburg. At that time Gottschalk was killed, while his widow, with her infant son Henry, took refuge with her father, King Sven Estridson of Denmark.

Only towards the end of the century was Gottschalk's son able to reassert the rule of his family over the Obodrites; he established his seat at Altlübeck, an old fortress where the Schwartau flows into the Trave. Protected by the castle, inside which was a small chapel, was a settlement of craftsmen and a community of Saxon merchants with a church of their own—the only one in Obodrite territory. This now provided a useful base for the revived mission from Bremen led by Canon Vizelin—a man imbued with ascetic ideals and missionary fervour, later venerated as 'apostle of the Wends'.

In 1126 Vizelin made his way to Altlübeck, but his first missionary attempt was short-lived, as in the following year Henry died—he was probably murdered—and disturbances broke out among the Obodrites. Vizelin transferred his activity to Holstein, close to the imperial frontier: here, a few years later, he founded the Augustinian canonry of Wippentorp, afterwards Neumünster, which was to provide a base for the renewed mission into Wagria.

To keep the peace in Wagria, soon after Henry's death Lothair enfeoffed it to the Danish prince Knut Laward, who resided in Schleswig as governor for his uncle King Niels. However, the union of Wagria with the territory on the Schlei was of short duration: in 1131 Knut was slain by Niels's son Magnus, who feared that Knut might challenge him for the succession.

The murder of his vassal compelled Lothair to intervene personally in Nordalbingia. In Denmark there ensued some twenty-five years of fighting for the crown, with rival claimants seeking and obtaining support in Germany. Both the German kings and the Saxon dukes were confronted during these decades with constantly changing circumstances. At this period Lothair already established the feudal suzerainty of the Empire over the Danish rulers. In 1131 he advanced to the Danewerk (Dannevirke) near Schleswig, obliging Niels and Magnus to submit and pay heavy indemnities. Three years later Magnus was formally enfeoffed with Denmark at a court held at Halberstadt. The suzerainty of the Empire over Denmark was confirmed under the next two kings, Eric Emune and Eric Lam.

The revival of the mission to Wagria also owed much to Lothair's aid. In 1134, at Vizelin's instance, he advanced into the country as far as the Segeberg area. On the Alberg, the calcareous rock near present-day Segeberg, he founded a castle and appointed one of his vassals to command it. Wagria, as part of the frontier march, was to remain directly under the king's authority and was not yet included in the countship assigned to Adolf II. Alongside the castle Lothair established a foundation of canons from Neumünster under Vizelin's direction. This once again provided a valuable base for the Wagrian mission; an attempt to found a mission in Altlübeck, however, proved unsuccessful.

How strong Lothair's position had become on the eastern borders of the Empire was shown at the last great diet held by him at Merseburg in Saxony in August 1135 and attended by representatives of several other rulers. Bolesław III of Poland came in person to pay twelve years' arrears of tribute and do homage for Pomerania east of the Oder. Among Lothair's objects was to promote trade between the Empire and the Baltic countries. By a privilege which is no longer extant, dated perhaps as early as 1134, he promised the merchants of Gotland extensive protection in his dominions. As king and as duke, by these measures in the northern and eastern parts of the Empire he pointed the way that was to be followed by his grandson Henry the Lion.

Lothair also made arrangements in the eastern part of central Germany which were of importance to later imperial history. Albert the Bear was given the Nordmark as a fief in 1134. Two years later the march of Lusatia went to Conrad of Wettin, who thenceforth held it and Meissen together. In this way the Ascanians and the Wettins acquired the basis for the expansion of their territorial domain. In particular Albert the Bear devoted himself to increasing his power and soon extended his influence to the Brandenburg area, so that before long he became a dangerous rival of the Welfs.

Although Lothair had risen to prominence as an opponent of the Salian dynasty, as king he conformed to the German royal tradition and endeavoured to strengthen the monarchy against the Papacy and the church. His policy in Italy was a reflection of this. His intervention was occasioned by a disputed election to the Holy See in 1130, when a majority of cardinals voted for Anacletus II, a representative of the older reformist Papacy, while a large minority of younger cardinals voted for Innocent II. Anacletus found support in Rome and central Italy and also with Roger II of Sicily, while Innocent was obliged to flee to France. However, Innocent was increasingly supported in the West thanks to the authority of Bernard of Clairvaux, and was supported by Lothair and the German clergy.

The reinstatement of the Pope was a principal object of Lothair's first expedition to Italy in 1132–3, in addition to receiving the imperial crown and re-establishing royal power in Italy. With his consort Richenza, he was crowned in Rome by Innocent in June 1133.

In the negotiations that accompanied this solemn act, the Pope granted the Emperor important privileges for the German church. A settlement was also reached concerning the Matildine lands, which had been a subject of dispute between the German king and the Curia since Henry V's time. Lothair recognized that the lands belonged to the church, but was granted possession of them for an annual payment of 100 pounds in silver. Innocent invested Lothair with the spiritual symbol of the ring, but did not formally exact homage. It was agreed, however, that Lothair's son-in-law Henry the Proud (who did not take part in the expedition) and his wife Gertrude should, after Lothair's death, inherit the lands as a fief from the Pope.

The acquisition of these extensive domains was a great accretion of power to the Emperor and also to the Welfs, who, in addition to their claim to the Este inheritance, now stood to inherit a large complex of possessions in northern and central Italy.

Soon after the Emperor left Italy, the Pope's fortunes again took an adverse turn. Roger II of Sicily advanced against the papal states, and Innocent had to take refuge in Upper Italy. Hence Lothair had again to intervene in Italy in the summer of 1136. This time Henry the Proud accompanied him with a strong military force. During the march southwards Lothair enfeoffed Henry with the imperial strongholds of Garda and Guastalla, the latter situated at an important crossing of the Po. During the autumn Lothair consolidated his position in Upper Italy, and at the beginning of 1137 he continued southward. He and Henry the Proud, advancing by different routes, reached and captured the important port of Bari. However, peace negotiations with Roger II were unsuccessful. The hot summer obliged the Emperor to abandon the campaign in south Italy without coming to terms with its Norman rulers. On the return march he conferred on his son-in-law the margraviate of Tuscany.

During the march through Italy the Emperor fell gravely ill. He managed to recross the Alps, but died on 4 December in the Tyrolese village of Breitenwang. Before his death he handed the imperial insignia to his son-in-law and also conferred on him the duchy of Saxony, though it is not certain whether this was done in legal form. Lothair was laid to rest in the monastery of Königslutter which he had founded.

Duke Henry was now certainly the mightiest prince in the kingdom. Besides his two duchies and the fiefs and imperial lands in Italy, he possessed the rich allodial estates and other rights of the Welfs in Swabia, Bavaria, and Upper Italy, held jointly with his younger brother Welf VI. In Saxony he combined Lothair's multifarious domains with the Billungs' possessions inherited from his mother Wulfhild. According to Bishop Otto of Freising, whose chronicle is the principal source for these years, he used to boast that his power extended from sea to sea, from Denmark to Sicily. Thus he might naturally regard himself as the future king of Germany, particularly as Lothair had, as it were, designated him by handing over the insignia.

However, Henry had made many enemies in the Empire by his arrogant, domineering manner, which earned him the sobriquet of 'the Proud' even in his lifetime. Innocent II was opposed to his election since, when in Italy, he had been a staunch upholder of imperial rights against the Curia. At this time the see of Mainz was vacant owing to the death of Adalbert and, as Archbishop Arnold of Cologne had not yet been enthroned, the election was conducted by Adalbero of Trier. The date had been fixed for Whitsun 1138, but meanwhile Adalbero summoned his supporters to Koblenz, where on 7 March 1138 Conrad of Hohenstaufen was elected king. A few days later he was crowned as Conrad III by a papal legate in Aachen. Conrad's election was the work of a minority: once again the principle of free election of the monarch had prevailed.

The new king soon obtained universal recognition. Henry the Proud handed over the imperial insignia to him but refused to do homage, as Conrad demanded that he surrender certain imperial fiefs. This brought the Hohenstaufen–Welf conflict to a climax. Conrad's attack on Henry was aided by the fact that at the beginning of 1138 Albert the Bear had come out as an opponent of the Welfs; as a grandson of Magnus Billung, he now formally presented to the king his claim to the duchy of Saxony. At a diet at Würzburg in July 1138 Henry, who failed to appear, was placed under the ban of the Empire and formally deprived of the fief of Saxony, which was assigned by the princes present to Albert the Bear.

Lothair III's energetic widow Richenza now became the champion of the Welf cause in Saxony. Despite her opposition and that of other Saxon princes, Albert the Bear at first achieved some successes. The conflict also extended to Nordalbingia. Adolf II refused to recognize Albert as duke and was obliged to take flight, while Albert conferred the countships of Holstein and Stormarn on Henry of Badwide, member of a knightly family from the Lüneburg district.

The conflict within the Empire entered a fresh phase when, at a diet held at Goslar in December 1138, Conrad deprived Henry the Proud of the duchy of Bavaria, which he transferred in the following spring to the Margrave Leopold IV of Austria of the house of Babenberg. Leopold was Conrad's half-brother, his mother Agnes having married the Margrave Leopold III after the death of her first husband, Frederick I of Swabia. In the internal German quarrels of subsequent times the Babenbergs were the chief allies of their close relatives the Hohenstaufens. Meanwhile Henry the Proud also forfeited the margraviate of Tuscany.

The rule of Albert the Bear in Saxony was of short duration. At the beginning of 1139 Henry the Proud left his younger brother Welf to fight the Staufens in south Germany and himself went to Saxony, obliging Conrad III, who was in the duchy at the time, to take refuge in flight. Albert was more and more thrown on the defensive: he was forced to give up both the duchy and his own margraviate, and to seek help from the king in south Germany.

The summer of 1139 seemed to bring a military settlement of the conflict. An imposing army assembled at Hersfeld under royal command for the attack on Saxony, opposed by Henry and his forces. The troops confronted one another for a time at Creuzburg on the Werra, till an armistice was arranged by the churchmen present.

Henry the Proud could consider himself the victor. Almost the whole of Saxony was now in his hands. As the armistice did not extend to Bavaria, he was able to make plans to recover his family's dominant position there also. But before he could put these into effect he died after a short illness at Quedlinburg on 20 October 1139. He was only 40 and full of vigour, and in Saxony there were rumours among his supporters that his death must have been due to poisoning.

The Welfs had lost their leader at the critical moment, and he had left no easy inheritance to his son of the same name, who was of tender years.

Henry the Proud—the name by which he is known to history— was occasionally referred to in the twelfth century as 'Henry the Lion'. In an age when the great dynasties were adopting individual coats of arms and animals to symbolize their race, the lion was an obvious designation for the Welfs, as this word was rendered in Latin not only as *catulus* but also as *leo*. Henry the Proud issued coins with the effigy of a lion; his brother Welf VI did the same, and used a lion-seal which no longer survives. But it was Henry the Proud's son who made the animal a permanent symbol of his race.

Henry's Youth and
First Beginnings in Saxony

THE historical writings of the early and high Middle Ages tell us little of the childhood and youth of even important rulers. Contemporary sources take notice of them only when they emerge as independent agents. This is equally true of the two personalities—Frederick Barbarossa and Henry the Lion—who gave a decisive stamp to German history in the twelfth century.

We do not know the exact date and place of birth of either the Emperor or the duke, his cousin. According to the chronicle of the Steterburg foundation near Wolfenbüttel, the compiler of which, Provost Gerhard, was close to the duke in the last years of his life, Henry died in his sixty-sixth year, so that he must have been born in the last months of 1129 or the first half of 1130. In that case his mother Gertrude, who was born on 18 April 1115, would have been barely 15 years old at his birth. As Henry was not baptized until Whitsun 1135 or 1136, it has been thought that he must have been born in 1134 or 1135; but it was not unusual in the twelfth century for a long interval to elapse between birth and baptism. Again, the fact that he first made his demand for the recovery of the duchy of Bavaria in 1147 does not justify the assumption that he had only just become twelve years old (the then customary age of majority).

Moreover, Henry's first independent acts of government in the mid-1140s show such personality that he can hardly have been a mere lad of some ten years old. Even if Gerhard made a mistake, we must place Henry's birth in 1130 or shortly after. He was thus some eight or nine years younger than Frederick Barbarossa, who was born in 1122, the eldest son of Duke Frederick II of Swabia and Judith, his bride of the Welf clan. We do not know the place of Henry's birth either: there is no source evidence for the supposition that it was the family's ancestral seat, the Ravensburg.

Henry undoubtedly received the knightly upbringing that was usual for children of the great dynasties unless they were intended for a church career. Skill in the use of arms played an important part. Henry grew up in the aristocratic culture that was taking shape at the beginning of the twelfth century. Regensburg, the old residence of the dukes of Bavaria, was in those decades the most important intellectual centre of south-eastern Germany, with its monasteries and other religious foundations, some of which, like St Emmeram, possessed a long tradition. We cannot say whether this urban culture had a strong influence on Henry's upbringing, as we do not know if he spent long in Regensburg while his father was duke of Bavaria. In any case he did not have direct access to the learned literature of his day: like most nobles of the time, he could neither read nor write Latin. But the strong encouragement his court later gave to literary and artistic activities suggests that as a youth he was not unaffected by the intellectual trends of the early twelfth century.

His adolescence was a period of agitation during which his family had to fight hard for its position. This no doubt caused him to mature early, with a good knowledge of the world and his fellow-men. The fact that the Welf party overcame all vicissitudes must have made him proud and self-confident: this shows itself in the way he fought ruthlessly for his own claims and despised the rights of others.

On his father's death young Henry received general recognition from the Saxon magnates. The regency was exercised by his mother Gertrude and his grandmother, the energetic Empress Richenza: the latter in particular carried on the fight for her dynasty in Saxony. In south Germany Welf VI became leader of the Welf party, having probably received a large part of the family's allodial lands in that area. He laid claim to Bavaria, and resorted to arms when King Conrad denied him satisfaction.

Albert the Bear, who had been unable to retain possession of Saxony during the lifetime of Henry the Proud, now sought to reassert himself there. On receiving the news of his rival's death he hastened to Bremen on All Saints' Day, 1 November 1139, and attempted to use the occasion of a large market to obtain recognition of his claim; however, he was driven out of the town by supporters of the late duke.

A number of Saxon princes, including Archbishop Conrad of Magdeburg, Count Palatine Frederick of Sommerschenburg, and Count Rudolf of Stade, now took the offensive against Albert, invading not only the Nordmark but the Ascanian patrimonial lands. Albert was again obliged to give up Saxony and take refuge with the king in south Germany. Conrad attempted to settle the Saxon dispute at two diets, held at Worms and Frankfurt in the first months of 1140; but the Saxon princes refused to attend, as the king refused them a safe conduct.

In south Germany the fighting continued with varying results. Welf defeated Leopold of Babenberg, the new duke of Bavaria, in the summer of 1140 at the castle of Valley on the river Mangfall. However, Conrad, aided by his brother Duke Frederick, took the offensive in Swabia and in November laid siege to the stronghold of Weinsberg near Heilbronn. Welf hastened to the rescue but was defeated, and Weinsberg finally surrendered.

This event is associated with the well known story of the 'loyal wives of Weinsberg'. The king, it is said, declared that the women only might leave the town but that they might take out with them anything they could carry on their shoulders. Thereupon a long procession of women emerged, each carrying her husband on her back, so that the men escaped captivity. Conrad, the story says, was taken aback but refused to go back on his word. The tale has often been decried as a legend of later origin, but it rests on a contemporary source and is entirely plausible.

The capture of Weinsberg was a clear success for the Hohenstaufen. However, Welf VI did not give up the struggle but entered into relations with Roger II of Sicily, the German monarch's chief opponent in Italy. Anxious that Conrad should be occupied in Germany by internal feuds and unable to intervene in Italy, Roger II promised Welf a subsidy of 1,000 marks a year: a very considerable sum, as the mark then was a unit of some 230–40 grams of silver. The date of this agreement is not quite certain, however: it may have been a few years later.

Roger's policy of expansion in the Mediterranean had already led to a *rapprochement* between Lothair III and the East Roman Emperor, John II Comnenus. Under Conrad these diplomatic ties became closer still, and it was planned to unite the dynasties by the marriage of Manuel, a son of the Byzantine Emperor, to Conrad's sister-in-law, Countess Bertha of Sulzbach. Bertha made the journey to Byzantium forthwith, but did not marry Manuel till 1146; he had meanwhile, in 1143, succeeded his father on the throne, his elder brothers having died. Thus in the early 1140s a new alliance had taken shape in the West and the Mediterranean area, which was to play a decisive part in the politics of the time.

Conrad's efforts to pacify Germany were at first unsuccessful. However, the death of the Empress Richenza in June 1141 created a new situation, especially as the Hohenstaufen–Babenberg party suffered an unexpected loss by the death of Duke Leopold of Bavaria. His brother Henry Jasomirgott succeeded him at first only in the march of Austria. A compromise between the two camps was reached in the spring of 1142 through the good offices of Markolf, the new archbishop of Mainz, who, like his predecessors, was on good terms with the Saxon ducal house. At a diet held by the king at Frankfurt in May and attended by many German princes, Henry the Lion was recognized as duke of Saxony and invested with the duchy, presumably jointly with his mother Gertrude. Albert the Bear finally gave up his claim to the ducal title, and in return received back his rights and possessions in Saxony. The compromise was sealed by a marriage which then took place between Gertrude and Henry Jasomirgott. Conrad, who arranged a great wedding feast, hoped in this way to exert some influence on events in Saxony. The agreements were formally confirmed at a diet at Goslar in Saxony at the beginning of 1143; Henry the Lion renounced his claim to the duchy of Bavaria, which Conrad conferred as a fief on Henry Jasomirgott. Welf VI maintained his own claim to Bavaria, but his attempt to secure it by invasion failed.

Meanwhile Gertrude had taken up the reins of government in Saxony on her son's behalf. In the few documents that have survived from the ensuing years she is seen acting jointly with the boy duke. Thus in September 1142 at Bremen they and Archbishop Adalbero made arrangements for the reclamation of the swamp-land of Stedingen on the left bank of the Weser, the archbishop preserving his own rights in that area. In the spring of 1143 Gertrude set out for Bavaria, where she died giving birth to a premature male child on 18 April, her twenty-eighth birthday. She was buried in the convent founded by the Babenbergs at Heiligenkreuz near Vienna.

Gertrude's early death broke the personal link between the two parties in the Empire and endangered the peace that Conrad had engineered. In the spring of 1143 her son took over the government of Saxony, aided by magnates and *ministeriales*, most of whom had served his father and grandfather before him.

The young duke's first public acts were concerned with Nordalbingia, where the order imposed by Lothair III had broken down owing to the contest for the duchy of Saxony and the dispute between Adolf II of Schauenburg and Henry of Badwide for the border county of Holstein–Stormarn. In the summer of 1138 Pribislav, a nephew of the Wendish prince Henry, who had succeeded in becoming the ruler of Wagria, attacked the first Saxon settlements around Segeberg and destroyed the church there; the canons found temporary refuge at Högersdorf west of the Trave. But Pribislav's own residence of Altlübeck was captured by his rival, the Wendish prince Race.

During the next winter Henry of Badwide led a punitive expedition against Pribislav and devastated large parts of Wagria. The stronghold of Plön was taken in summer 1139 by a levy of Holsteiners under their leader Marcrad. Meanwhile Count Henry had had to evacuate the territory, as Adolf II recovered possession of his county with the help of Henry the Proud. As he withdrew he destroyed the castles of Hamburg and Segeberg. However, he was able to ensure that after the duke's death his widow Gertrude granted him the fief of Wagria in return for a money payment.

In this confused situation Henry the Lion saw it as an urgent task to bring the two counts to a compromise and restore peace in the German–Slav frontier area. He achieved his object in 1143. Count Adolf, in return for a large sum of money, regained his previous countship, to which Wagria was now finally united; the fortress on the Segeberg, which he rebuilt, became his chief stronghold in the area.

Henry of Badwide received as compensation the newly created county of Ratzeburg, the Polabian territory subsequently known as Lauenburg. He used as his residence the castle of Ratzeburg, which had been built in the Wendish period. Only the district of Sadelbande in the south-west was under the duke's direct control.

The political settlement of Nordalbingia in 1143 made it possible to begin the colonization and Christianization of Wagria. The Chronicle composed some twenty years later by Helmold of Bosau in his parish on the Plöner See gives a vivid picture of these events, such as we do not possess for any other German territory. Count Adolf sent out messengers to recruit settlers for the regions that were still underpopulated, appealing not only to inhabitants of nearby Holstein and Stormarn but also to more distant parts of the Empire, to Flanders, Holland, Frisia, and Westphalia. As Helmold tells us in quasi-biblical language, 'an innumerable multitude of different peoples rose up at this call, and they came with their families and their goods into the land of Wagria to Count Adolf that they might possess the country which he had promised them'. The first region to be settled was that between the Plöner See and the lower course of the Trave. The Slavs under Pribislav retreated to the north-eastern part of Wagria and the coast and became tributaries of the count. It was now possible for Vizelin to resume the missionary activity that had been checked since the death of Lothair III and to establish the first parishes.

One of Adolf's first aims was to revive the old trading-post on the lower Trave that had ceased to exist with the destruction of Altlübeck. He refounded it not on its previous site but somewhat further upstream on the Werder, a peninsula at the junction of the Wakenitz and the Trave. The new trading settlement, which retained the name of Lübeck, was thus well protected by nature, and a fortress was built to defend the narrow land passage in the northern part of the peninsula. The exact position of the fort is not known, but it was probably on the flat ground between the later Marienkirche and the Trave. It has recently been suggested that an outpost of the trading settlement of Altlübeck already existed on the peninsula in Lothair III's time, but there is no first-hand evidence for this. The new settlement developed rapidly and soon became a serious rival of the older trading posts in north-eastern Saxony, especially Bardowick. Although Lübeck possessed no written municipal law, it was topographically a city according to contemporary ideas. To protect the new settlements in Wagria from external attack Adolf concluded a treaty of friendship with Niklot, the ruler of the Obodrites in Mecklenburg.

Duke Henry took no part in Nordalbingian affairs immediately after 1143, as he was fully occupied with other troubles in Saxony. On 15 March 1144 Count Rudolf II of Stade was murdered by peasants in Ditmarsh, where he had asserted his rule with a heavy hand. As he left no children it became a crucial question who should inherit the extensive domains of the Stade family, from the lower Weser to the Eider. Rudolf's nearest heirs were his brother Hartwig, canon of Magdeburg and provost of Bremen, and his sister Liutgard, who, shortly before his death, had married King Eric III of Denmark, having previously divorced her husband, Count Palatine Frederick of Sommerschenburg.

Soon after Rudolf's death Hartwig made an agreement with Archbishop Adalbero of Bremen, transferring to him the whole of his patrimony in that diocese; in return he was invested for life by the archbishop not only with these allodial lands but also with the countship rights of the house of Stade. The family possessions on the middle Elbe were transferred by Hartwig and his mother partly to the bishopric of Havelberg, the religious foundation at Jerichow, and the Marienstift in Magdeburg; the remainder they sold to the see of Magdeburg, whose archbishop in return promised to help Frederick recover Ditmarsh.

The transfer of the Stade inheritance to the Bremen church would have greatly enhanced the latter's already strong position in north-eastern Saxony and given it a preponderance over the duke himself. To prevent this Henry laid claim to Rudolf's inheritance and took it into his possession in the same year.

It is not certain on what grounds he based his claim. According to the Stade annals, which admittedly date only from the middle of the thirteenth century, he relied on an alleged promise by the archbishop to his mother Gertrude that he should have the countship after Rudolf's death. Nothing else is known of such a promise, and it seems unlikely that Adalbero should have disposed of Rudolf's inheritance in this way during the latter's lifetime.

Helmold of Bosau, who is closer in time to these events, states that the duke claimed the Stade estates partly by right of inheritance and partly under feudal law. But Henry had no valid hereditary or feudal claim to the county of Stade, and it remains doubtful whether he had any legal basis for his demands.

A diet held by Conrad at Magdeburg at Christmas 1144, at which both the duke and Hartwig were present, confirmed the latter's agreement with the Bremen church. Henry, however, refused to accept the decision or surrender the estates. The matter was to be debated next year in Corvey at a further royal diet, but Adalbero did not appear for fear of being attacked by the duke. When Henry again complained the king appointed a court of arbitration consisting of Albert the Bear and other Saxon princes, which was to meet at Ramelsloh near Lüneburg at an early date and settle the matter finally.

Both parties appeared at Ramelsloh, Adalbero desiring this time to defend his cause in person. The duke, seeing little hope of a favour-able verdict, resorted to force. Soon after the proceedings began his supporters created a disturbance, took the archbishop prisoner and brought him to Lüneburg, where he was set free in return for renouncing his claims. Hartwig escaped capture at Ramelsloh but was later taken by a vassal of the duke's. He was released to Albert the Bear for a large ransom and was soon back in Bremen.

Henry's behaviour over the Stade inheritance shows that the young duke was already prepared to flout the law ruthlessly for the sake of power. The sanctity of places where justice was administered was generally recognized in the Middle Ages, yet he did not scruple to use force even there.

The acquisition of the Stade rights and possessions meant a considerable increase in Henry's power. Stade itself was the most important trading centre on the lower Elbe. With it he probably also became advocate over the Bremen church, a right that had belonged for a time to the house of Stade, and thus gained a strong influence over the archbishopric. His high-handed action was bound to exacerbate the old antagonism between it and the duchy. The *coup de main* at Ramelsloh also revived the tension between the Welfs and the king, especially as Conrad was unable to vindicate the archbishop's right.

In the same year as the Stade crisis an important territorial change became imminent in southern Saxony. On 27 April 1144, a few weeks after the murder of Rudolf of Stade, the death occurred of Count Siegfried IV of Boyneburg, the last male scion of the prominent Northeim family. His domains, which were little less extensive than those of his grandfather Otto of Northeim, lay for the most part between the middle Leine and the upper Weser as far as the region of Eschwege. However, Siegfried possessed not only a large part of the family's allodial estates but also nearly all the countships and advocacies that his predecessors had amassed in the course of time.

His nearest heirs were his widow Richenza, his sister of the same name, and his only daughter Guda. But Henry the Lion could also put forward a claim as Siegfried's great-nephew, his grandmother the Empress Richenza having been a member of the Northeim family. If he did not do so at once it was no doubt because he was engaged in fighting for the Stade inheritance, which he probably thought still more valuable. His position in Saxony was not yet strong enough to enable him to claim two such important estates at the same time.

The Boyneburgs' possessions went first to the other dynasty which had occupied a strong position in southern Saxony. These were the counts of Leinegau, who had originally resided south of Göttingen in Reinhausen and on the Gleichen mountains, but since the beginning of the twelfth century mostly styled themselves after the Winzenburg, which they held as a fief from the diocese of Hildesheim. The head of the family was at that time Count Herman II, who had played an important part in imperial politics since the time of Lothair III but had constantly changed sides between the Hohenstaufen and the Welfs. His younger brother, Henry of Assel, married Siegfried's widow Richenza soon after the latter's death and thus received part of the succession; the lion's share of it, however, was purchased by the wealthy Herman from Siegfried's heirs. Between them the brothers also acquired the extensive Boyneburg fiefs. In the same year Conrad, in order to attach the Winzenburgs firmly to the crown, conferred on them the countships and advocacies that Siegfried had held as a vassal of the Empire. The family were also able to acquire the fiefs that Siegfried had held from the archbishopric of Mainz and other churches. How important the Mainz fiefs in particular were to them is shown by the fact that they surrendered to the archbishopric in exchange their ancestral monastery of Reinhausen and that of Northeim which had just become theirs. While Conrad had had to give way in the matter of the Stade inheritance, he could count as a success the territorial settlement in southern Saxony after the extinction of the Boyneburg family. Henceforth the Winzenburgs formed a strong counterweight to the Welfs in that area.

Soon afterwards the king was able to assert his influence in Saxony in another way also. In 1146 a new abbot had to be chosen for the imperial monastery of Corvey, and Conrad was able to ensure that the monks elected Wibald of Stablo, one of his closest advisers. Wibald was expected to take measures to revive the state of religious life, which had fallen into decline not only at Corvey but in other foundations. Accordingly at the beginning of 1147 Conrad placed under his care the nearby communities of canonesses at Fischbeck and Kemnade, which were also directly under the Empire.

This step aroused violent opposition in the communities themselves and also on the part of Duke Henry, who saw it as an interference with the right of patronage that he and his ancestors had exercised over them. Wibald was prevented from taking possession of Fischbeck by Count Adolf of Schauenburg, representing Henry's rights as advocate, and Welf *ministeriales*. After holding a diet at Frankfurt in March 1147 Conrad summoned the duke to receive both advocacies at the archbishop's hands. Henry complied only in respect of Kemnade, the advocacy of which he accepted from Wibald as a fief during the summer. Apart from this the dispute continued for years. Wibald tried in vain to persuade the Curia to allow him to incorporate the two foundations in his own abbey of Corvey. Only in the spring of 1151 was a compromise reached. The king once again made over Kemnade to Corvey, but the advocacy was retained by Duke Henry; Wibald was obliged tacitly to renounce his claim to Fischbeck. In this way Henry the Lion was able to consolidate the rights he already possessed on the middle Weser.

The tensions that were becoming more and more evident throughout the Empire in the mid-1140s were soon eclipsed by an event in the Near East which caused great alarm. In 1144 Zengi, the Seljuk ruler of Mosul and Aleppo, conquered the greater part of the county of Edessa, including its capital. The disappearance of their eastern bastion placed the other Crusader states in a precarious position. Unable to resist the Turks by themselves, they sought help from the West and particularly from the newly elected Pope Eugenius III. The Pope appealed for a crusade, in the first instance to Louis VII of France and the French nobility; at Christmas 1145 Louis made known his intention to lead an army to the Holy Land.

The fact that this developed into a general crusade was due to Bernard of Clairvaux. The dominant and often fateful role that he played in the history of the West first became evident at this time. With his well-known eloquence he stirred up a crusading movement that extended well beyond France and also led to savage pogroms in Rhineland cities.

Bernard himself came to Germany, partly to put a stop to these excesses but mainly to persuade Conrad to join the crusade. The king was at first reluctant owing to the tense situation in the Empire, but under the influence of a powerful sermon by the abbot he resolved to take the cross at Christmas 1146. Many German princes followed his example. They included his nephew Frederick III of Swabia, who had succeeded his father Frederick II, and Henry Jasomirgott of Bavaria. Welf VI had already joined the crusade. Roger II was inclined to do so if Louis VII would lead his armies via Sicily; like the First Crusade, the second would thus be favourable to Norman plans of conquest in the eastern Mediterranean.

Before starting on the crusade Conrad had to settle affairs in the Empire. For this purpose he held a solemn diet at Frankfurt in March 1147, which proclaimed a general truce (*Landfrieden*) within the Empire for the duration. To ensure the succession in case of need,

Conrad had his ten-year-old son Henry elected king. Archbishop Henry I of Mainz was to be regent in Conrad's absence. At this diet Henry the Lion for the first time demanded the return of the duchy of Bavaria, of which he claimed his father had been illegally deprived. Conrad left the legal question undecided, but persuaded Henry to defer his claim until after the crusade.

The Saxon princes, to serve their own political ends, declared that they would rather crusade against the heathen Slavs on Germany's eastern frontier than join the forces in the Levant. To this the diet agreed, and Bernard of Clairvaux promised that those who took part in such a crusade would earn the same indulgence as those in the Holy Land. He declared specifically that the purpose of the northern crusade was to convert the heathen or combat them ruthlessly, and forbade the conclusion of treaties with the Slavs which might allow them to pay tribute while remaining pagans. Bernard's conditions were expressly confirmed by Eugenius III in a bull appointing Bishop Anselm of Havelberg as Papal representative for the crusade against the Wends. While Conrad went from Frankfurt to Regensburg to begin the land journey to the Orient, the Saxon army was to assemble at Magdeburg on 29 June, the feast of SS Peter and Paul. The appeal for a crusade against the Wends was also welcomed in Denmark. Prince Sven and his cousin Knut, who had been contending for the throne since the death of Eric III in 1146, now made peace for the time being and fitted out a fleet with which to fight the Slavs.

These preparations did not escape the Wends, and their prince, Niklot, caused the fortress of Dobin at the northern end of Lake Schwerin to be strengthened as a refuge for the surrounding population. He also asked Count Adolf to mediate in view of the treaty of friendship between them. The Count, who had himself taken the cross at Frankfurt, was unable to promise neutrality; however, he advised Niklot to keep the peace but to warn him if the Slavs intended to take the offensive.

Niklot gave this promise, but decided to forestall the crusaders by advancing into Wagria. In the last days of June he sailed with a fleet into the Trave estuary while sending messengers to Segeberg to warn Adolf according to his promise. Adolf being absent, the defenders could do little. Although the inhabitants of Lübeck received warning from the castle garrison, they allowed themselves to be surprised by Niklot's troops on the night of 26 June, having held a great feast in honour of the martyrs John and Paul. Their ships lying at anchor were burnt; more than 300 men are said to have died in the fighting. Only the castle offered effective resistance. At the same time Niklot's mounted troops scoured the countryside, destroying most of the recent settlements. Only Segeburg and one or two other fortified places survived. When the count mustered his forces for a counter-attack Niklot withdrew his fleet, taking with him prisoners and much booty.

The crusaders, who had meanwhile assembled on the Elbe, divided into two armies. The larger, led by Albert the Bear and Conrad of Meissen and accompanied by Anselm of Havelberg, set out from Magdeburg not against the heathen Liutichi east of the Elbe, but against Hither Pomerania. This attack on a region where Christianity had been gradually gaining ground since the time of Otto of Bamberg showed clearly that the idea of a crusade was a pretext for other designs. Albert the Bear saw the possibility of making good his claims on territory promised him by Lothair, while Anselm of Havelberg wanted to extend his diocese northwards. However, the advance was checked at Demmin, which the crusaders besieged unsuccessfully, and at Stettin (Szczecin), which Bishop Adalbert dissuaded them from attacking. The army dispersed after negotiating with Prince Ratibor at Stettin concerning the further Christianization of his subjects.

The same discrepancy between the idea of a crusade and the political aims of the Saxon princes is seen in the behaviour of the second army, which marched against the Obodrites under the command of Henry the Lion, Conrad of Zähringen, and Archbishop Adalbero of Bremen. At Dobin it joined forces with the Danish crusaders, who had landed from a fleet near Wismar. The Danes suffered severe losses in attacking the fortress; the Ranians of Rügen, coming to the Obodrites' aid, attacked the fleet and destroyed some of its ships. The Saxon magnates soon realized that the crusade was doing them more harm than good, as it was devastating land which was otherwise a rich source of tribute: as Helmold represents them saying, 'Is not the land we are devastating our land, and the people we are fighting our people?' The magnates thus carried on the battle half-heartedly, in sharp contrast to the Danes and the bulk of the crusaders. When the Obodrites undertook to embrace Christianity and release their prisoners, the siege of Dobin was raised.

This token baptism meant, according to the ideas of the time, that the crusaders had performed their vow; but it could not disguise the fact that their enterprise was basically a failure. The methods hitherto used to fight the heathen had proved unavailing, and the good relations between Saxons and Wends that had prevailed in Nordalbingia in the first years of Adolf II were temporarily destroyed, although there was a subsequent *rapprochement* between the count and Niklot.

A year later we again find Duke Henry in the region north of the Elbe. In the summer of 1148 he led a large expedition against Ditmarsh to avenge the death of Rudolf of Stade; among its members were Albert the Bear, the counts of Holstein and Ratzeburg, and many Holstein knights. Archbishop Adalbero and Provost Hartwig of Bremen were also obliged to join the force. The self-confident inhabitants of Ditmarsh were defeated in battle; the duke imposed a tribute and placed them under the authority of a certain Count Reinold. Thus another part of the Stade inheritance was brought under Henry's control.

At about this time Holstein was involved in the quarrel between Sven and Knut for the Danish succession, which had flared up again after the conclusion of the Wendish crusade. Each of the rival princes tried to get Count Adolf on his side. Adolf decided for Knut, who in return enfeoffed him with lands, probably in the Schleswig area. Sven countered with a plundering foray into Wagria; Etheler, an exiled inhabitant of Ditmarsh, assisted him and won over a part of the Holstein nobility. Oldenburg was set on fire and the whole coastal area devastated; the settlement at the foot of the Segeberg was again sacked. How weak the position of Adolf of Schauenburg was in his own county is shown by the fact that he had temporarily to quit his lands and seek refuge with the duke. The latter's authority, on the other hand, was so great that by merely ordering that the peace be kept he was able to confirm Adolf's rule over the county without himself having to intervene there. Adolf proceeded to counter-attack Sven and Etheler. Fighting continued for a time in the region between Schleswig and Rendsburg, until Etheler was killed in battle.

Duke Henry took no personal part in these disputes in Nordalbingia, as another matter of crucial importance for him arose at this time. Archbishop Adalbero of Bremen died on 25 August 1148. The chapter first wished to elect as his successor Abbot Wibald of Corvey, but in the end the appointment went to the ambitious Provost Hartwig. This was tantamount to a defiance of Henry.

Hartwig's aim was to rescue the archbishopric from its unhappy condition and regain the respect it had enjoyed in the middle of the eleventh century. For this purpose he took up a plan of his predecessor's to recover the metropolitanate of Scandinavia, which had been lost at the beginning of the twelfth century owing to the creation of the archbishopric of Lund. Hartwig also saw an opportunity of refounding the bishoprics of Oldenburg, Ratzeburg, and Mecklenburg in Wendish territory, to which no appointment had been made since the catastrophe of 1066, and thus restoring the ecclesiastical lordship of Bremen over the Slavs.

During his stay in Rome in the spring of 1149 to receive the pallium (the sign of his dignity as archbishop) from Eugenius III, Hartwig no doubt attempted to obtain the Pope's approval for these designs, but without success. The Curia was not disposed once more to grant Bremen primatial rights in the North, while as to refounding the three missionary sees, it was thought advisable first to consult Duke Henry. For this purpose Cardinal Guido set out in 1148 on a journey that took him first to Moravia and Poland and then to Saxony. In the summer of 1149 he met with the duke at Königslutter, but nothing is known of what took place. No firm agreement seems to have been reached, and presumably it was only a preliminary exploration.

Hartwig now tried to hasten matters by making appointments to the vacant bishoprics. In September 1149, at the monastery of Harsefeld near Stade, he consecrated Vizelin bishop of Oldenburg, and a monk named Emmehard, of whom practically nothing else is known, as bishop of Mecklenburg. The conferment of regalia, which was a royal prerogative, did not take place. No bishop was yet appointed for Ratzeburg, as the bishop of Verden had claims on the Polabian territory.

The archbishop was certainly entitled to effect this consecration, as the three bishoprics had never been abolished; but he could not provide them with the necessary economic foundation, which could only be done by the holders of secular power in their areas. It was thus a diplomatic blunder, if not a calculated affront, to take this step without consulting Henry. The unilateral appointment of the bishops was bound to reopen the old conflict between the archbishop of Bremen and his old rival Henry the Lion.

The duke saw how dangerous it might be for him if ecclesiastical domains in the north-east of his duchy were subject only to the Bremen archdiocese. Claiming the right of investiture for himself, he ordered Count Adolf to stop the payment to Vizelin of tithes from his bishopric, which for the time being were of small amount.

The account by Helmold of Bosau clearly brings out the differing views of the legal position. The duke declared to the bishop that he alone was competent to settle the issue in the land his forefathers had conquered and bequeathed to him. This, however, was not a valid ground for claiming the right of investiture, which the archbishop—quite correctly, in accordance with the law at that time—forbade Vizelin to accept from anyone but the king. Vizelin had to decide whether to comply with the duke's demand or give up the possibility of working in his see. At first he obeyed the archbishop and refused investiture at Henry's hands. This virtually paralysed his activity in the diocese, and his energies were at this time diminished by a stroke. He had to confine himself to consecrating a few churches in his bishopric from Neumünster. Having tried in vain to induce the archbishop or Henry to relent, he gave up the struggle and in the winter of 1150–1—probably December 1150—was invested by the duke, who presented the crosier to him at Lüneburg. Henry of Weida, one of the duke's chief *ministeriales*, had urged Vizelin to submit on the ground that the duke was sole lord of the territory.

Henry and Count Adolf now set about the initial endowment of the bishopric. Vizelin was presented with the village of Bosau on the Plöner See together with a dependent locality; in this area the count waived his right to one half of the tithe which, here as in other colonial districts, was regarded as a state tax and not merely a church levy. As the old episcopal residence at Oldenburg had lost its earlier importance, Vizelin settled in Bosau and carried on vigorous missionary activity from there until incapacitated by a second stroke in 1152.

Emmehard of Mecklenburg seems to have refused the duke's demand and therefore probably never set foot in his bishopric. As in the matter of the Stade inheritance, Henry had once again firmly asserted his will against the Bremen church.

It may appear strange that Conrad III did not intervene in these disputes affecting the rights of the crown. This, however, was due to the unhappy state of the German kingdom after the Second Crusade.

This, like the expedition against the Wends, had begun with a reverse. The army under Conrad III had reached Constantinople in September 1147 but had had to abandon the march through Asia Minor after heavy fighting with the Turks. Part of the force was almost wiped out, while the remainder attached itself to the French crusaders who were following behind. Conrad himself fell gravely ill and remained in Constantinople till the end of the winter, arriving in Palestine by sea in the spring of 1148. There he fell in with Louis VII, whose army had also suffered heavy losses on the march through Asia Minor. There was no hope of recapturing Edessa, and two attempts in the direction of Damascus and Ascalon were unsuccessful. In September 1148 Conrad returned to Constantinople, whence he set sail on the homeward journey early in 1149. Louis VII remained in Jerusalem till Easter 1149 and then returned to France by way of Sicily.

During the crusade itself there were differences among the Western leaders, and after its inglorious end the old tensions in Western Europe and the Mediterranean, which had been patched over with difficulty, broke out again in all their violence. Roger II had used the crusade to despoil the Byzantine Empire. In the summer of 1147 he occupied Corfu, whence he made plundering raids on Greece. Manuel, faced with hostilities on the northern borders of his Empire, could not effectively resist the Normans and tried to secure allies against them. During Conrad's second stay in his dominions—probably in Salonika in October 1148—the two rulers agreed upon joint action against the Normans. Conrad was to take up arms against Roger in Italy, Manuel aiding him with troops and money in return for parts of the Norman kingdom to be ceded to him after victory. The maritime powers of Venice and Pisa were to be included in the coalition. The alliance was cemented by a marriage between Henry Jasomirgott of Babenberg, who was in Conrad's retinue, and Manuel's niece Theodora. A marriage between Conrad's son King Henry and a Byzantine princess was also contemplated.

Roger II had for some time perceived the threat to his kingdom and tried to form a counter-alliance. In the summer of 1148 Welf VI visited Sicily on his return from Palestine and the two princes renewed their former agreements. The king tried to make contact with Henry the Lion, Conrad of Zähringen, and Frederick of Swabia, but his messengers were taken prisoner in Italy. Louis VII, who landed in Calabria in July 1149, was also won over to Roger's cause. The latter had as an ally King Géza II of Hungary, and Louis now approached Pope Eugenius III. It looked as if the Second Crusade would end in a Mediterranean war, which was prevented only by the Pope's refusal to join the coalition against Conrad and Manuel.

In Germany too the rival groups again came more clearly into view. Conrad of Zähringen was, as far as we know, the only South German prince to take part in the crusade against the Wends. The link this created with Henry the Lion was strengthened shortly after the end of the campaign, probably in 1148 or the following year, when Henry married Conrad's daughter Clementia, who brought with her as dowry the castle and lordship of Badenweiler with 500 hides of land and 100 *ministeriales*. Henry had inherited from his father a considerable part of the Welf patrimony in Upper Swabia, though this cannot be identified in detail, and thanks to his wife's dowry he was able to extend this dominion in south-west Germany as far as the valley of the upper Rhine. Here, for a time, Welfs and Zähringer formed a common front against the Hohenstaufen.

Conrad III set foot in Germany after two years' absence in the early summer of 1149, by which time Welf VI had already begun hostilities in Swabia. Anxious to prevent the conflict spreading to Saxony, the king summoned the Saxon princes to a diet at Würzburg. Henry the Lion, who was then negotiating with Cardinal Guido about the re-establishment of the Nordalbingian sees, did not attend this diet or later ones held by the king in 1149.

At the beginning of 1150 a decisive event took place in southern Germany. In the first days of February Welf attacked the Hohenstaufen fastness of Flochberg near Nördlingen, but was defeated in battle by the young King Henry and barely escaped being taken prisoner. Wibald and others advised Conrad III to exploit the victory, but Conrad of Zähringen and Frederick of Swabia persuaded him to compromise. Welf submitted to the king and promised to keep the peace; in return Conrad released his prisoners. This was the first clear example of Frederick endeavouring to reconcile the two families of which he was a descendant.

After the submission of Welf VI the most urgent internal problem in Germany was the Bavarian question, which had been shelved at the beginning of the crusade. Henry the Lion regarded himself as the rightful ruler of the duchy, and in letters and documents from 1150 onwards repeatedly styled himself duke of Bavaria and Saxony. We know little of the further dealings between him and the king, who once again resorted to a formal process of law. The matter was presumably intended to be raised at the diet of Würzburg in July 1150, but as Henry did not appear there a further diet was set to be held at Ulm on 13 January 1151.

The duke, however, tried to reach a decision beforehand by force of arms. Towards the end of 1150 he led his troops south from Lüneburg, where he had been holding court, to take up the fight for Bavaria. Clementia remained in Saxony as regent with Count Adolf of Holstein as her adviser, responsible in particular for ensuring peace in Nordalbingia. Adolf led a large force to the aid of the Obodrite prince Niklot, who was fighting the Kessiner and Circipani in eastern Mecklenburg.

Henry disregarded the king's summons to Ulm, but matters did not come to an open conflict. Certain princes—probably again Conrad of Zähringen and Frederick of Swabia—arranged a peaceful settlement, after which a fresh diet at Regensburg in June 1151 held out hope that Henry's claim would be met. However, Henry did not attend either this or a further diet at Würzburg in September.

A peaceful solution having thus failed, the king decided to advance into Saxony so as to attack the centre of the duke's power during his absence. This seemed a promising course, as Henry had made many enemies in Saxony by his harsh regime. In November numerous Saxon princes, headed by Albert the Bear, assembled at Altenburg, where the king was making preparations for the campaign. Conrad advanced to Goslar at the beginning of December and moved thence towards Brunswick. To prevent Henry's return northwards he had a strict guard placed along the borders of Swabia.

However, Henry had word of the king's plan and was able to outwit him. Christmas was at hand, and he invited his supporters in Swabia to celebrate it with him. Instead, however, he disguised himself and with a few attendants rode rapidly to Brunswick to prevent Conrad's intended *coup de main*. The king therefore broke off the campaign and returned southward before the year's end.

In Saxony the contest between Henry the Lion and Albert the Bear continued, as their antagonism was fed by fresh causes. Count Bernard of Plötzkau, who was the last of his race, had met his death on the Second Crusade, and the duke and the margrave both laid claim to his estates on the eastern side of the Harz mountains. Then, on the night of 29–30 January 1152, Herman II of Winzenburg was murdered by some *ministeriales* with whom he was unpopular on account of his arrogance; they also murdered his wife Liutgard of Stade, widow of King Eric III of Denmark (Herman being her third husband). The couple left only two small daughters. Herman's brother Henry of Assel was already dead. For reasons unknown to us, the hereditary claims of Henry's putative son Otto and of Herman's daughters were passed over. The disposal of this huge estate was of the greatest importance to the balance of power in Saxony. Again both Henry the Lion and Albert the Bear advanced their respective claims, on what legal grounds we do not know. No decision was reached during Conrad III's reign.

In the last years of the reign external problems were completely overshadowed by these internal disputes. The plan for a campaign against Roger II in alliance with the Emperor Manuel had to be abandoned. The position of the Papacy in Rome had grown more and more precarious since 1143, when the revolutionary citizens had set up a senate of their own to govern the city. Eugenius III, like his predecessors, could only reside there safely for short periods. He appealed to Conrad for help, offering him the prospect of an imperial coronation. The king agreed to make an expedition to Rome, which was to take place in the autumn of 1152.

Meanwhile the quarrel between the rival Danish princes Sven and Knut continued. Sven was successful in the contest for the throne; Knut had to go into exile in Saxony, where he sought help from Henry the Lion and then from Hartwig of Bremen. His repeated attempts to gain possession at least of Jutland were a failure. In 1151 he was again defeated on the Mildau near Husum by Sven and his new ally Prince Valdemar, son of Knut Laward. Knut then repaired once again to Henry's court, while Sven on his side approached Hartwig of Bremen and the Ascanians. Both claimants also appealed by letter to Conrad III, addressing him by the imperial title to curry favour. The king, however, was no longer able to settle the problem of the Danish succession and thus formally restore the imperial suzerainty over Denmark which had existed since the time of Lothair III.

Conrad was a sick man when he returned from the Orient, and in these years his power to govern was more and more impaired. He fell ill again at the beginning of 1152, and died at Bamberg in February. His eldest son Henry had died two years earlier; his second son Frederick was now aged six. Realizing that the boy would be unable to govern the Empire, Conrad on his deathbed designated his nephew Frederick, duke of Swabia, who was probably then aged twenty-nine, handing to him the imperial insignia and entrusting him with the care of his young son. This designation, however, was not as yet binding in law.

Conrad, whom the chroniclers depict as a man of praiseworthy qualities, made many new departures at the beginning of his reign. Above all, his consistent territorial policy succeeded in expanding the Hohenstaufen power base in Swabia and Franconia. Yet at his death the Empire was in a lamentable condition. Internally it was torn by quarrels and feuds, and in the great decisions of the Western world the German kingdom had forfeited its leading role. In the long line of German rulers since Otto the Great, Conrad was the first king not to have attained the dignity of Emperor, though in his diplomatic correspondence he repeatedly used the imperial title so as to emphasize his equality with the ruler of Byzantium.

Contemporaries were fully conscious of the change of fortunes, as we may see from the *Chronicle* by Conrad's half-brother, Bishop Otto of Freising, which dates from about the middle of the 1140s and is probably the best-known medieval work of philosophical history compiled in the West. After contrasting God's eternal kingdom with that of the transitory and ever-changing world, the chronicler ends on a note of gloomy apprehension. He foresees the end of the world and the imminent coming of Antichrist, while firmly believing that Christ as the judge of all the earth will finally triumph over his enemies.

Conrad's adversary Roger II died two years after him; Bernard of Clairvaux in 1153. During his lifetime the Cistercian abbot had almost played the part of an uncrowned king in the West. In the coming decades, new men and new forces were to shape its destiny.

3

Reconciliation with the Hohenstaufen: the Duke in the Service of the Empire

ON 4 March 1152, a few weeks after Conrad's death, Duke Frederick of Swabia was elected king—the first of his name—at Frankfurt by a large assembly of German princes. Five days later, in accordance with tradition, he was crowned in the minster church at Aachen by Archbishop Arnold of Cologne and was installed on the throne of Charlemagne. The details of the election are not wholly clear. Otto of Freising, whose second work *Gesta Friderici I Imperatoris* is our principal source for the early part of the new king's reign, gives a notably brief account of the proceedings, which he depicts as unanimous. Frederick, a scion of the two great rival families of the Empire, 'linked the two walls in the fashion of a cornerstone'. However, in sources dating from the end of the century we find hints of a stratagem on the Hohenstaufens' part. The negotiations in which Frederick engaged before his election included a meeting with his cousin Henry the Lion in or near Mainz at the end of February or the beginning of March; Henry was also a candidate for the kingship, and Frederick no doubt made substantial promises in return for his acquiescence. The consent of Welf VI was probably gained in a similar fashion. Both princes certainly took part in the election and attended the coronation, though there is specific evidence only for their presence at the latter ceremony. On the other hand, Henry Jasomirgott of Bavaria attended neither event.

The new king lost no time in making known, from Aachen, the main lines of his policy, embodied in the notion of the 'reformatio Imperii'. Announcing his election to Pope Eugenius, Frederick declared that the Roman Empire was to be restored to its former power and glory. It is noteworthy that, while protesting his devotion to the Holy Father, Frederick emphasized that he held his power directly from God; he informed the Pope of his election, but did not ask for confirmation of it.

Frederick, whom the Italians afterwards nicknamed 'Barbarossa' on account of his reddish-blond hair, set about 'restoring the Empire' with all his native energy. The first requirement was peace in Germany, and for this purpose Frederick undertook a royal progress through his dominions. He went first from Aachen to the lower Rhine district and Saxony, accompanied by Henry the Lion and Welf VI, and spent a few days at the beginning of May in the palatinate of Goslar. There, in all probability, he enfeoffed the Saxon duke with the imperial advocacy of Goslar, which was a rich source of income owing to the Rammelsberg silver mines. The sources do not confirm that he did so, but we find that Anno of Heimburg, the duke's treasurer and one of his principal *ministeriales*, exercised the advocacy for more than a decade from that time on. It is more likely that the advocacy was granted to the Welf prince, who then entrusted it to his servant, than that the king would have bestowed it on the latter direct. The palatinate itself, on the other hand, remained directly subject to the king.

Soon afterwards, at Whitsun, Frederick held his first great diet at Merseburg, its chief purpose being to regulate the disputes in Denmark and Saxony. However, the king did not succeed in settling the conflict between Henry the Lion and Albert the Bear over the Plötzkau and Winzenburg estates, or the dispute over the right of investiture of the Nordalbingian bishoprics. Archbishop Hartwig, who attended the diet together with Vizelin, urged the latter to accept investiture once again at the king's hands, implying that that conferred by the duke was not valid. The bishop, however, refused to make a lifelong enemy of the duke in this fashion.

The diet at Merseburg did bring about a settlement of the Danish royal succession. Both claimants obeyed the summons to attend: Sven with Archbishop Hartwig, and Knut under the protection of Henry the Lion. Knut, who had lost the contest in Denmark, handed over a sword to Frederick in token of the renunciation of his claim; Sven was enfeoffed with the kingdom with the same sword and did homage to the German ruler, who placed a crown on his head. In the solemn Whitsun procession Sven then bore the imperial sword before the king. Thus the suzerainty of the Empire over Denmark was formally renewed. Knut was compensated with some lands in Denmark, especially in Zealand. Prince Valdemar, who also attended the diet, received a Danish province, probably the Schleswig district. Henry the Lion, who had till then taken Knut's part, agreed to the award. Another action of Henry's at the Merseburg diet was, with the consent of his Welf uncle, to issue an important *privilegium* for the Premonstratensian canonry of Weissenau south of Ravensburg, founded by his *ministerialis* Gebezo of Peissenberg–Ravensburg. Frederick I and the king of Denmark are cited as witnesses to the *privilegium*, which shows that Henry intended to exercise independent rule in the ancestral lands of the Welf dynasty.

Some months later, in October, the king held his second important diet at Würzburg, where he arbitrated between Henry the Lion and the Margrave Albert concerning the two Saxon inheritances, assigning the Winzenburg rights and estates to Henry and those of Plötzkau to Albert. This settlement was preponderantly in Henry's favour. True, it added considerably to Albert's possessions on the eastern border of the Harz mountains, but Henry's gain was much greater, as the Winzenburg inheritance included a large part of the original Northeimer estates.

At the beginning of his rule Henry had been able, thanks to the Stade inheritance, to add appreciably to his patrimony in the northern part of the duchy, and now he had acquired an important power base in the south. Henceforth he possessed almost all county rights and numerous advocacies in the region between the upper Weser and the Leine, for instance over the imperial monasteries of Corvey and Heimatshausen and that of Heiligenstadt in the Eichsfeld, a dependency of the archbishopric of Mainz. In addition he owned a large number of proprietary lands, concentrated especially in the area from the middle course of the Leine southward to the Eschwege district, but also extending in a scattered form westward of the Weser and far into Westphalia. Moreover Henry refused to recognize the transfer, by the Winzenburgers, of the monasteries of Northeim and Reinhausen to the archbishopric of Mainz; they were soon both reabsorbed into the Welfs' sphere of power, which from then on no Saxon dynasty was able to rival.

Also at Würzburg, or shortly before, the Welfs recovered the imperial rights they had previously enjoyed in Italy, as Frederick enfeoffed Welf VI with the duchy of Spoleto, the margraviate of Tuscany, Sardinia, and the Matildine lands. By endowing his uncle with these possessions, which had once been held by the latter's brother Henry the Proud, Frederick hoped to gain Welf's support for the imperial power in northern and central Italy. Perhaps also at this time, Frederick granted to Henry the Lion the advocacy of the monastery of Reichenau, of which the Welfs had been deprived by Conrad III.

It was intended at Würzburg to settle the long-standing dispute over the duchy of Bavaria, to which Henry the Lion frequently laid claim in charters of these years by styling himself duke of Bavaria and Saxony. However, Henry Jasomirgott, though summoned to Würzburg, did not appear, and the dispute lasted for years longer, as he made free use of the right of remonstrance allowed him by the rules of medieval litigation. Finally, after two invitations, a diet was set for Whitsun 1153 at Worms. The duke of Bavaria and Henry the Lion were present, but the former contested the legality of the summons; this he did again when a further diet was called for December of that year at Speyer.

The king, who needed Henry the Lion's aid for his planned expedition to Rome, decided on a final summons to a diet at Goslar in June 1154. As Henry Jasomirgott failed to appear, judgment was given against him by default and Bavaria was assigned to Henry the Lion. The judgment did not take immediate effect, as the duchy was to remain for the time being in the Babenberger's possession, but the important thing for the Welf was that the legal dispute had been settled in his favour. The problem was, however, also an eminently political one, given the Babenberger's power and rank—he was married to a Byzantine princess—and, whatever the legal position, Frederick had if possible to find a solution that did not involve a breach with the Babenberg family.

The diet at Goslar brought about another important success for Henry the Lion, as the king, in the bishop of Bremen's absence, decided in Henry's favour the long-standing dispute over the Nordalbingian bishoprics. A solemn privilege authorized Henry, in territory beyond the Elbe bestowed on him by the king, to establish bishoprics and churches for the propagation of the Christian faith and to endow them with imperial lands as he might see fit. The duke and his successors were given the right to invest bishops of Oldenburg, Mecklenburg, and Ratzeburg; the conferment of regalia on them by Henry was to have the same validity as if they had been enfeoffed directly by the king, and the same was to apply to any further bishoprics Henry might establish in the area. Whereas hitherto Henry had claimed the right of investiture on the ground of conquest, the privilege made clear that it was a right belonging to the king and only delegated to the duke. The legal position of the crown was safeguarded; but the territory on the north-eastern border of the Empire was recognized as belonging to the duke's sphere of interest, and the latter from this time on largely assumed the functions of a representative of the imperial power.

Thanks to the king's decision the duke was able in the same year to appoint a bishop to re-establish the see of Ratzeburg. This marked the beginning of a new phase in Henry's policy towards the Slavs, which will be considered in its context in due course.

Despite his concessions to Henry, the king was at pains to maintain the royal authority in Saxony with the aid of the church. Thus in the spring of 1154 he was able to settle the dispute over the vacant archbishopric of Magdeburg by securing the pallium for his candidate, Bishop Wichmann of Naumburg. At an earlier date the king had been able to appoint his own men to the archbishopric of Mainz and the bishoprics of Hildesheim and Minden, having deposed the previous incumbents.

The diet at Goslar marked the successful conclusion of the king's attempts to reach an understanding with the Welfs in place of the old hostility. For twenty years or so this had a decisive effect on the history of the Empire; at the same time it provided the most important precondition for the success of the Hohenstaufen's external policy.

The deliberations at Goslar were no doubt also much concerned with the king's forthcoming visit to Italy and Rome. In 1152 his departure had been fixed for the autumn of 1154, and thorough diplomatic preparations were made for the journey. In March 1153, after long negotiation with the Curia, Frederick signed a treaty at Constance with the legate of Eugenius III, which was to regulate long-term relations between the German monarchy and the Holy See. The king undertook not to conclude any separate peace with the Normans, to subject the Romans to the papal authority, and to defend the sovereign rights of the Papacy against all comers. In return the Pope promised the king an imperial coronation if he came to Rome, and undertook to use ecclesiastical sanctions against any who might seek to infringe the rights of the Empire. Finally both parties agreed to make no territorial concessions in Italy to the 'king of the Greeks', as the Byzantine Emperor was styled in the treaty.

The restoration of imperial rights and the guarantee of territory in

Italy was one of the most important points in the treaty of Constance. The Normans and the insurgent Romans were the enemies of the king and Pope alike; but the compact also marked a change in Hohenstaufen policy towards Byzantium. As yet there was no actual breach: Frederick continued to maintain diplomatic relations with Manuel, but unlike Conrad III he was not willing to concede any Italian territory to the Eastern Empire.

In October 1154 Frederick set out from Augsburg via the Brenner on his first expedition to Italy. The Saxon knights under Duke Henry formed the largest contingent in his comparatively small army, a sign of the new understanding between Swabian and Welf. Once again Henry entrusted the regency of Saxony to the Duchess Clementia. His retinue included Swabian vassals besides his own *ministeriales*, and the royal expedition provided an opportunity of asserting old Welfic claims in Upper Italy. Immediately after the army reached Italy at the end of October Henry held a meeting in the camp near Verona with the Margraves Bonifazio and Fulco of Este, grandsons of Azzo II of Este by his second marriage. An agreement was reached concerning the estates of the house of Este which Welf IV had vainly tried to secure for himself after his father's death. The two margraves, on their own behalf and that of their absent brothers Albert and Opizo, recognized the duke's right to Este and other neighbouring places, and were enfeoffed by him with these localities for themselves and their descendants in the male and female line; they also paid 400 silver marks by way of compensation. Welf VI, who was not on the expedition, concluded a similar agreement with the margraves in 1160.

The position in imperial Italy had altered to the king's disadvantage during the past decades. Since the days of Henry V the German rulers had seldom visited Italy, and this had much encouraged the independence movement in the towns. The latter's economy had been boosted by trade with the Orient, and they had increasingly usurped imperial rights and possessions. In this way powerful city states had arisen in Upper Italy, sometimes in a state of feud with one another. The most important was Milan, which in Henry IV's time had already been the spearhead of the anti-imperial party in Lombardy. For the time being Frederick could not contemplate a showdown with the powerful communes: the main object of his journey was to receive the imperial crown in Rome. At the beginning of December 1154 he held a diet, which was also a display of military strength, on the plains of Roncaglia in the Po valley near Piacenza.

Here the king received the homage of those cities that accepted his authority and confirmed an ordinance of Lothair III forbidding vassals to dispose of their fiefs without their lords' consent. Milan was compelled to make peace with Pavia, the main support of the German monarchy in Upper Italy. Later Milan fell under an imperial ban for breaking this peace, but Frederick was not strong enough to enforce it.

The diet of Roncaglia also witnessed a decision of importance to Henry the Lion. Archbishop Hartwig of Bremen and Bishop Ulrich of Halberstadt, another of Henry's adversaries, were deprived of the regalia for their own persons, though not for their churches, as a penalty for having violated their feudal duty by failing, without sufficient cause, to take part in the expedition. Hartwig had also taken advantage of the duke's absence to encroach upon his rights in Saxony. He seized the fortified places of Stade, Bremervörde, Freiburg on the Elbe, and Harburg, which had been in the duke's hands since 1145, and soon afterwards held a meeting in the Bohemian Forest with other Saxon opponents of the Welfs and some Bavarian notables. His purpose was no doubt to organize military action against the duke, but this did not come about; Henry's supporters were even able for some time to prevent Hartwig returning to his own parish. The verdict of the diet was thus an important success for Henry.

Early in the new year (1155) Frederick besieged Tortona, which was a close ally of Milan and a constant threat to the loyal city of Pavia. Henry the Lion rendered stout service during the siege; in a short time he and his knights captured the lower part of the city, but the heavily fortified citadel for a long time resisted all attack, even by engines of the most modern kind. Finally after nine weeks and the cutting off of its water supply the garrison was forced to surrender on 18 April. The city was then sacked and destroyed. A few days later Frederick celebrated his victory at Pavia, where he received the iron crown of Lombardy.

Pope Eugenius III, who had died in July 1153, was succeeded by the aged Anastasius IV, who himself died in the following year. In December the cardinals elected Nicholas Breakspear—the only Englishman who has ever been Pope—who had distinguished himself chiefly by a visit to Scandinavia as papal legate, and who now took the name of Hadrian IV. He appointed as his chancellor Roland, who before being made a cardinal had been, at Bologna, one of the chief canon lawyers of his day. Hadrian soon became a vigorous champion of papal claims in the West, but for the time being his position in Rome was very difficult. The insurgents had found an ally against the Pope's temporal sovereignty in Arnold of Brescia, a pupil of Abelard, who was active in Rome as a preacher of the ideal of ecclesiastical poverty. William I, the new Norman ruler of Sicily, also advanced against the papal territory, as Hadrian refused to recognize him as king.

The Pope therefore had a strong interest in reaching prompt agreement with the king in Germany. In January 1155 he sent envoys to confirm the treaty of Constance, and at the beginning of June he met Frederick at Sutri north of Rome. Here a significant incident took place. Hadrian demanded that the king perform the so-called 'marshal's service' of holding the Pope's stirrup and leading his horse for a certain distance. Frederick at first refused, considering that the action might imply that the kingdom was subordinate to the Papacy. The Curia, however, argued that it was an ancient custom and purely complimentary in character, whereupon the king consented after taking counsel with the German princes.

As the king and Pope proceeded towards Rome they were met by an embassy demanding in arrogant language that Frederick receive the imperial crown from the Roman people and that he pay 5,000 pounds silver for the privilege. Frederick, regarding this as a presumption, retorted that the power and dignity of the Roman Empire had now passed to the Germans. The effect of his reply was that if he were crowned by the Pope it could only be against the opposition of the Roman people. On 18 June, with the German army surrounding St Peter's, a solemn ceremony was held in which Hadrian conferred the imperial crown on Frederick in the presence of the German princes, including Henry the Lion. On the same day, as soon as this became known in Rome, there broke out a general rising which threatened to endanger the Pope and the small German army, as the citizens advanced on the church itself. The insurgents were defeated in a fierce struggle which lasted till after nightfall, and in which Henry the Lion and his troops seem to have delivered a decisive attack on them from the rear.

The Pope rewarded Henry by a special display of favour. Vizelin, who had been gravely ill for many years, died in December 1154. The Duchess Clementia wished him to be succeeded as bishop of Oldenburg by Canon Gerold of Swabia, a noted scholar who was chaplain to the ducal court and director of the school attached to St Blaise's collegiate church in Brunswick. However, Archbishop Hartwig refused to appoint Gerold, regarding the manner of his promotion as uncanonical. At the beginning of 1155, at the duke's wish, Gerold came to Italy and accompanied Henry from Tortona to Rome. During the meeting at Sutri Henry had asked the Pope to consecrate Gerold, but Hadrian hesitated to interfere in the rights of the metropolitan of Bremen. Now, in Rome, he granted Henry's request, however, and performed the consecration on the day after the coronation ceremony.

With the coronation, Barbarossa had achieved the main purpose of his expedition to Italy. According to the Constance agreement he should now have proceeded against the Normans. The circumstances were not unfavourable, as King William was hard pressed by a rebellion of barons in Apulia; but the German army was too small for lengthy operations, and the lay princes urged Frederick to turn back. Henry the Lion in particular was no doubt anxious to return to Saxony after a year's absence and repair the damage caused by Hartwig's machinations. In midsummer Frederick reluctantly decided to break off the campaign. On the return march through Upper Italy he found it impossible to establish peace among the Lombard cities. The German army was endangered by a Veronese attack as it crossed the Adige river and made its way through the narrow gorge; Otto, the count palatine of Wittelsbach, distinguished himself in this fighting. In September 1155 Frederick and Henry the Lion were once again on German soil.

The Emperor's return from Italy ahead of time did not mean that he had abandoned the policy agreed at Constance: there was nothing to prevent it being carried out at a later date. However, the Curia now changed course. As William I of Sicily succeeded in consolidating his position on the mainland, Hadrian felt compelled to make peace with him. By the treaty of Benevento in June 1156 he recognized William as king and invested him with all Norman territory in Sicily and southern Italy. William also obtained far-reaching concessions in the ecclesiastical sphere in Sicily. The treaty of Benevento marked the final conclusion of peace between the Papacy and the Normans. The Curia gave up once and for all its opposition to the existence of a large Norman realm in the Mediterranean area. This put a severe strain on relations between the Emperor and the Pope.

At the same time there was an estrangement between Frederick and

Byzantium. The long negotiations for a marriage between the Emperor and a Byzantine princess broke down at the beginning of 1156. In 1158 Hadrian actually arranged a thirty years' peace between Manuel and William I. Byzantium and the Normans, who had been sworn enemies for generations, drew together in opposition to the Western Empire. The political constellation in the Mediterranean area had radically altered in the space of a few years.

Frederick's main concern after his return to Germany was the Bavarian problem. In September 1155 he had a meeting near Regensburg with his uncle Henry Jasomirgott, who had not joined in the Italian expedition, and endeavoured without success to persuade him to give up Bavaria in return for compensation. A further meeting between the Emperor and Henry Jasomirgott's representatives was also fruitless, although this time the latter's brother, Bishop Otto of Freising, was at great pains to reconcile the two. Then, at a diet at Regensburg in mid-October, Frederick decided to install Henry the Lion as duke of Bavaria. The Bavarian magnates had to do homage and take the oath of fealty to their new ruler, and the citizens of Regensburg had to provide bail as a guarantee of their loyalty.

However, Henry Jasomirgott still regarded himself as the rightful duke. Only after long discussions and a further meeting with the Emperor at the beginning of June 1156 did he agree to waive his claim in return for the creation of a separate duchy of Austria, the Babenbergers' original domain. By this compromise Frederick was at last able to close the long dispute at a diet at Regensburg, attended by many princes. At a solemn ceremony on 8 September—held, out of consideration for the ex-duke, not in the town itself but outside its walls—the Babenberger surrendered seven flags to the king in token of his renunciation of the duchy. The king handed these over to Henry the Lion, thus conferring on him once again the fief of Bavaria. Henry then returned two of the seven, signifying his relinquishment of all claim to the Austrian march. By the royal decision, the march and the counties that had belonged to it from of old were elevated into a duchy which was granted in fee to Henry Jasomirgott and his wife Theodora and to their descendants in the male and female line.

An important document of 17 September 1156 granted special privileges to the ducal couple. If they should die without issue, they could bequeath the duchy at will. Jurisdiction within the duchy was to be exercised only with the duke's consent. His feudal duties were confined to attending diets in Bavaria and taking part in military expeditions to neighbouring territory such as Hungary. This famous *privilegium minus*—so called to distinguish it from the *privilegium majus*, a fourteenth-century forgery—is not only the birth certificate of the duchy of Austria, but also an important landmark in the process of constitutional development in Germany from the old type of tribal duchy to the new territorial princely state. Frederick's diplomacy had achieved a solution which satisfied Henry the Lion's claims while at the same time avoiding injury to the Babenberger's rank and prestige.

A part may have been played in these negotiations by Reinald of Dassel, who was the king's chancellor from the spring of 1156 onwards and in July of that year stayed at Henry the Lion's court in Brunswick. We do not know the reason for his journey, but it is likely that the Bavarian question was discussed. The descendant of a prominent Saxon line of counts from the region of Einback, Reinald had enjoyed an intellectual and clerical education in France, though without being deeply affected by thenew trends of the age. His world was still that of the great imperial bishops of the tenth and eleventh century, who regarded service to the Empire as their supreme duty and saw no conflict between their spiritual and secular obligations. He had been dean of Hildesheim before entering the imperial chancery, and was now the Emperor's chief adviser and the principal statesman of the Empire. Extremely able but often headstrong, he was not an *éminence grise* as has sometimes been suggested, but exercised a considerable influence over Frederick's policy for about a decade until his death in 1167. We know little of his relations with Henry the Lion during those years. On general questions of imperial and church policy they probably saw eye to eye at the outset, but it soon appeared that Henry did not approve of Reinald's increasingly brusque methods. After the Emperor made Reinald archbishop of Cologne in 1159, the chancellor and Duke Henry clashed violently over territorial policy in Westphalia in the first half of the 1160s.

Henry returned to Saxony from the Regensburg diet in the autumn of 1156, and was soon involved again in the dispute over the Danish succession. The settlement pronounced by Frederick at the diet of Merseburg in 1152 had not brought peace to the country. Sven, it soon appeared, was not equal to his royal duties. Already in 1153 he had to seek help from the duke of Saxony against the Slavs who were plundering the Danish coasts. He hoped for military aid in return for a payment of 1500 pounds in silver, but Henry was too much occupied by the Bavarian dispute to render assistance. Sven's position was further weakened by an unsuccessful campaign against Sweden in the winter of 1153-4 and by the unpopularity of his government. His rivals Knut and Valdemar joined against him, aided by the powerful Archbishop Eskil of Lund. In 1154 Sven fled from Denmark and took refuge with his father-in-law, the Margrave Conrad of Meissen. Only after two years' exile did he attempt to recover his kingdom by force of arms.

For this purpose he sought and obtained the aid of Henry the Lion. Abandoning his previous policy of non-intervention in the dispute, Henry advanced into Jutland towards the end of 1156 with a large army including some Slav auxiliaries. Apart from Sven's promise of a further large sum of money, Henry was no doubt acting with the consent of Frederick I, who since 1154 had to a great extent left him a free hand in northern Germany. Moreover Hartwig of Bremen and other Saxon princes had, since Henry's return to Saxony, urged him to support Sven's cause. The frontier rampart of the Danewerk fell into the army's hands, perhaps through treachery or bribery, and the town of Schleswig was also captured. Henry levied on it a sum which indemnified him for the campaign, while Sven inflicted severe injury on the city's trade by plundering Russian ships in the harbour which were laden with furs. Henry and Sven continued their advance, capturing the town of Ripen and reaching the vicinity of Hadersleben. Their success was not lasting, however, as, contrary to Sven's promises, the army found no local support. Knut, Sven's adversary, seems even to have had friends among the Slavs in Henry's army. To avoid danger, Henry in January 1157 returned to Saxony after taking hostages from the two captured towns.

Henry took no further direct part in the Danish dispute. During the next few months Sven decided to invade Denmark with a Wendish fleet, whereupon Henry commanded the Slavs of Wagria and Mecklenburg to assist the enterprise. In August 1157 Knut was murdered by Sven at a meeting of the three rival claimants which took place at Roskilde. Valdemar escaped, raised an army in Jutland, and in October inflicted a crushing defeat on Sven on the Gratheheide near Viborg. Sven fled and was killed; Valdemar's claim was now generally recognized in Denmark, and the dispute over the succession thus came to an end.

As Sven was a vassal of the king of Germany, his death made it necessary for Frederick to take a hand in the country's affairs. Valdemar in 1158 sent an embassy requesting Frederick to confirm the succession and invest him with the kingdom. Frederick, who was engaged in preparations for his second expedition to Italy, agreed on condition that on his return Valdemar would do homage and receive the kingdom of Denmark at his hands.

The understanding between Frederick and Henry the Lion which characterized imperial policy during these years was seen in another important case, that of the king's action against Poland in 1157. During the reign of Conrad III, Duke Władysław II, who was married to a stepsister of the German king, was expelled from Poland by his brother Bolesław IV. In 1146 Conrad had unsuccessfully tried to reinstate his brother-in-law. In the summer of 1157, as Bolesław and his other brothers refused to do homage for Poland and pay the customary annual tribute of 500 marks, the Emperor decided on an invasion. He set out at the beginning of August from Halle on the Saale with a large army including Henry the Lion, Albert the Bear, and numerous other secular and ecclesiastical princes, and advanced rapidly through Silesia to the neighbourhood of Posen (Poznań). Bolesław was obliged to submit and do homage; he promised to pay large fines to the Emperor and the other princes and to provide 300 knights for the next expedition to Rome. He also agreed in advance to accept arbitration between himself and his brother Władysław.

The Polish campaign marked the successful conclusion of Barbarossa's first five years of Empire. In the same year Frederick's uncle, Bishop Otto of Freising, began to compile his *Gesta Friderici* at the Emperor's request; he was able to say that affairs had improved since Frederick came to the throne and that his deeds had increased the prestige of the Roman Empire. In this success Henry the Lion played no small part. The Hohenstaufen–Welf compromise had in a few years proved of great benefit to both sides.

In the autumn of 1157, after his return from Poland, the Emperor made his way to Burgundy. He had been divorced in 1153 from his first wife, Adela of Vohburg, and, the plan for a marriage to a Byzantine princess having come to nothing, he had married Beatrice, heiress of the county of Upper Burgundy, in the summer of 1156. Henry the Lion was present at the wedding celebrations, held with great pomp at Würzburg in June. The Emperor and his bride then proceeded to Besançon to receive the homage of the Burgundian nobles.

There an incident occurred which throws a vivid light on the growing tension between the Curia and the German court. At the beginning of the year Pope Hadrian had appointed Archbishop Eskil of Lund primate of the Swedish church. Eskil had been taken prisoner by bandits in Burgundy on his way back from Rome, and despite papal requests Frederick had done nothing to secure his liberation. A group of legates headed by Cardinal Roland now appeared at Besançon with a letter complaining violently of the Emperor's behaviour. In it, Hadrian took the opportunity to raise the basic question of the relationship between Pope and Emperor. He reminded Frederick of how readily he had conferred on him the imperial crown and complied with his other wishes. He then continued: 'Nor do we regret that we fulfilled in all respects the ardent desires of your heart; nay, if your highness had received still greater benefits [*beneficia*] at our hands [. . .] we would have rejoiced, not without reason.'

The ambiguous term *beneficia* was certainly used on purpose. In everyday language it was a general term for favour or benefit; in church law it meant a living, while in feudal terms it was synonymous with 'fief'. Reinald, translating the letter aloud to the German nobles, no doubt intentionally gave the word its feudal interpretation; this provoked a storm of indignation, which was increased when one of the cardinals exclaimed: 'From whom then does he hold the Empire, if not from our lord the Pope?' Otto of Wittelsbach drew his sword upon the legates, and the Emperor had to intervene personally to prevent violence. Documents were found in the legates' baggage revealing the Curia's intention to interfere in German church matters; the legates were obliged to return home, and appeals and journeys of German clerics to Rome were for the time being forbidden.

In a circular letter describing these events to the German princes, Frederick energetically rebutted the idea that the Empire was a papal fief. He himself was king and Emperor by God's will and the princes' choice. Hadrian for his part wrote to the German bishops to enlist their support, but in a collective reply at the beginning of 1158 they espoused the Emperor's viewpoint and urged the Pope to be conciliatory.

Henry the Lion, who at this time made his first long stay in his newly acquired duchy of Bavaria, did not attend the diet at Besançon but soon took a hand in the conflict between Pope and Emperor. He sent envoys to Rome, probably before the end of 1157, to ask the Curia for privileges on behalf of the newly founded bishopric of Ratzeburg and the church at Ranshofen on the Inn, which was under the protection of the duke of Bavaria. However, the envoys' principal task was no doubt to persuade the Pope to yield in his quarrel with the Emperor. Faced with universal opposition to his action in Germany, Hadrian decided to give way. In a letter to Frederick in which he expressly mentioned Henry the Lion's attempt to mediate, he explained that he had meant *beneficium* only in the sense of *bonum factum* or kindness. Provost Gerhoch of Reichersberg, who was always well informed of contemporary events, praised Henry's efforts as a mediator in a letter he wrote to the duke soon afterwards.

This episode for the first time brought Henry to some extent into conflict with Reinald of Dassel, who had gone with Otto of Wittelsbach to Upper Italy to consolidate the Emperor's position and prepare the way for his second Italian campaign. In their report in the spring of 1158 both men urged the Emperor not to give in to the Curia or let anyone persuade him to give a friendly reception to the Pope's envoys; this has all the appearance of a warning against Henry the Lion's advice.

Cardinals Henry and Hyacinth, bearing the Pope's letter to Frederick in the spring of 1158, were attacked and taken prisoner in the valley of the upper Adige by the local Counts Frederick and Henry of Eppan, who refused to set them free until a brother of Hyacinth took his place as a hostage. Henry the Lion, however, was not prepared to tolerate such an act of violence against papal legates in his dominions. He took punitive action against the two counts, probably in the course of a visit to Upper Italy in 1159, forcing them to release the prisoners and pay compensation.

The Emperor received the two legates at a diet in Augsburg at Whitsuntide in June 1158. Although not all issues between him and the Pope were satisfactorily settled, peace was restored for the time being by the Pope's letter of excuse. Henry the Lion, who had played a decisive part in the reconciliation, was present at the diet, as were the princes who were to accompany Frederick on his second Italian expedition.

As the Emperor expected his absence to be a fairly long one, he endeavoured to compose differences at home before setting out. A violent dispute had broken out in Bavaria between Duke Henry and

Bishop Otto of Freising. In the autumn of 1157 the duke had broken up the market and toll station near Föhring on the main trade route between Salzburg and Swabia, which had for many years belonged to the see of Freising, and had destroyed the bridge over the Isar. The market, mint, and customs station were removed about a mile upstream to an old monastic settlement named Munichen, where a new bridge was built to convey the produce of the salt mines.

The significance of this measure will be discussed in the general context of Henry's policy in Bavaria. Otto of Freising complained to the Emperor against the duke's illegal act. On 14 June in Augsburg Frederick pronounced a decision involving a compromise between the disputants, both of whom were his close relations. The duke's conduct was sanctioned, but he had to allow the bishop a third of the customs and mint receipts and to permit him to share in the administration of these regalia.

In Saxony too the Emperor tried to establish a firm peace between the duke and his old adversary, Archbishop Hartwig of Bremen. After returning from the first Italian expedition Henry had gone to Bremen in the autumn of 1155 to administer justice, in accordance with ancient custom, on 1 November, the day of 'St Willehad's market', in his capacity as advocate over the archbishopric. He had inflicted severe punishment on the inhabitants of the Rüstringen district, who had shown hostility towards him: their merchants attending the Bremen market were taken prisoner and their wares confiscated. Since at the same time an imperial official was engaged in sequestrating the estates of which the archbishop had been deprived at Roncaglia, the duke was able to gain possession of some of these, including the city and archbishopric itself. This was the nadir of Hartwig's power: according to the Stade annals, Henry 'rated him no higher than a chaplain'. At this time also Henry expelled Bovo, an official whom the archbishop had put in charge of the colonists in the Weser marshland.

Fearful of losing all influence in his see, Hartwig again sought the favour of the Emperor and duke. He first came to terms with Bishop Gerold of Oldenburg, who recognized him as his metropolitan. When Henry supported Sven's claim to the Danish throne in 1156 the archbishop approached the duke in the hope of recovering influence on church affairs in Denmark. From the beginning of 1158 onwards he also stayed repeatedly at the Emperor's court and gradually regained the latter's favour. In the spring Frederick conferred on him several important privileges, the effect of which was to place the Bremen church under imperial protection and to confirm the rights and possessions granted to it by Frederick's predecessors, in particular the metropolitan authority in Scandinavia.

The diet of Augsburg was intended to seal the peace settlement between the duke and the archbishop. The Emperor enjoined both of them, in the event of further disputes, not to take the law into their own hands but to accept his judgement. He also granted the archbishop exemption from the duty to take part in royal campaigns and perform other feudal services. While all causes of tension between Henry and Hartwig were not yet removed, the Emperor could at any rate hope that they would not attempt to solve their differences by force of arms.

After the Augsburg diet the Emperor set out for Italy with a large army. Henry the Lion did not take part in this second expedition from the outset, being fully occupied with affairs in north-eastern Saxony. The expedition, undertaken to restore imperial power in Italy, unexpectedly kept Frederick out of Germany for about four years, until October 1162. His purpose was to settle all questions that he had not been able to regulate on his first, short Italian expedition, and above all to recover the rights and possessions in Upper and Central Italy that the Empire had lost in recent decades, especially to the cities. Reinald of Dassel and the Count Palatine Otto of Wittelsbach had prepared the ground by skilful diplomacy during their stay in Italy. Several communes had sworn oaths of loyalty to them, and when the imperial army entered Italy it obtained further support. Only Milan continued to resist, but was subdued at the beginning of September after a siege of several weeks; all its citizens were then forced to swear fealty to the Emperor. The city had to pay a large indemnity and to surrender its regalia. It retained the right to elect its consuls, but they had to be confirmed in office by the Emperor.

After the defeat of Milan Frederick could proceed to the political and legal reorganization of Upper Italy. This was the work of a great diet held in the first half of November on the fields of Roncaglia, where Frederick on his first Italian expedition had met with representatives of the legal school of Bologna which was then coming into prominence. He now set up a commission consisting of leading jurists from Bologna and twenty-eight representatives of the communes, to define the extent of the Emperor's regalia. The commission declared that they included rights over duchies, margraviates, and counties, the right to appoint consuls, authority over communications and tolls, coinage and market rights, the creation of palatinates, and the whole complex of imperial and royal possessions. All local lordships and cities were to renounce these regalia unless they could point to specific grants in support of their claim. To these decrees were added other laws, chiefly concerning imperial jurisdiction. Finally the diet proclaimed a general truce (*Landfrieden*) and a feudal law reinforcing the provisions of 1154.

Although the Roncaglia decrees showed the influence of Roman law in some respects, in essence their effect was only to restore the royal power as it had existed in Italy in the eleventh century. The customs that had developed in the last few generations were largely reversed, resulting in a tremendous increase in the power of the Hohenstaufen monarchy. Rahewin, Otto of Freising's notary, who continued his master's *Chronicle* after the latter's death in 1158, and who is an important source for the events of this year, estimated the annual revenue from these regalia, to be directly administered by the Empire, at 30,000 silver marks, an enormous sum for the time.

The cities initially accepted these provisions, which would have meant the end of their self-government and the liberties they had acquired over the centuries. Their conception of law was in fact contrary to the Emperor's, and the execution of the Roncaglia decrees was bound to lead to further sharp clashes between him and the North Italian communes.

Immediately after the diet, imperial envoys were sent to the cities to define the extent of the regalia and to appoint rectors or *podestàs* whom the Emperor could trust. Several cities which had previously sided with Frederick, such as Pavia, Cremona, Piacenza, and Lodi, showed obedience, but the envoys met with strong resistance in Milan and its small ally Crema, which were therefore placed under the ban of the Empire.

Again the matter was put to the test of arms. Early in 1159 Frederick, who had already disbanded part of his army, called upon Henry the Lion, Welf VI, and other German princes to supply military aid. Before complying, Henry endeavoured to secure peace on the north-western border of Saxony. He met Valdemar I of Denmark and concluded a treaty of friendship with him, and exacted an oath from the Slav princes that they would undertake no hostilities against the Saxons and Danes during his absence. Around Whitsun, at the end of May, Henry set out for Italy at the head of 1,200 knights;

he was accompanied by Count Adolf of Holstein and other Saxon and Bavarian magnates, and took under his escort the Empress Beatrice, who was bringing reinforcements on her own account. On the way through Upper Italy he destroyed the castle of Peschiera near Garda, whose garrison had attacked his army.

On 20 July Henry and Beatrice reached Crema, to which Frederick had laid siege shortly before. Despite the Emperor's military superiority the small city held out for nearly seven months. Henry's strong force took a decisive part in the fighting, which was conducted on both sides with relentless vigour and cruelty. The Emperor caused prisoners to be hung in baskets from the great siege-towers that were moved up to the city, so that they fell victim to their fellow-citizens' weapons, while the townsfolk executed their prisoners on the city walls in the sight of all. Not until the end of January 1160 did their resistance cease. They negotiated terms of surrender with the Emperor through Henry the Lion and the patriarch of Aquileia, but the Emperor exacted a heavy punishment: the townsfolk escaped with their bare lives, but the city was razed to the ground. Meanwhile the battle for Milan had begun. Here again Duke Henry took part, advancing boldly to the very gates of the city, but it soon appeared that Milan was even harder to overcome than its small neighbour.

During the fighting in Lombardy a new situation had arisen in Rome. The antagonism between Frederick I and Hadrian IV was intensified by the fact that the regalia legislation applied to Tuscany as well as Lombardy and did not even stop short at papal territory. The Pope's complaints were met by recriminations over the treaty of Benevento. Hadrian entered into relations with the Lombard communes, while Frederick approached the Roman city authorities through Otto of Wittelsbach. Such was the tense situation when Hadrian died on 1 September 1159.

For some time there had been divergent policies in the college of cardinals, and these now produced a disputed election to the Papacy. A majority who had supported Hadrian's policy towards the Emperor now elected the prime mover of that policy, the chancellor Roland. The pro-imperial minority, mostly members of noble families, voted for Cardinal Octavian, a Monticelli and hence a kinsman of the Hohenstaufen: his election was supported by Otto of Wittelsbach, who was near Rome at the time. Riots broke out at the enthronement of the new Pope; Octavian seized the papal mantle from his opponent, placed it on himself and was consecrated as

Victor IV. Roland had to leave the city together with his supporters, and was consecrated under the name of Alexander III.

It was imperative for Frederick to put an end to the schism, which threatened his whole policy of restoring imperial rights in Italy. Outwardly he observed neutrality, while secretly favouring Pope Victor, since Alexander would clearly follow the same policy he had pursued as Hadrian's chancellor. Cardinal Boso relates in his life of Alexander III that Frederick was so enraged by Alexander's election when it was announced to him by papal legates in the camp before Crema that he wanted to have the legates hanged, and was only dissuaded from this sacrilegious act by Henry the Lion and Welf VI. However, there is no confirmation of this report, which, like other statements by Boso, is tendentious and improbable.

The dispute over the papal election was to be settled in a manner appropriate to Frederick's conception of the Empire. As advocate of the Roman church he claimed the right to summon a general council for the purpose, which was to meet at Pavia in January 1160. The question, however, was whether the Emperor's claim to exercise authority in church matters would still be acknowledged throughout the Western world. Victor IV agreed to attend the council, but Alexander III refused on the ground that, as he was Pope, his cause could be judged by no one.

Owing to the siege of Crema the council could not assemble till the beginning of February. It was then clear that it could not be regarded as fully representative of the West. Only about fifty archbishops and bishops from Germany and the pro-imperial Italian territories were present, together with envoys from the kings of England, France, Denmark, Bohemia, and Hungary; the French, English, and south Italian clergy were scarcely represented at all. After a short debate Victor IV was declared the rightful Pope, and the imperial ban was proclaimed against Alexander III for refusing to appear at the council. Henry the Lion, who attended with other German princes, concurred in these decisions. Alexander III retorted by excommunicating the Emperor and his chief advisers. Western Christendom was thus split by a schism which lasted eighteen years. The quarrel with the Papacy gave its stamp to Frederick's policy for a long time to come and obliged him to find new ways of achieving his 'reformatio imperii'.

Alexander III's position in the struggle was by no means unfavourable. From the outset he had on his side a majority of the cardinals, the kingdom of Sicily, and many of the North Italian communes. He was recognized by the peripheral Western states of Hungary, Spain, Norway, and Ireland, as well as by the Levantine rulers, and he sent an embassy to the Emperor Manuel. Above all he scored a great success in the summer of 1160, when the rulers and clergy of England and France declared for him. Victor IV could claim as his supporters only the countries dependent on the Emperor: Germany, Denmark, Poland, and imperial Italy. Even the German church was not unanimous in his support. One of the chief ecclesiastical princes, Archbishop Eberhard of Salzburg, took Alexander's side, while his subordinate clergy either followed suit or remained neutral. However, this attitude on the part of the Bavarian clergy did not influence their duke, who continued to take the Emperor's side after the council of Pavia, though for some years he took no steps against the Alexandrine party in Bavaria. Welf VI, on the other hand, soon established contact with Alexander.

In Saxony the Pavia decisions gave Henry an opportunity to move against his old opponent Bishop Ulrich of Halberstadt. Ulrich, like Hartwig of Bremen, had been deprived of regalian rights at Roncaglia in 1154 but had subsequently regained the imperial favour. On the return journey from a pilgrimage to Jerusalem, probably in the winter of 1159–60, he met Eberhard of Salzburg and seems to have openly espoused the cause of Alexander III. This gave Henry the Lion a welcome pretext to institute ecclesiastical proceedings against Ulrich. In the early summer of 1160 Victor IV sent Cardinal Gerard as his legate to Saxony. In Halberstadt Gerard deposed and excommunicated the bishop, who was still abroad and was given no opportunity to answer the charges. The sources emphasize that Henry the Lion was the instigator of this highly uncanonical proceeding, which was no doubt endorsed by the Emperor. Dean Gero, a loyal servant of the duke's, became the new bishop of Halberstadt.

Soon after Ulrich's deposition, at the end of July 1160, a great assembly of princes was held at Erfurt. Besides Reinald of Dassel, the archbishops of Trier and Magdeburg and several other bishops, it was attended by Henry the Lion, the young Duke Frederick of Swabia, Albert the Bear, and others. Probably at Reinald's initiative, the princes swore to give military aid to the Emperor, who had just resumed the fight against Milan. Later that summer, as the Slavs had broken their promise to keep the peace during the duke's absence, Henry and Valdemar of Denmark conducted a successful campaign against the Obodrites; then, towards the end of the year, Henry prepared to march southward.

He reached Como by the end of January 1161, and there had a meeting with the Emperor. Though the sources do not expressly say so, we may assume that he again supplied a military contingent as agreed at Erfurt. Despite strong reinforcements from Germany, Barbarossa's siege of Milan was long and difficult, as the city was heavily fortified. The intensity of the struggle is illustrated by the story that the Emperor took a vow not to withdraw from the city walls until it was captured. In case he should be killed in battle, he nominated as his successor Frederick of Swabia, the son of Conrad III, and after him Henry the Lion. The fact that Barbarossa, who was as yet childless, envisaged Henry as his successor shows clearly how close an accord there was between them.

At the beginning of July Henry was still in the camp before Milan, but soon afterwards he returned to Germany and took no further part in the siege. Despite its desperate resistance the city was forced to capitulate at the beginning of March 1162 and to accept humiliating terms. The famous *carroccio*, the proud symbol of municipal freedom, was laid at the Emperor's feet. The city walls were torn down so that the imperial army might make its ceremonial entry. As at Crema two years before, terrible punishment was meted out to the citizens. At the request of Milan's hostile neighbours the city was destroyed and its inhabitants settled in surrounding villages. The other Lombard communes now surrendered to the Emperor.

The overthrow of the city which had been the champion of resistance throughout Upper Italy made a profound impression in the West. When Duke Henry and Archbishop Hartwig of Bremen, shortly afterwards, granted two privileges to the see of Ratzeburg, the documents referred to 'the Emperor's brilliant victory over the famous city of Milan'.

Faced with the Emperor's superior power, Pope Alexander III was constrained to leave Italy. In April 1162 he came to France with the purpose of arbitrating between Louis VII and the latter's vassal, Henry II of England. The Emperor for his part saw the Anglo–French dispute as a means of ending the schism in the church. Accordingly he broke off preparations for a campaign against the Normans in Italy and negotiated an agreement with Louis whereby the two rulers and the two Popes were to meet on 29 August at Saint-Jean-de-Losne on the frontier bridge over the Saône between

Burgundy and France, in order to decide on equal terms between the two claimants to the Papacy. However, under pressure from the French clergy Louis began to hesitate, especially as Alexander refused to submit to the proposed arbitration. The meeting failed to take place, as the Emperor did not reach the Saône from Italy till the evening of the appointed day. A date three weeks later was agreed, but meanwhile, at the beginning of September, Frederick prejudged the issue by holding a synod at Saint-Jean-de-Losne at which Victor IV was once again formally recognized and Alexander III excommunicated.

Henry the Lion, who was in Bavaria during the summer, was present at the synod, as was Valdemar I of Denmark. The latter took the oath of fealty to the Emperor as he had promised years before and received his kingdom as a fief; he also reaffirmed his recognition of Victor IV. The firm loyalty of the king of Denmark to the Emperor's policy continued in subsequent years and helped to strengthen Henry the Lion's position in the Baltic area.

The proceedings at Saint-Jean-de-Losne deepened the rift between Frederick I and the supporters of Alexander III. Reinald of Dassel gave deep offence by declaring that the 'provincial kinglets' (reguli) of the West had no right to a voice in determining the papal question. The meeting, which was intended to be a triumph for the Emperor's policy, ended in failure. Frederick returned to Germany in the autumn, his purpose unaccomplished.

At the end of November Frederick held a diet at Constance which was attended by Henry the Lion and at which the latter's marriage to Clementia of Zähringen, which had lasted about fifteen years, was dissolved. The couple had a son, who died of an accident in tender years, and probably two daughters. One of these, Gertrude, some years later married Conrad III's son, Frederick IV of Swabia, on whom Barbarossa had conferred that duchy in 1152. The other daughter, whose name is not certain but may have been Richenza, was shortly afterwards betrothed to Knut, the son of Valdemar of Denmark, but died young.

Henry the Lion's lack of male heirs at the time was no doubt a reason for his divorce; as frequently in the Middle Ages, the pretext for annulment was that the couple were too closely related. However, political reasons probably also played a part. The old antagonism between Hohenstaufen and Zähringen, which was partly assuaged at the beginning of Frederick I's reign, had flared up again as the two families' territorial interests on the upper Rhine and in Burgundy once more conflicted. In 1158 Frederick persuaded Henry to make over to him Clementia's extensive dowry of estates around Badenweiler in Swabia, in exchange for several imperial strongholds in the southern Harz area.

Henry's divorce from Clementia marked the end of his long alliance with the Zähringer. The initiative for this step may have come from the Emperor himself; in any case the duke acted in full agreement with Frederick. As in the major issues of imperial and ecclesiastical policy, a close understanding between the Emperor and the duke can be observed in these years as regards territorial issues in Germany.

4

Policy in Nordalbingia
and the Baltic

FOR about a decade, from the time of Frederick I's accession in 1152 to the end of his second Italian expedition, Henry the Lion's person and resources were largely devoted to the service of the Empire. During those years he participated actively, by deeds or by counsel, in almost every important undertaking by the Emperor. In so doing he became acquainted with the forces and tensions that governed political affairs in the West at that time.

However, Henry's firm support for the Staufen monarchy was not given at the expense of his tasks in Saxony and Bavaria. Thanks to the understanding he had reached with Frederick I and to the latter's assistance, he was in a better position to pursue his interests than he had been in Conrad III's time, when conflict with the Crown repeatedly prevented him from building up a strong ducal power in Saxony.

The change was felt above all in Nordalbingia, the area in which Henry had been especially active in the first years of his rule. The decision of the diet of Goslar in June 1154, conferring on him the right to invest the Nordalbingian bishops, did not merely resolve the dispute with Hartwig of Bremen in his favour. The fact that royal powers were thus delegated to him and that he could in future take action in the area as a representative of the Empire was bound considerably to reinforce his position *vis-à-vis* the local wielders of authority, both German and Slav.

In the summer of 1154, soon after the Goslar diet, Henry—as we have briefly mentioned—took a decisive step towards refounding the see of Ratzeburg by installing a bishop there. He chose Evermod, provost of the important Premonstratensian canonry of St Mary's in Magdeburg, in order that church work in Nordalbingia should receive the benefit of the wide experience gained by the Order in recent decades in missionary work east of the middle course of the Elbe. Evermod was no doubt recommended to Henry by Archbishop Wichmann of Magdeburg, who was present at the diet of Goslar and by whom he was consecrated.

Count Henry of Ratzeburg placed the island in the Ratzeburger See near the castle at Evermod's disposal as a residence for the bishop and canons and a site for the new church. He made over to the duke from his own fief 300 hides of land for the endowment of the diocese, and made an agreement with the bishop concerning tithes. These, as was usual in colonial territory, were to be divided between the church and the count as the wielder of secular power: the diocesan tithe was the bishop's property, but he granted half of it to the count as a fief, except for the tithe on the 300 hides. The foundation of the see was sanctioned by Hadrian IV in a *privilegium majus* granted at the duke's request to the bishop and chapter a few years later, in January 1158. The Pope extended his protection to the diocese, which included the Polabian territory and the Sadelbande district towards the Elbe, and confirmed its rights and possessions. He sanctioned the Augustinian rule for the chapter and gave it the right to elect its bishop, though this for the time being was without effect in view of the duke's right of investiture.

Despite all this support from the duke, the count and the Pope, Evermod's task was not an easy one. The Christianization of the Polabian territory was in its first stages. The bishop took up residence in the monastery on the Georgsberg on the western shore of the lake, which had been founded in the eleventh century but destroyed in the great Wendish uprising of 1066 and only rebuilt when the county was established. From here Evermod ruled the diocese for a considerable time. There was some delay before the diocese received its endowment of land: this may have taken place during an expedition of the duke's into Obodrite territory in 1158, which took him through the county of Ratzeburg. The church's principal estate was that of Boitin east of the Ratzeburger See, together with scattered possessions in other parts of the diocese.

Conditions in the see of Oldenburg were scarcely more favourable. While Vizelin was still alive (he died in 1154), Count Adolf had promised to follow the example of the count of Ratzeburg and make over 300 hides to the duke out of his own fief, but here again the transfer did not take place at once.

The difficulties encountered by Gerold, the new bishop of Oldenburg, on his return from Italy are vividly described by Helmold of Bosau, who accompanied him on his first visitation in the

winter of 1155–6. The feast of the Epiphany (6 January) was celebrated at Oldenburg, the bishop's former residence, but the town
was practically empty. Gerold held a service in a small wooden chapel
in the icy cold, but the Slav population of the surrounding area failed
to appear except for Prince Pribislav, who invited Gerold to visit him
and partake of a twenty-course banquet. In the course of their further
journey the bishop and his suite destroyed the sacred grove of the
Slav god Prove, but were nevertheless received hospitably, a few days
later, by another Wendish chief. On this occasion they saw captive
Danish priests with the fetters and instruments of torture that had
been used on them; Gerold attempted to secure their release, but in
vain.

Next Sunday the bishop, preaching in the market-place of Lübeck,
urged the assembled Slavs to renounce their idolatry and become
Christians. In reply Pribislav complained bitterly of the almost
unendurable oppression of his people by the new rulers. In the past
year alone they had had to pay 1,000 marks to the duke and hundreds
to the count, and every day fresh burdens were imposed. If this went
on the Slavs would be driven from their own territory and would
have to live as pirates. If, however, they were granted the same rights
as the Saxons in regard to their possessions and revenues, they would
gladly become Christians, build churches, and pay tithes.

Shortly afterwards Niklot made an even clearer reply to Henry the
Lion, who held a diet at the Ertheneburg, the site of an old Elbe
crossing to the west of the subsequent settlement of Lauenburg.
When Henry, at Gerold's instance, urged the Slav princes to accept
Christianity, Niklot answered: 'Let the God in heaven be your God
and you shall be ours—that is enough for us. You worship him, and
we will worship you.'

Helmold's account of these events, and the words he ascribes to the
Obodrite ruler, are a severe criticism of the behaviour of the German
princes, whose rapacious demands for tribute did much to impede
the work of the Christian mission. Helmold speaks even more
severely of Henry's policy when he states that all the duke's
campaigns in Wendish territory from his youth upwards were
undertaken not for the sake of religion but for money. The harsh
pressure inflicted on the Slavs alienated them from Christianity, a fact
of which the missionaries were well aware.

Gerold as yet had no economic basis for fruitful work in his
diocese. He applied to the ducal court in Brunswick but obtained

little assistance, as Henry's participation in the Emperor's first Italian expedition had involved him in heavy expense. Count Adolf had still not made over the 300 hides to the diocese. Only when Gerold complained of this to the duke did the count cede the locality of Eutin and a village on the Eutiner See; at the same time he enlarged the episcopal estate at Bosau and added some further land near Oldenburg. The total area, however, amounted to only 100 hides, as it included marsh and forest and was surveyed with a measure smaller than the standard one. The duke ordered it to be reassessed, but this was not done for some time. A decade later Helmold noted with resignation that the diocese was still not in possession of its full endowment.

The core of the bishopric was the area between the Plöner See and the Eutiner See. Gerold made his residence not in Bosau but in Eutin, where he founded a market and built himself a house. The progress of German settlement in Wagria also enabled him to press on with church-building. The canons of Segeberg, who had taken refuge at Högersdorf after the destruction of their foundation, were able to return to Segeberg east of the Trave, where an imposing church was built in the next few decades. Gerold also began to build a large new church at Oldenburg, and in other parts of his bishopric he created new parishes with the count's assistance.

Count Adolf's chief reason for promoting colonization and missionary activity in Wagria was that whereas in the original Holstein territory his power was disputed by the local nobility, the new lands provided him with a political and economic power base. His good relations with the duke were also an important adjunct to his position. Only once, as far as can be seen, was there a serious conflict between him and the duke, to whom he otherwise proved a loyal vassal.

Adolf's trading centre of Lübeck, with its favourable situation on the lower Trave, soon developed in importance and attracted many merchants from Bardowick, the old market town and trading post on the north-east border of Saxony, which was the duke's property. In the same way the duke's saltworks at Lüneburg suffered serious competition from those established by Adolf at Oldesloe, south-west of Lübeck. On this account, probably in the early 1150s, Henry demanded that the count cede to him half the revenue from the Lübeck market and the Oldesloe saltworks. When Adolf refused, the duke resorted to violence in his customary way: he ordered the

Lübeck market to be closed except for trade in foodstuffs, and had the Oldesloe saltpits filled in.

The market ban at Lübeck was probably not strictly enforced, and the merchants stayed on there in the hope that it would be lifted. However, when the town was destroyed by fire in 1157 they appealed to the duke to provide them with another settlement, as the ban and the fire had made it impossible to go on living there. Henry once again asked the count to give them the area between the Trave and the Wakenitz, but Adolf again refused. Thereupon in the autumn of that year Henry decided to found a new town in his own land of Ratzeburg on the Wakenitz, to be called Löwenstadt. We do not know its exact location, which may have been near the present-day village of Herrenburg south-east of Lübeck.

However, the new locality was quite unsuited for trading. It had none of the natural protection afforded by the river island known as the Lübecker Werder, and the Wakenitz was too shallow for ships of any size. In reply to a further insistent demand from the duke, Count Adolf now agreed to make over to him the stronghold of Lübeck and its peninsula in return for substantial compensation, probably of a financial kind.

The new town of Lübeck no doubt dates from the spring of 1159. Henry the Lion himself spent only a short while in the area at that time: as we have seen, he set out at the end of May for Italy, to join the Emperor at the siege of Crema. Accordingly he confined himself to giving the first orders for the rebuilding of the town and the revival of commerce. Only some years later did he formally bestow a municipal charter, the terms of which were negotiated with the confederation of citizens.

In order to make town planning possible on a broad scale, the duke ordered the local peasantry to clear the dense forest that covered the ridge of high ground along the peninsula. The citizens were granted an area on both banks of the Trave for their communal use. They themselves no doubt decided upon the layout of the streets and built their houses and the first churches, with the aid of craftsmen from the older parts of the Empire. In the centre of the new city was the spacious market-place with the merchants' stalls, and the Marienkirche beginning to rise on its northern side.

The rapid development of the new town, however, was only possible because of a large accession of population as compared to the original city. Among the newcomers were probably German merchants from Schleswig, whose trade had suffered badly during the conflict over the Danish succession. The duke may have encountered these merchants for the first time when he moved into Schleswig in 1156, when the ships in harbour were destroyed by Sven of Denmark's troops. Much more important, however, was the influx of enterprising long-distance traders from Westphalia and the Rhineland, amply provided with capital, who soon recognized the economic advantages offered by the city on the Trave.

The duke for his part did all he could to encourage commerce. According to Helmold he sent envoys to the towns and kingdoms of the north—Denmark, Sweden, Norway, and Russia—offering peace and free trading opportunities in his city of Lübeck. We also hear of commercial treaties with King Knut Eriksson of Sweden, Duke Birger of that country, and probably also an unidentified prince of Novgorod. These treaties have unfortunately not survived, and we do not know when they were signed. The upsurge of Lübeck was also much benefited by the exemption of its citizens from tolls throughout the duchy of Saxony, except for the old ducal toll at the Ertheneburg.

For the duke himself the fiscal aspect was the main feature of these arrangements. As lord of the city he enjoyed the revenue from market and tolls and from the mint established there. This soon amounted to a very large sum, as is seen from the fact that as early as 1162 Henry made a grant to the chapter of Ratzeburg of twenty-seven marks a year, a substantial figure for those days, out of the Lübeck customs receipts.

The duke's rights in the city were administered by his bailiff (*Vogt*), who resided in the castle that had formerly belonged to the count. The first of these officials whom we encounter by name is one Reinold, in 1161. He is also referred to as count of Lübeck, but there can be no doubt that he was a *ministerialis* of the duke's; he is probably identical with the Reinold who is mentioned not long afterwards as castellan of the Ertheneburg.

Although the foundation of Lübeck was not completed in every detail in 1159, the achievements of that year are nevertheless of great historical importance. Lübeck became the centre of German navigation in the Baltic and set an example for the foundation of many new towns that were to give the Baltic area a distinctive character within the next hundred years. A fortunate combination between the political power of the duke of Saxony and the enterprising commercial spirit of the Low German bourgeoisie made possible the development of the city which was for centuries to play such a brilliant part as the chief of the German Hanseatic towns.

The refounding of Lübeck was a visible sign of the intense political activity that Henry the Lion undertook from the late 1150s onwards in Nordalbingia and the neighbouring districts. His intention was to subdue the Obodrites and bring the rest of the Saxon borderland under his rule, making the Peene river the frontier of his dominions. This policy was much aided by the settlement that Frederick I brought about between him and Hartwig of Bremen in the summer of 1158. Personal relations remained uneasy, but it was an advantage to the duke that the archbishop ceased to oppose his ecclesiastical policy. Hartwig had to recognize Henry's measures in Nordalbingia if he wished to preserve his own spiritual supremacy in that area.

The archbishop even hoped to revive the old claims of his church to the metropolitanate of Scandinavia, which had been confirmed to him by Frederick I in March 1158 as a move against Archbishop Eskil of Lund. However, Pope Hadrian IV, who had served in Scandinavia as a legate, in February 1159 defined the metropolitan diocese of the church of Hamburg as comprising only the Slav territory as far as the Peene. Victor IV, the imperial anti-Pope, was also not disposed to grant Hartwig's wishes: he was anxious to secure the allegiance of Valdemar I of Denmark, and in February 1160, after the council of Pavia, confirmed the archbishop's authority only over the sees of Oldenburg, Mecklenburg, and Ratzeburg. In view of Hartwig's approaches to the Curia it was of importance to Henry the Lion that the Emperor, perhaps also at the beginning of 1160, once again confirmed his right of investiture to the three Nordalbingian bishoprics. This was probably in part a reward for the valuable help Henry had rendered in the siege of Crema. It is uncertain, however, whether Frederick issued a further charter on the subject at this time.

Henry's Baltic policy was also affected by the fact that the long dispute over the Danish succession had come to an end with Valdemar I's victory over his opponents in 1157. In reconstructing a strong royal power the king had a shrewd adviser and ally in Bishop Absalon of Roskilde. His aim was not only to consolidate the position of his dynasty at home but to make the country secure from foreign enemies. From the beginning of his reign he undertook expeditions to Mecklenburg and Hither Pomerania, not only to discourage the raids of Slav pirates on the Danish coasts but also to increase Danish power in the Baltic area.

Initially the king and the Saxon duke were drawn together by their common hostility to the Slavs; but as their territorial ambitions in Hither Pomerania began to conflict, they frequently became rivals instead of allies. Henry the Lion adapted his policy in Slav territory to changing conditions, and more than once allied himself with the Slavs against the Danes instead of vice versa. Valdemar, however, was bound to seek good relations with Henry as long as he was endeavouring to obtain recognition of his rights by Frederick I.

Henry's first foray into Slav territory took place in the summer of 1158, but practically nothing is known of this brief expedition against the Obodrites via the county of Ratzeburg. It is possible that Niklot was captured at this time and imprisoned at Lüneburg. Next year the duke led a sizeable levy to Italy, and his Nordalbingian policy was interrupted for about a twelvemonth. Before departing he did his best to ensure peace in the border area. He met Valdemar, concluded a treaty of friendship and, in return for a promise of 1,000 marks in silver, undertook to mediate between the Danish king and the Slavs. He summoned Niklot and the other Slav princes and made them take an oath that they would remain at peace with the Saxons and Danes until his return and would surrender their ships to his agents in Lübeck. Count Adolf also warned Niklot not to embark on any hostilities during his absence.

However, these measures had no effect, as the Obodrites only handed over old and unserviceable vessels and, after the duke's departure, resumed their raids on the Danish coasts. With great difficulty Bishop Gerold brought about an armistice and dissuaded the Danish king from advancing into Wagria. Instead Valdemar decided in the course of the year to undertake two expeditions against the coastal part of Hither Pomerania and the island of Rügen, which were important bases of the Slav pirates.

After his return to Saxony, at the beginning of August 1160, Henry held a diet at Barförde on the Elbe north-east of Lüneburg; at the nearby Ertheneburg he met King Valdemar, who complained of the Slavs' breach of faith. The Slav princes, who had disobeyed the duke's summons to appear, were outlawed, while Henry and Valdemar planned a joint attack on the Obodrites at harvest-time. As in the case of the Wendish crusade in 1147, Niklot sought to forestall the attack by a coup against Lübeck. However, as Helmold tells us, the vigilance of a priest made it possible to bar the bridge over the Wakenitz and prevent a surprise attack on the city.

In the late summer Henry invaded the Obodrite country with a large army, while a Danish fleet under King Valdemar and Bishop Absalon landed opposite the island of Poel and ravaged the Mecklenburg coast. Niklot could not stand up to the twofold attack. He gave up most of his territory, and as he withdrew set fire to the fortresses of Ilow near Wismar, Mecklenburg, Schwerin, and Dobin. He managed to hold out in Werle, a stronghold protected by the river Warnow, whence he carried on guerrilla warfare against the slowly advancing Saxon army. When his sons Pribislav and Vratislav suffered a reverse near Mecklenburg, Niklot made a sortie and attempted to ambush the duke's servants as they were collecting fodder. However, he was outwitted and slain by Saxon knights disguised as foragers, who carried off his head as booty—a measure of the ferocity of the conflict.

Niklot was the last important prince of the Obodrites, and there is something tragic about his career. His aim was to maintain the political independence of the Obodrite territory east of Lübeck Bay and also to preserve the pagan religion. He hoped to do this thanks to an understanding with Count Adolf of Holstein, to which he adhered even after the Wendish crusade of 1147. However, the cause of Slav independence conflicted with the ambition of the duke of Saxony, and he could not withstand the latter's military superiority.

After Niklot's death Wendish resistance soon collapsed. His sons abandoned Werle, set fire to the castle, and withdrew into the trackless interior. Later in the year they made peace with the duke and surrendered the whole area conquered by him, keeping only the districts of Kessin and Circipania with the fortress of Werle, which they received as a fief from Henry.

A few days after the Danish landing Henry the Lion held a meeting in his camp at Werle with Valdemar and Absalon, which was followed by further negotiations with the bishop. After the capture of Werle, Henry led his army northwards along the Warnow and had a second meeting near Rostock with the Danish king, who had meanwhile reached the river-mouth by sea and had plundered Rostock itself. Nothing is known of what passed, but it may be supposed that Valdemar put forward territorial claims in return for his aid against the Wends. Henry, however, was able to prevent the Danes settling in Mecklenburg. Instead, Valdemar sailed eastwards to the coast of

Hither Pomerania opposite Rügen, and by taking hostages obliged the inhabitants of the island to recognize his suzerainty.

Henry the Lion could now embark on the the conquered territory. For this purpose he made use of the existing Slav system of castle-guards. The damaged fortresses were rebuilt and became strongholds of the new Saxon lords, who were responsible not only for defence but also for the administration of the surrounding lands. One large area was commanded by Gunzelin, a member of the noble family of Hagen, whose ancestral home was on the Elm river east of Helmstedt; his descendants were the counts of Schwerin, and he was also lord of the fortress of Ilow. Liudolf, member of a family of Welf *ministeriales*, was appointed to Quetzin on the Plauer See, having previously been a ducal *Vogt* in Brunswick; another of the duke's servants, Liudolf of Peine, was given the fortress of Malchow in the Müritzgau. To the important stronghold of Mecklenburg Henry appointed a Dutch nobleman, Hendrik van Schooten—an indication that the castellans in this region were also in charge of its colonization. Van Schooten brought many settlers from Flanders to the Mecklenburg region. In this way Henry's measures were designed to bring the conquered lands firmly under Saxon rule.

Shortly before the conquest there had already been a settlement of Saxon merchants under the protection of the stronghold of Schwerin. This became the basis for the first German municipal foundation in Obodrite country. We have no details of the early stages, but it is recorded that Henry the Lion raised Schwerin to the rank of a city in 1160 or soon after. The earliest municipal seal shows him to be its founder: it is a replica of the seal he used in the 1160s, bearing his name and depicting him on horseback. Presumably he bestowed municipal rights on the merchant colony and thus promoted the development of the city.

These political steps were followed by reorganization in church matters. Bishop Emmehard, whom Hartwig of Bremen had appointed to Mecklenburg, could not function there effectively as he refused to accept investiture from the duke. He died in 1154, after which missionary work among the Obodrites was begun by the Cistercian Berno from Amelungsborn near Holzminden, a monastery founded by Siegfried IV of Boyneburg. Thus the Cistercians found a fresh sphere of activity in Mecklenburg. Berno's part in establishing the Christian church in Mecklenburg is comparable with that of Vizelin in Wagria; however, no contemporary recorded his life as Helmold did for Vizelin, and we know practically nothing of his first missionary work except that it was approved by Hadrian IV, who presumably gave him a general licence for the purpose. We do not know when he began his mission to the Obodrites, but given Niklot's hostility to Christianity it cannot have been very successful. It seems likely that Henry the Lion appointed him bishop of Mecklenburg some years after Emmehard's death and invested him with the see.

After the conquest of the Obodrites and the appointment of Gunzelin as governor, Schwerin was the obvious ecclesiastical centre of the region. Unlike Mecklenburg, it enjoyed natural protection thanks to its surrounding lakes. In 1160 Henry had already designated it as the new seat of the bishopric, to be endowed, like Oldenburg and Ratzeburg, with 300 hides of land.

In the same year a corresponding change was made in the Oldenburg diocese. Oldenburg itself, the bishop's original residence, had lost its importance in the twelfth-century refoundation. Vizelin had resided at Bosau, Gerold at Eutin. With the rise of Lübeck and the increase in its population, the centre of gravity in Wagria shifted also. Lübeck, with its situation on the Trave, had the advantage over Eutin for purposes of communication. Accordingly, at Gerold's request Henry in 1160 transferred the seat of the bishopric to Lübeck, assigning an area in the southern part of the city for a cathedral and canons' offices.

The transfer of the two episcopal residences marked the accomplishment of the first phase of church organization in Wendish territory. Archbishop Hartwig had to be content with recognizing the situation created by the duke. In 1160 he made the three bishoprics—officially designated for the first time as Lübeck, Ratzeburg, and Schwerin—subordinate to Hamburg as their metropolitan authority. The seniority of the churches of Bremen and Hamburg was to be preserved, but the three suffragan bishops east of the Elbe were obliged only to attend the provincial synod in Hamburg and not the general synod in Bremen. At this time Henry the Lion also expressly recognized the metropolitan authority of the church of Hamburg in Nordalbingia.

The extent of Henry's power in the Baltic area at this time, well beyond the borders of Nordalbingia, was clearly shown by a diet that he held at the Ertheneburg in October 1161. This was attended by representatives of the Swedish merchants in Gotland and the German merchants' guild which had established itself on that island in the course of time, its governor Odelrich being an appointee of Henry's. Disputes had arisen between the two groups, and Henry now arbitrated between them. In doing so he confirmed the Gotlanders' trading rights in the Empire, originally granted by Lothair III in a charter that has not survived. Whereas the Emperor had apparently confined himself to issuing a privilege in general terms, the new charter spelt out the provisions and sanctions that were to ensure the Gotlanders' personal safety and the protection of their wares in ducal territory. In addition Henry exempted them from tolls in his cities. At the same time—and this illustrates the change in the conditions of Baltic trade in the past few decades—he made these concessions subject to German merchants being granted the same rights in Gotland. He also invited the Gotlanders to make frequent use of Lübeck, and instructed Odelrich to apply to merchants under his authority the same regulations concerning the protection of traders and their goods. These measures were intended to promote trade with Lübeck, in the same way as the treaties, now lost, with the Swedish rulers and the prince of Novgorod. In confirming and extending an imperial privilege granted by his grandfather Lothair, as in his use of the right of investiture in Nordalbingia, Henry was acting as a representative of imperial authority in the Baltic area.

In the following years, Henry and Archbishop Hartwig continued with the organizational development of the sees of Lübeck and Ratzeburg. In 1162 they defined the boundaries of the latter diocese, and the proportion of its revenues that should go to the cathedral chapter. The half-tithe to which the church was entitled was to be divided equally between the bishop and the chapter. Accordingly the canons in the district of Boitin were to receive one half of the whole tithe, and in the rest of the diocese one quarter of it. These revenues could not provide an adequate livelihood for the chapter until the country was opened up by German settlers. For this reason, as already mentioned, the duke assigned to it an annual share of twenty-seven marks from the Lübeck tolls.

A year later, in July 1163, the first cathedral in Lübeck was consecrated by Archbishop Hartwig and Bishop Gerold in the presence of Duke Henry and Count Adolf. A modest wooden building, it was dedicated to the Virgin Mary, John the Baptist, and St Nicholas. At the same time the question of the chapter's endowment was settled. Gerold granted the provost all tithes on existing and prospective cultivation in the city and its district. Henry confirmed this gift and granted the provost a plot of land for the chapter's offices on the eastern side of the cathedral. The question of the chapter's share of the tithes was settled differently than at Ratzeburg: canons were to draw tithes from specified areas of the diocese up to a stated amount, any surplus going to the bishop. Like the Ratzeburg chapter, that of Lübeck was to receive twenty-seven marks a year from the city tolls. The duke and count also endowed it with certain villages. Finally Hartwig and Gerold granted the chapter pastoral rights throughout the city; the church that had meanwhile been built on the market-place was also incorporated with it.

During his stay in Lübeck the duke probably also conferred important privileges on its citizens direct. No documentary evidence has survived, but the great charter issued by Frederick I in 1188 expressly refers to a *privilegium* granted by Henry. Unfortunately we only possess this charter in a forged version of 1225, so that the legal purport of Henry's document cannot be stated with certainty: it may either have been a detailed grant of privileges or a more general confirmation of rights on the lines of those granted to Soest, which served as the model for Lübeck.

After the Soest pattern Henry granted to Lübeck the privilege of *Kore*, i.e. the right to make regulations for internal order and peace-keeping. No doubt the lost ducal charter also embodied the principle of *Stadtluft macht frei* ('city air makes a man free')—one of the most important features of municipal charters in the twelfth century, whereby within a twelvemonth every citizen became a free man, able to dispose of his property at will.

The earliest civil community of Lübeck already had institutions of its own. The first municipal authority was a sworn confederation or corporation and was the predecessor of the later town council. The regulation for the election of the council, drawn up in Low German and allegedly granted to the citizens by Henry the Lion, is a thirteenth-century forgery; the first council in Lübeck probably dated from about 1200.

The presidency of the corporation, which was composed of merchants, administered the town's share of the revenue from fines and probably also supervised the market trade in provisions, independently of the duke. The citizens may also have had the right to appoint a priest to serve the market church.

While the rights conferred by the duke on the citizens were not as yet very extensive, they mark an important stage in the development of municipal self-government in Lübeck. Also at this time, Henry probably enlarged appreciably the city's holding of land outside its walls.

Shortly before the settlement in the summer of 1163, the question of the tithes in the bishopric of Lübeck had led to a dispute between Bishop Gerold and the Holstein settlers in his diocese, which throws light on the difficulties attending the church's work. The Holsteiners refused to pay the whole tithe, claiming that when they came to settle in Wagria they had been exempted from part of it in return for military service in the border area. Count Adolf declared that this was not the case and that German settlers in the Polabian and Obodrite country paid the regular tithe, whereupon Gerold demanded that the Holsteiners do likewise. He approached their leader (*Landesälteste*) Marcrad, who resided at Bornhöved, but without success: the Holsteiners still refused to pay the whole sum, on the ground that it was being used for secular instead of ecclesiastical purposes. Gerold appealed to the duke, who ordered the Holsteiners in Wagria to pay the bishop the full tithe. At first the settlers threatened to emigrate to Denmark, but finally they agreed—probably in the spring of 1163—that they would sign an agreement with the bishop in the duke's presence in which the amount of the tithe should be clearly laid down in terms of payment in kind. This agreement was never confirmed by the duke in writing, however, as the Holsteiners refused to pay the usual chancellery fee of one gold mark.

The agreement over tithes and the consecration of Lübeck cathedral were Gerold's last official acts. He died at Bosau on 13 August 1163, after a short illness in the course of a visitation, and was laid to rest in the cathedral. Although he had been bishop for only eight years, church work had made much progress in the time thanks to his good relations with the duke and Count Adolf. Several new parishes were created under his rule, a proof of the rate of German colonization of Wagria during those years.

In February 1164, after a fairly long vacancy, the duke, despite opposition from Archbishop Hartwig and the Lübeck chapter, appointed as the new bishop Gerold's brother Conrad, abbot of the Cistercian monastery of Riddagshausen near Brunswick. His object in appointing a member of the Brunswick clergy was to maintain his own influence in Nordalbingia. Archbishop Hartwig had to content himself with consecrating the new bishop.

In the bishopric of Schwerin there could at first be no question of developing church organization in this way. The campaign of 1160 had by no means ensured peace in the Obodrite country, as Niklot's sons Pribislav and Vratislav fought on for their father's inheritance. They planned an assault in the spring of 1163, but Henry got wind of their designs and anticipated them by attacking the stronghold of Werle. With the aid of siege machines that he had seen in action at Crema and Milan—a battering-ram and a tall wooden tower—he captured Werle and took Vratislav prisoner with many of his chief followers. Vratislav was deported to Brunswick, whereupon Pribislav gave up resistance and agreed to a peace.

Henry realized, however, that the Obodrite country could only be pacified if he were also able to assert his rule in Hither Pomerania, where the two chieftains had repeatedly taken refuge and recruited help. Accordingly, after capturing Werle he pressed on into the Wolgast area and compelled the Rügian leaders to acknowledge his suzerainty. Chiefs from Rügen attended the consecration of Lübeck cathedral in July 1163 to do homage to the duke. However, Valdemar of Denmark saw Henry's action as an encroachment on his sphere of interest, and soon afterwards compelled the Rügians to recognize him as their overlord.

The peace concluded in 1163 did not last long: Pribislav renewed the struggle in February 1164 with the help of the Pomeranian chiefs, at the instance of his captive brother Vratislav. He overran the fortress of Mecklenburg—its commander, Hendrik van Schooten, being absent—slaughtered the male Flemish population and led the women and children into captivity. Bishop Berno of Schwerin himself barely escaped being taken prisoner when he attempted to bury the dead a few days later. Pribislav also captured Quetzin and Malchow without a fight, after promising the garrisons safe conduct. Only Ilow and Schwerin, defended by Gunzelin of Hagen and his men, offered successful resistance.

As in 1160, the duke now allied himself with Valdemar of Denmark against the Slavs. The link between them was sealed by the betrothal of a daughter of Henry's—perhaps Richenza, who died not long afterwards—to Valdemar's son Knut, who was then one year old.

The duke proceeded to counter-attack the Slavs in the summer of 1164 with a large army including not only the great nobles of Nordalbingia but also many princes from the rest of Saxony. Albert the Bear also responded this time to his appeal for help. At Malchow the captive Vratislav, whom Henry regarded as the instigator of the Slav rising, was publicly hanged. The advance guard, led by Count Adolf and Count Reinold of Ditmarsh, then marched eastward towards the border fortress of Demmin. A battle took place on 1 July to the west of Demmin, at Verchen on the Kummerower See. Despite the enemy's superior numbers the Saxons, after abandoning their camp, were finally victorious, though with heavy casualties, including Counts Adolf and Reinold and many knights. But the Slavs too suffered heavy losses, and Pribislav and the Pomeranian leaders had to surrender Demmin.

The death of Count Adolf II was a grievous loss to the duke. For over thirty years he had been a loyal champion of the Welfic cause in Nordalbingia. In addition, especially at the beginning of Henry's career, he had constantly been close to the duke as one of his chief helpers and advisers.

King Valdemar had meanwhile sailed to Rügen with his fleet and had occupied the Wolgast district. He and the duke met near Stolpe at the mouth of the Peene and agreed on terms of peace with the Slavs. The Wolgast district was divided among several Slav chieftains but remained under Danish suzerainty. Henry retained the conquered Obodrite territory. At this time or soon after, the Pomeranian princes Casimir of Demmin and Bogislav of Stettin (Szczecin) acknowledged themselves his vassals. The overlapping of Danish and Saxon interests in Hither Pomerania was to cause friction from time to time between Henry and Valdemar. In 1166, however, they again campaigned jointly against the Pomeranians.

Also in 1166, as we shall see in another context, new and violent conflict broke out in Saxony between the duke and the league of Saxon princes, and in consequence he had radically to alter his policy towards the Obodrites. To keep his hand free for the domestic quarrel in Saxony he restored Pribislav to favour and, probably at the beginning of 1167, made him once more ruler of most of the Obodrite country except the Schwerin area. Pribislav, who chose Werle for his residence, thus became the founder of the dynasty that reigned in Mecklenburg till 1918. He received his territory as a fief from the duke, to whom he promised military service. Pribislav, who probably became a Christian at this time, remained from then onwards a loyal vassal of Henry the Lion. To reconcile him with Saxon suzerainty Henry subsequently gave his illegitimate daughter

Matilda in marriage to Pribislav's eldest son, the young Henry Borwin. Pribislav also accompanied the duke on his pilgrimage to the Holy Land in 1172.

With the change of policy in 1167 Henry gave up his original plan of taking the Obodrite country under his direct rule with the help of Saxon lords and *ministeriales*. Instead, as in Wagria and the Polabian lands, he contented himself with feudal overlordship. He also transferred the county of Schwerin to Gunzelin as a hereditary fief.

After Adolf II's death the county of Holstein was administered by his widow Matilda of Schwarzburg on behalf of her under-age son Adolf III. Soon afterwards the duke, anticipating armed conflict in Saxony, appointed Matilda's brother Count Henry of Schwarzburg to be the boy's guardian and commander of the levy. At the beginning of the 1160s there was also a change of ruler in the county of Ratzeburg. Count Henry, the former rival of Adolf II, died soon after 1163; his eldest son, Bernard I, carried on his father's work vigorously by founding new villages and parishes in the area under his authority.

From 1167 onwards the situation in Nordalbingia was for the time being much less important to Henry the Lion than the grave internal conflict in Saxony. Meanwhile Valdemar of Denmark seized the opportunity to strengthen the position of his dynasty at home by successes in the foreign sphere. In 1168 he undertook an expedition against the island of Rügen; Henry could not take part owing to the troubles in Saxony, but saw to it that Valdemar received help from Pribislav and the Pomeranian chiefs Casimir and Bogislav. Bishop Berno also joined in the campaign, hoping to include parts of Rügen in his diocese. Valdemar rapidly subdued the island after conquering the fortified shrine of Arkona and destroying the statue of the heathen god Svantevit. Bishop Absalon of Roskilde, who accompanied Valdemar on this campaign also, was able to have the whole island added to his diocese, thus frustrating Berno of Schwerin's plan. With the conquest of Rügen the power situation in the Baltic shifted markedly in favour of Denmark.

A breach now ensued between Henry and Valdemar as the latter, contrary to their agreement, refused to surrender half of the Rügen hostages and of the tribute paid by the defeated tribes. Instead of the traditional Saxon–Danish alliance, the next few years saw an alliance between Henry and the Slavs against Denmark. Probably as early as 1168, the Obodrite and Pomeranian chiefs began again to harry the

Danish coasts. Valdemar beat them off and counter-attacked: in 1170 a Danish fleet sailed as far as the Wollin area, and in the following year the Mecklenburg coast and Wagria were plundered. However, these reprisals had no lasting effect. Valdemar made peace with Henry at a meeting on 24 June 1171 on a bridge over the river Eider: Henry was careful to mark his equality of status by advancing only mid-way across. Valdemar agreed to Henry's terms, promising to hand over half the hostages and tribute and a proportion of the treasures of the conquered shrine. The inhabitants of Rügen declared themselves willing to pay tribute to Henry, thus recognizing his suzerainty. As Henry's daughter, who had been betrothed to the Danish prince Knut in 1164, had meanwhile died, it was agreed that Knut, now aged eight, should be married to Henry's daughter Gertrude, whose husband, Duke Frederick of Rothenburg, had met his death at Rome in 1167. Gertrude went to Denmark in the winter of 1171–2, and the marriage to Knut was solemnized some years later.

The agreement of 1171 was another important success for the duke of Saxony, and brought peace to the Baltic for several years. After the reinstatement of Pribislav considerable advances were made both in agriculture and in the organization of the three Slav bishoprics.

In the Lübeck diocese, however, progress was temporarily held up by a conflict between the duke and Bishop Conrad, who had made many enemies by his arrogant rule. Initially his relations with the duke were smooth, but in the great rebellion of the Saxon princes in 1166–7 he sided with Henry's opponents and persuaded Hartwig of Bremen to do likewise. Henry summoned him and demanded that he take an oath of fealty, which he had not done since his appointment to the see. At a meeting at Stade Conrad refused to do this, whereupon Henry forbade him to enter his bishopric and cut off his revenues. On Hartwig's advice the bishop appealed first to Archbishop Wichmann of Magdeburg and then to the general council of the Cistercian order in France. When he returned to Germany he was still excluded from his bishopric until after Hartwig's death in October 1168, when Frederick I succeeded in reconciling him with Henry and the ban was lifted.

After the fighting in Saxony was over, Henry turned again to the affairs of Nordalbingia. In 1169 and 1170 he regulated legal conditions in the sees of Ratzeburg and Lübeck: identical privileges for the two churches are still extant, though they may date from a somewhat later time. The duke was concerned to preserve the old margravial rights in their fullness. The bishop's vavasours (rear-vassals) had to serve in the ducal armies and contribute to the building and maintenance of fortified places. Only ten villages in each diocese were exempt from these obligations. The bishops for their part were relieved of secular dues and the 'ducal tribute', an old impost that went back to the Slav period. They thus possessed fiscal immunity, but not immunity from judicial proceedings. The duke insisted on the margravial right to summon any inhabitants of the march to his court, the *Markding*. Minor judicial matters were left to the bishops to administer themselves or through their agents. Major offences belonged to the jurisdiction of advocates (*Stiftsvögte*); in the case of capital crimes, the bishop was to receive only two-thirds of the indemnity.

The senior advocates (*Hochvögte*) for the diocese of Lübeck were the counts of Holstein; in Ratzeburg they were the counts resident there. The duke, however, was at pains to protect the bishops against encroachment on the advocates' part. A similar arrangement was later made for the diocese of Schwerin, where the counts likewise came to occupy the position of senior advocate. As the duke was their feudal overlord, the uniformity of the judicial system was preserved as it always had been in frontier areas.

This form of judicial organization constituted an essential difference between the three bishoprics founded by the duke and all other German dioceses. They are, as far as we know, the first bishoprics in Germany to have been subject to a territorial prince.

In the Schwerin diocese the first German settlements had for the most part been destroyed in the heavy fighting of 1164. Only after the peace of 1167 between the duke and Pribislav could Bishop Berno begin missionary activity with any prospect of success. He did not confine himself to Obodrite territory, but took in Circipania—the region south-east of Werle, then considered part of Pomerania—and also the Tribsees district.

In view of the special position of the Schwerin bishopric and its ambition to extend beyond the Obodrite territory, Henry thought it desirable to obtain a confirmatory privilege from Frederick I, especially as he could get no charter for the see from Alexander III during the schism. At a diet in Frankfurt in January 1170 Frederick issued a diploma for the bishopric, which has survived only in a revised form dating from the beginning of the thirteenth century. The lost original presumably confirmed the foundation of the bishopric by the duke and defined its territorial extent; it is not certain, however, whether it endorsed the bishop's claim in respect of Rügen and Hither Pomerania. It would have been a great advantage for the duke in his dispute with King Valdemar if the Emperor had recognized Rügen as coming under Saxon overlordship, as the document expressly states in its extant form.

A year later, on 9 September 1171, in the presence of the duke and several princes, Bishop Berno consecrated the first cathedral at Schwerin, which was probably a wooden building like its counterpart at Lübeck. Among those who attended the solemnity were Pribislav, designated as lord of Kessin, Casimir of Demmin, and the counts of Ratzeburg and Schwerin. At this time the duke made over to the diocese the promised 300 hides of land, situated for the most part in the Bützow and Ilow districts. Part of the grant was earmarked for the cathedral chapter, then in process of formation, which was also assigned a share of the tithes from certain parts of the diocese. The duke expressly ordained, however, that this should be only a temporary measure. After the land was cleared by the German settlers the then reigning duke and the bishop were to carry out a redistribution of the tithe revenue in agreement with the counts of Schwerin and Ratzeburg, in whose county the diocese was granted some scattered holdings.

This last provision points to the special task imposed on the bishopric. As yet there were few German settlers in the Obodrite country; Schwerin was to be primarily a missionary diocese and at the same time to promote agriculture. Berno, as a former Cistercian monk, desired to give the Order fresh opportunities in his diocese by founding monasteries, and the two oldest in the region were created by his efforts. In 1171 the monastery of Doberan was founded by Pribislav in the Kessin district in the north-eastern part of the Schwerin diocese; a year later Dargun in eastern Circipania was founded, endowed by three Wendish lords, and taken under the protection of Casimir of Demmin. Bishop Berno of Schwerin granted important tithe privileges to the two new monasteries. Both were occupied by Cistercian monks: these came to Doberan from Berno's former monastery of Amelungsborn, and to Dargun from Esrom in Denmark.

With the consolidation of political and ecclesiastical life in Nordalbingia, Duke Henry intervened in its affairs on exceptional occasions only. Bishop Conrad of Lübeck, who had accompanied him on his pilgrimage to the Holy Land, died at Tyre in July 1172. The question of his successor could not be settled until Henry's return to Saxony at the beginning of 1173. The course of events is fully described by Arnold of Lübeck in the *Chronicle* with which he continued Helmold's work at the beginning of the thirteenth century. According to him, the initiative for the new appointment to the diocese came from the chapter. In accord with the close personal relations that had existed since Gerold's day between the Brunswick and the Lübeck clergy, the canons chose Abbot Henry of St Giles's monastery in Brunswick to be their new bishop. He was a close confidant of the duke and had also accompanied him to Jerusalem, so that the proposal could be expected to receive his assent. Henry, though at first reluctant to lose the abbot from his own entourage, finally agreed to the appointment, no doubt seeing the advantage of having a bishop in Lübeck on whose loyalty he could rely. The messengers from the chapter proceeded to Brunswick to inform the abbot of their choice and the duke's decision. After the usual protestations of unworthiness, the abbot accepted. He was invested with his see by Henry the Lion at Lüneburg, and solemnly enthroned at Lübeck in the duke's presence on 24 June 1173. The order of consecration shows that Henry the Lion wished to exclude the influence of the archbishop of Bremen: Hartwig's successor Baldwin was not present, the consecration being carried out by the bishops of Havelberg, Ratzeburg, and Schwerin.

One of the new bishop's first official acts was to lay the foundation stone of a new cathedral. The exact date of this ceremony is not known. However, we are told that the initiative for a new building came from the duke and that he and Bishop Henry laid the stone jointly, so it is probable that they did so at the time of the bishop's consecration in the summer of 1173. Henry the Lion did not again visit Nordalbingia for several years thereafter.

As the diocese was not yet able to bear the cost of a new building on a grandiose scale, the duke promised an annual contribution of 100 silver marks, a very considerable sum for the time. The new church, made of brick, was built on the site of the original, smaller wooden church in the southern part of the city.

At about the same time, or perhaps a little earlier, work began on the building of a cathedral at Ratzeburg at the northern tip of the island belonging to Count Henry's bishopric; this was also built of brick and dedicated to the Virgin Mary and St John the Evangelist. Here again the initiative came from the duke, and, as at Lübeck, he contributed 100 marks a year to defray the cost, which was beyond the diocese's slender resources.

The beginning of these two cathedrals, on which generations worked before they were completed, was not only a visible sign of the great progress made in both dioceses in the past decades. Given the close association in Nordalbingia between church organization and secular rule, the two buildings were also intended to constitute a monument to ducal power in the area. A gallery was constructed at the west end of both cathedrals for the duke to occupy when he attended services.

Concluding his *Chronicle* in 1172, Helmold of Bosau described the work he had witnessed in Nordalbingia during the past thirty years in the proud words: 'All the country of the Slavs, beginning at the Eider which is the boundary of the kingdom of the Danes, and extending between the Baltic Sea and the Elbe river in a most lengthy sweep to Schwerin, a region once feared for its ambuscades and almost deserted, was now through the help of God all made, as it were, into one colony of Saxons. And cities and villages grew up there and churches were built and the number of the ministers of Christ multiplied.' This is certainly much exaggerated: there were still large areas scarcely touched by German colonization. But it can clearly be seen that the face of the land had profoundly changed in the three decades since the beginning of Henry the Lion's rule. Though the duke did not himself take a direct part in the work of colonization, he laid the political foundation for it.

It would be wrong, however, to seek to explain Henry's actions in Nordalbingia purely by national motives, as has often been done. Such ideas were not characteristic of him or of his age. His object was rather to bring firmly under his own control, politically and militarily, the large borderland eastward of Saxon territory as far as the Peene, over which his predecessors had only managed to assert a loose form of domination by occasional military expeditions and demands for tribute.

While Henry repeatedly appealed to inherited margravial rights, his actions were those of a power-seeker with little concern for the rights of others. He knew how to exploit the changing political situation to his own advantage, and he used harsh measures to achieve his ends. While he promoted the organization of the church in the

Slav territories, this too was designed as a measure of political penetration.

Despite many setbacks, on the whole he succeeded in creating in Nordalbingia a compact, unified dominion such as could not be achieved in the ancestral Saxon territory owing to the many forms of lordship that already existed there. The progress of German settlement in the new territory, supported by the lay and ecclesiastical authorities which he had established, did much to strengthen his power by means of military aid and other feudal services; and the Baltic trade based on Lübeck brought steadily increasing financial profit.

The almost royal position that Henry the Lion created for himself in Nordalbingia and the western Baltic contributed greatly to his prestige and self-confidence. This power and his awareness of it go far to explain his actions in the Saxon duchy itself.

5

The Development of
Ducal Rule in Saxony;
Henry's Conflict with his
Opponents

REVIEWING the first decade of Henry's rule in Saxony, from his instatement at the diet of Frankfurt in May 1142 to the diet of Würzburg in October 1152, it can be said that despite strong resistance he had effectively asserted his power over a vast area between the Weser and the Elbe, extending from the Baltic to the Eichsfeld and the northern part of Hesse. His success in claiming the large Winzenburg inheritance marked the conclusion of the first phase in a very consistently pursued territorial policy in Saxony.

He did not, however, as yet possess a homogeneous or self-contained territory, but rather a conglomeration of lands based on a variety of legal titles. It has become customary to refer to the manifold entities of which the medieval Empire was composed as 'lordships' (*Herrschaften*), a term which reflects the fact that they only constituted a unity through the person of their lord, to whom the rights belonged and who made them politically effective. In some areas—especially around Lüneberg, in the region between Brunswick and Königslutter, or in southern Saxony around Northeim and Göttingen—the duke's rights and possessions were closely concentrated from the territorial point of view, but still lacked any firm external delimitation.

This geographical and legal situation explains Henry's further actions in Saxony, which were devoted to enlarging his dominions and consolidating them internally. The most promising field of expansion lay in the extensive border areas, but here he encountered the rights and claims of others, including lay and ecclesiastical princes, who were also desirous of increasing their loosely-knit domains. This led to constant tension and conflict, which repeatedly broke out into open warfare and dominated Saxon politics in the ensuing decades.

A brief account of Henry's territorial rivals will help to explain his policy. In the north of Saxony the archbishops of Bremen had long been his chief adversaries owing to the quasi-ducal status they had come to enjoy in their dioceses since the middle of the eleventh century. However, Henry's acquisition of the rich Stade inheritance had firmly altered in his favour the political balance of power between the lower Elbe and the lower Weser. He tightened his control over this region by building strongholds and appointing *ministeriales*, especially in the region of the Oste river. His rights of advocacy over the archbishopric and the city of Bremen enabled him to exert strong influence in that area. Archbishop Hartwig had to bow to the duke's wishes regarding church policy in Nordalbingia, and in territorial matters too his opportunities were much circumscribed. Although Frederick I was able to bring about an ostensible settlement between the archbishop and the duke, Hartwig continued to regard Henry as his chief rival.

The duke, in addition, endeavoured to enlarge his domain on the left bank of the lower Elbe, where he possessed scattered estates from the Northeim inheritance. For example, he acquired the manor of Hittfeld near Harburg, which was of importance as the seat of an old 'hundred court' (*Gobezirk*). Siegfried IV of Boyneburg had ceded the manor to his proprietary monastery of Amelungsborn, from whom Henry bought it in 1156. According to later sources the purchase was agreed with the abbot without the community's knowledge, and Henry afterwards cheated the monastery out of half the price.

The duke also gained a strong position in the diocese of Verden, which included the Bardengau with Lüneburg. Herman of Verden, who occupied the see for nearly twenty years, from 1148 to 1167, belonged to a family of Welf *ministeriales* and was always on the best of terms with the duke. Like the Billungs and his grandfather Lothair, Henry possessed extensive patrimonial lands and county rights in this area, and also the advocacy of the cathedral chapter and of the monastery of Walsrode. Until his downfall the bishops were unable to build up a territorial power of their own. Herman, at the beginning of his pontificate, attempted to use a forged charter, purportedly issued by Charlemagne, to extend his diocese to the neighbouring districts east of the Elbe before the duke could finally settle the question of church organization there. Henry, however, prevented his efforts, refusing to agree to any curtailment of the territory of the Ratzeburg diocese. In the negotiations of 1158 for the endowment of that see Herman's claims were only met to the extent of two large islands in the Elbe near Hamburg, where the river divides into separate channels.

Henry was also in an advantageous position *vis-à-vis* the east Saxon bishoprics of Hildesheim and Halberstadt. The former was largely surrounded by territory that belonged to the Welfs or in which they had rights of suzerainty. Initially the duke's own lands within the diocese were not very extensive. The Winzenburg inheritance added considerably to them, although the castle itself continued to be a fief of the bishop's. Hildesheim became more and more dependent on Henry's territorial policy. The noble families and the bishop's *ministeriales* increasingly cultivated relations with the duke, in whose charters they often figure as witnesses. It took all the skill of Bishop Bruno and of Herman, who succeeded him in 1161, to preserve the independence of the diocese.

In the see of Halberstadt, comprising the north-eastern foreland of the Harz mountains, Henry was well entrenched owing to the possessions and rights he had inherited from the Supplinburgers. Ulrich, who became bishop in 1150, was before long a keen opponent of the Welfs. At the diet of Roncaglia in 1154 he was deprived of his regalia for failing to provide the Emperor with a military force, and on his return to Saxony Henry executed this judgement. Ulrich was soon restored to the imperial favour, but Henry allied himself with the *ministeriales* of the bishopric and the citizens of Halberstadt against the bishop, whose position they regarded as irregular.

When the schism broke out in Rome Ulrich declared for Alexander III and, as we have seen, this enabled the duke to institute church proceedings for his deposition and to oust him from the diocese. The new bishop Gero, hitherto dean of the chapter, acted throughout as a loyal instrument of Henry's. He enfeoffed the duke with possessions of the Halberstadt church and granted him other revenues of the diocese, which became completely subordinate to ducal policy. Henry erected the strategically placed stronghold of Gatersleben near Quedlinburg in the episcopal domain.

The Haldersleben district was the most easterly part of the Welf dominions in central Germany. Here the duke's interests clashed with those of the archdiocese of Magdeburg, which owned exten-sive lands between Magdeburg and Haldersleben. Archbishop

Wichmann, the most prominent of the twelfth-century archbishops of Magdeburg, strove to enlarge its possessions throughout his long pontificate (1154–92). This brought him into conflict with the duke, who developed the fortress of Althaldersleben into a stronghold of his power in eastern Saxony. It was also an important communications centre, and with Henry's encouragement the trading settlement of Neuhaldersleben came into existence close by. Wichmann saw this as a threat to his authority, so that, whereas he had previously been on good terms with Henry, he now became more and more hostile and sided with Henry's adversaries.

Henry's chief opponent in eastern Saxony was without doubt Albert the Bear. The quarrel over the duchy of Saxony after the death of Lothair III had led to years of dissension and fighting between the Ascanians and the Welfs, and even after Albert renounced his claim their antagonism in territorial matters remained undiminished. Albert had with great energy enlarged his patrimonial dominions, which originally comprised only the eastern foreland of the Harz in the Ballenstedt–Aschersleben–Bernburg area. After the Nordmark the Ascanians acquired a further important base in the eastern parts of what was later the Altmark, around Stendal and Tangermünde. However, the decisive factor in the rise of the Ascanian dynasty was the agreement concluded by Albert with Pribislav-Henry, prince of Brandenburg, whereby on the latter's death in 1150 he inherited the Havelland, which he proved able to defend against all comers. While the centre of gravity of his power was thus shifting eastward of the Elbe, Albert also had his eyes fixed on the west. Though his claim to the Winzenburg inheritance was unsuccessful, to the north of the Harz he not only acquired the advocacy of the monastery of Ilsenburg east of Wernigerode, but was also installed by Conrad III as advocate of the cathedral chapter of SS Simon and Jude in Goslar. In this way Albert advanced directly into the duke's sphere of interest north of the Harz.

Between these major territorial powers lay the estates of the Sommerschenburg family, who had been counts palatine of Saxony since the end of the eleventh century. Their rights and possessions were also widely dispersed, but two main concentrations can be discerned: the region around the family seat of Sommerschenburg south of Helmstedt, and the Quedlinburg area. In addition to these allodial lands they possessed important rights of advocacy, for instance over the imperial foundations of Gandersheim and

Quedlinburg and several monasteries, in addition to exercising county rights in the Hassegau and in Seehausen, the latter as vassals of the bishops of Halberstadt. The location of their holdings obliged them to pursue a policy of neutrality as between the Welfs and the Ascanians, but they were unable to avoid friction and conflict with the duke's expansionist policy.

On the southern border of Henry's dominions, on the upper Weser and in the region of the Reinhardswald, his territorial interests impinged on those of two powers that played a major part in twelfth-century history in that area. The first of these was the see of Mainz, whose archbishops had striven since the beginning of the century to increase their power in the Saxon and Thuringian parts of their great diocese, while taking care to keep on good terms with the dukes of Saxony. This was still the case in Henry the Lion's time. After the Winzenburg line died out, Archbishop Henry I regranted to the duke the possessions of the archdiocese that had been enfeoffed to the Winzenburg brothers Henry and Herman. The duke was also able to regain possession of the richly endowed monasteries of Northeim and Reinhausen, which the Winzenburgers had ceded to Mainz in exchange for the fief.

Archbishop Arnold, who succeeded Henry I after the latter's deposition in 1153, soon found himself at odds with the *ministeriales* and citizens of Mainz, and was consequently unable to pursue an active territorial policy to the north of his diocese. In 1159 an open rebellion broke out, and in the following year Arnold was prevented from returning to Mainz from the Council of Pavia. He appealed to Henry the Lion for help but was murdered by the citizens in June, before Henry could intervene.

The next few years, in which Conrad of Wittelsbach at first governed the archbishopric, were overshadowed by the great ecclesiastical dispute in the West. Conrad took the side of Alexander III in 1165, whereupon Frederick I deposed him and appointed Christian of Buch, of the imperial chancery, in his stead. Archbishop Christian I was a zealous supporter of the Emperor's policy, especially in Italy, but paid little attention to the administration and territorial problems of the archdiocese. Neither Conrad nor Christian pursued an active territorial policy in the northern part of their diocese, and they remained strictly neutral in the quarrels of the 1160s between Henry the Lion and his opponents.

Quite different were Henry's relations with the Ludolfingers

(Ludowingers), who, since the second half of the eleventh century, had gradually built up a large domain centred on the Thuringian Basin, and had extended it to the north and west. A skilful marriage policy brought the county of Hesse into their hands. Ludwig I, the first member of the family to attain the office of landgrave, was for a time made count of the Leinegau by the Emperor Lothair. However, Henry the Lion's new acquisitions on the Werra projected like a wedge between the Ludolfinger lands in Thuringia and Hesse. In Thuringia itself Henry possessed the important monastery of Langensalza, founded by the Brunonian dynasty, which had come to him by inheritance. Many documents show that he devoted especial attention to this monastery from the beginning of his reign.

In 1140 Ludwig II succeeded his father Ludwig I as landgrave of Thuringia. Relations between him and Henry seem to have been smooth at first, both being opponents of Albert the Bear; but later the landgrave joined Henry's enemies, as he felt threatened by the duke's ambitions south of the Harz.

By the early 1150s Henry occupied a strong position in eastern Saxony, and with the help of Frederick I he was able to improve on this especially in the Harz foreland and in the mountain territory itself. Here too he derived benefit from the accommodation between Staufen and Welf interests. As we have seen, for about a decade from 1152 onwards Henry's treasurer, Anno of Heimburg, exercised the advocacy over Goslar, which Lothair III had established as part of the organization of the imperial domains in the northern foreland of the Harz. As already mentioned, it is not certain whether Anno was appointed directly by the king or whether Frederick invested Henry with the office as a fief and Henry then entrusted it to his *ministerialis*, though the latter seems more likely. In any case, the entrusting of the advocacy to a Welf *ministerialis* did much to strengthen the duke's position in and around Goslar. The palatinate itself continued to be subject to the king, who frequently held court at Goslar during his reign. The advocacy of the cathedral chapter remained in the hands of Albert the Bear, thus providing a counterweight to unduly strong Welf influence in the area.

How strong the duke was in Goslar can also be seen from the fact that in June 1154—at the same time as the diet at which Frederick I ruled in Henry's favour concerning the duchy of Bavaria and the founding of, and appointments to, the Nordalbingian bishoprics— Henry himself held court on a grand scale at Goslar in token of his newly acquired power. The names of those who attended are known to us from a charter whereby Henry granted certain estates to the religious foundation of Riechenberg, just outside the city: it lists the unusual number of 122 witnesses. Besides some ecclesiastics from the Goslar area, the charter mentions several members of families of counts and other free-born nobles from all over Saxony; also thirty-five ducal *ministeriales*, the largest number that we find at any time in the duke's entourage, and sixty-four citizens of Goslar, their occupation indicated in each case. This array of witnesses to an insignificant legal transaction testifies to Henry's strong position in the city at that time. It is also significant that, then or somewhat later, members of two prominent Goslar families became *ministeriales* of the duke. Henry also had close relations with other church foundations in Goslar.

In the 1150s the duke was able to extend his influence in the Harz district still further. Probably in 1154 or shortly after, Frederick I conferred on him the hunting rights (*Wildbann*) including general rights over uncultivated land, though this extended not to the whole mountain area but only to its western part.

Still more important were the agreements that Henry made at a further meeting with the Emperor in Goslar at the turn of the year 1157 and that were confirmed by Frederick in two great privileges of 1 January 1158. The first of these provided for a major exchange of property. Henry made over to the Emperor the dowry of his wife Clementia of Zähringen, consisting of the castle of Badenweiler with 100 *ministeriales* and 500 hides of land; in exchange he became master of three imperial strongholds south of the Harz—Herzberg, Scharzfels, and Pöhlde—and also the imperial *ministerialis* Adelhard of Burgdorf with his family and all his goods. It was expressly stated that the exchange was taking place because these estates were well situated from the point of view of rounding off the duke's possessions. The transaction was also important from the point of view of improving the Staufens' position on the upper Rhine. To make it possible, Frederick had first acquired from the Empire the property that he made over to Henry, purchasing it with extensive Staufen lands in the Mulde and Pleisse area which thus became part of the imperial domain.

On the same day, by an agreement equally profitable to the duke, the Emperor invested him, as heir to Count Udo of Katlenburg, with the countship of the Lisgau in the south-western foreland of the Harz and with forest rights in the mountains—again probably in the western part only. Although both agreements distinguished clearly between the lands that became Henry's property and those that were imperial fiefs, for practical purposes he now held the whole south-western part of the Harz district from Seesen to Lauterberg. In the 1160s he also held advocate's rights over royal estates in the Nord-hausen area, but we do not know how he acquired them.

To the north of the mountains Lothair III, both as duke and as king, had strengthened the position of his dynasty in the Harzgau with the help of *ministeriales* whom he appointed to the Blankenburg and the nearby Heimburg. Here Henry continued his grandfather's policy. In both cases the appointees belonged to his principal families of *ministeriales*, members of whom we constantly encounter in his service. The counts of Wöltingerode and Blankenburg–Regenstein, whose countships were conferred on them by Lothair, were for a long time faithful servants of the duke in this area. The two important forests of Bodfeld and Hasselfelde at the top of the mountain range were in the duke's hands and formed a link between his possessions north and south of the Harz.

This great accession of power in the Harz area was bound to increase tension between Henry and his rivals in eastern Saxony, but initially there was no open conflict.

To the west of the middle and upper Weser, the territorial picture was substantially different. Here the Billungs had during the eleventh century acquired not only important county rights but—on the middle Weser in particular—considerable allodial possessions, so that their domain included a large part of the see of Minden. These rights and possessions had passed to Henry the Lion, who thus enjoyed a strong position in the diocese, though not the advocacy over the bishopric itself. He was on friendly terms with Bishop Werner of Minden, who held office till 1170; in 1168 Henry's second marriage (to Matilda of England) was celebrated in Minden cathedral.

Thanks to the Northeim and Winzenburg inheritances, Henry also gained a firm footing in the region of the Diemel river, westward of the upper Weser. He thus acquired influence in the Paderborn diocese, whose bishops were frequent visitors to his court. This influence was increased by the rights of advocacy that he obtained over the Weser monasteries: not only the proprietary ones, including Bursfelde and Amelungsborn, but the especially lucrative imperial monasteries of Corvey and Helmarshausen, which he acquired from the Northeim inheritance after the extinction of the Winzenburg line.

However, the limits of the sees of Minden and Paderborn were also those of Henry's power base in Westphalia; further west, his influence was small. True, a later source represents him as claiming that his dukedom in Westphalia extended 'as far as Deutz, and a spear's cast further into the Rhine'. But if these proud words were really spoken they in no way reflected the actual state of affairs, but only Henry's ambition to extend his power to the region between the Teutoburger Wald and the Rhine. This led to acute differences with the archbishops of Cologne, who pursued a determined territorial policy in the area. Among the magnates of the Cologne diocese, Henry's only vassals were the lords of Lippe; nor do we find any of the great nobles of the see of Münster in Henry's entourage at any time. It was a success for Henry that he obtained possession, at an uncertain date, of the advocacy over the see of Osnabrück; but among the noble families of the bishopric only the counts of Ravensberg became Welf supporters.

The Billungs had exercised their rights of lordship on the middle and upper Weser through feudal counts. Among the families that came to prominence at that time were the counts of Schwalenberg, whose ancestral home lay north-west of Corvey. With the vice-advocacy over that monastery, which they exercised for the Northeim and later for the Winzenburg dynasty, as well as the advocacy over the see of Paderborn and certain territorial acquisitions, the Schwalenbergs had since the beginning of the twelfth century attained a position of power far exceeding that of any other counts who were Henry's vassals. This was bound to lead to friction with Henry when he began to interest himself actively in the area after acquiring the Winzenburg succession. Moreover, the aggressive behaviour of the Schwalenberg brothers Volkwin and Widukind towards the monastery of Corvey made it necessary for Henry to take action. His moves to defeat the two brothers make clear the manner in which he asserted his overlordship.

From the late 1140s onwards we find in the letters of Abbot Wibald of Corvey repeated and vehement complaints of grave encroachments by the two brothers against the monastery and its possessions, and his failure to obtain redress from the bishop of Paderborn. In 1152 the brothers attacked the town of Höxter, which belonged to the monastery, destroyed its fortifications and extorted a ransom from its rich citizens. At Wibald's suit Frederick I summoned the miscreants to court, at the same time charging Duke Henry to call them to account and see that full justice was done. Nothing is known of the sequel, and it remains a question whether any process of law took place.

Meanwhile Widukind, who was notorious for his violence, continued to harry the monastery from his castle of Desenberg near Warburg. In 1156 he even murdered the *Stadtgraf* (bailiff) Dietrich of Höxter, a *ministerialis* of the monastery, while he was dispensing justice in front of the consecrated wall of the church. This time Henry intervened, perhaps again at the Emperor's bidding, and brought Widukind to trial at Corvey in May 1157. The sentence was on the whole a light one. Widukind had to promise an indemnity to the abbot and to the murdered man's widow and children; in addition the duke deprived him of all his fiefs, in particular the castle of Desenberg, and banished him under provincial law (*Landrecht*) to the left bank of the Rhine, whence he was forbidden to return without the duke's permission. However, it is very doubtful whether he actually went into exile. A letter of the duke's to Abbot Wibald, written before he joined Frederick I's Polish campaign in August 1157, indicates that Widukind had not complied with the sentence by that time. At the beginning of the 1160s he reappears at the ducal court, showing that he was once more in favour. However, the episode is evidence that Henry regarded the public peace (*Landfrieden*) as his personal responsibility throughout the territory of the duchy.

Henry intervened once again to keep the peace in Westphalia in 1164. Around 1160 a violent quarrel over inheritance matters had broken out between Count Henry of Arnsberg and his younger brother Frederick. It seems probable that the latter brought the dispute before Henry the Lion, as he was present at the solemn diet at the Ertheneburg in October 1161 and in the ensuing years both brothers appeared at the ducal court on two occasions, one being a diet at Hanover in 1163. No settlement was reached, however, and in the end Frederick was taken prisoner by Count Henry and starved to death. On hearing of this frightful deed Henry the Lion, Reinald of Dassel (the archbishop of Cologne), and the bishops of Münster, Paderborn, and Minden exacted retribution by capturing Arnsberg, destroying the castle, and expelling Count Henry from the land. Later, perhaps at the Emperor's instance, he was reinstated after making over his possessions to the diocese of Cologne, of which he became a vassal. In consequence of this, Henry the Lion lost all influence in the Arnsberg area, and Count Henry was afterwards one of his fiercest opponents. One of the duke's chief purposes in taking part in the punitive expedition may have been to vindicate his right to enforce the *Landfrieden*.

Meanwhile opposition was growing between the duke and his adversaries in eastern Saxony. As we have seen, in the autumn of 1154, while Henry was with Frederick I on the latter's first Italian expedition, a conspiracy against him was formed by the Saxon princes and some Bavarian magnates, the moving spirits being Archbishop Hartwig of Bremen and Albert the Bear. The plotters held a meeting in the Böhmerwald and sought the aid of Duke Vladislav of Bohemia, but the enterprise was soon foiled. Hartwig, on his way home from the meeting, fell into the hands of some of Henry's *ministeriales*, who kept him in captivity for a year. When the Emperor, on return from Italy, held his first diet on German soil at Regensburg in October 1155, Vladislav of Bohemia, Albert the Bear, and other nobles made their appearance to sue for pardon and regain the imperial favour.

We know nothing of any similar movement against the duke in the next few years. However, a letter from Bishop Albert of Freising to Archbishop Eberhard of Salzburg in the spring of 1163 shows that joint military action against Henry was planned by Albert the Bear, the Count Palatine Adalbert of Sommerschenburg, Bishop Udo of Naumburg, and Ludwig, landgrave of Thuringia. This time the plot was defeated by the Emperor himself, who dissuaded some of the chief leaders from joining in the coalition: these apparently were Vladislav of Bohemia, Duke Frederick of Swabia, Duke Henry Jasomirgott of Austria, and the Margrave Ottokar of Styria.

The Obodrite rebellion of 1164 for the time being eclipsed internal dissensions in Saxony. Duke Henry called on Albert the Bear for aid, which was most probably granted. The following year, however, saw the first actual hostilities in Saxony, as Albert the Bear and the Count Palatine Adalbert of Sommerschenburg agreed to combat Henry's expansionist policy. Adalbert, however, may have taken the field ahead of time; in any case Albert left him in the lurch. The count palatine had to submit to the duke, yielding to him the important fortress of Lauenburg south-west of Quedlinburg and also a fief which he held from the bishop of Halberstadt, the location of which is unknown. The defeat of the count palatine and above all the acquisition of Lauenburg greatly strengthened Henry's position *vis-à-vis* the Ascanian dynasty in the eastern Harz area.

This skirmish with the lord of Sommerschenburg was only a prelude to the severe fighting that broke out in 1166 and convulsed the whole of Saxony for years to come. In the late summer of that year, while the duke and Valdemar of Denmark were campaigning in Pomerania, a league of Saxon princes was formed comprising almost all Henry's opponents; its leading members were Archbishop Wichmann of Magdeburg, Bishop Herman of Hildesheim, and Albert the Bear. The latter's sons joined in the alliance, as did the Landgrave Ludwig II of Thuringia, Margrave Otto of Meissen, and the Count Palatine Adalbert of Sommerschenburg; also Count Otto of Assel, Count Christian of Oldenburg, and Count Widukind of Schwalenberg. Archbishop Hartwig of Bremen remained neutral for the time being.

Many of Henry's opponents were present at a diet held at the end of August at the Boyneburg by Frederick I, who was then preparing for his fourth Italian expedition. The Emperor may on that occasion have attempted, unsuccessfully, to dissuade them from hostilities. The princes even succeeded in winning over Archbishop Reinald of Cologne before he left with a contingent of knights to support the Emperor's cause in Italy.

To meet the growing threat, Henry strengthened the fortifications of his towns and castles and placed reliable garrisons at key points. In particular he saw to the defences of Brunswick, which had increasingly become his residence during the past two decades. It was at this time that he erected the statue of a lion in the courtyard of Dankwarderode castle, as a symbol of his power and resolution in time of crisis.

To safeguard his rear during the anticipated conflict in Saxony, he took the measures in Nordalbingia that we have already mentioned. He transferred the guardianship of the young Count Adolf III of Holstein from Matilda, the boy's mother, to her brother Count Henry of Schwarzburg, a seasoned warrior who would, it was hoped, ensure peace in the territory north of the Elbe. More important still, Mecklenburg was finally pacified by the reinstatement of Pribislav as prince of the Obodrites. When this occurred is not certain; it may not have been till the beginning of 1167.

Towards the end of 1166, a few weeks after the Emperor set out for

Italy, the fighting in Saxony broke out in all its violence. The first action took place in the east of the duchy. On 20 December Wichmann of Magdeburg, Albert the Bear, and the Landgrave Ludwig attacked the ducal fortress of Althaldensleben, but were unable to take it despite the use of siege engines. Henry the Lion hastened to the scene with a reserve army and plundered his enemies' lands as far as the gates of Magdeburg. Through the mediation of some bishops and abbots a pitched battle was averted and a truce brought about whereby the duke undertook to hand over Haldensleben to the archbishop of Magdeburg at the next court session, to be held soon after Easter (6 April 1167).

Henry had reason to set store by a truce in eastern Saxony, as Count Christian of Oldenburg had meanwhile taken up arms in the north-western part of the duchy. With the aid of troops raised in Frisia he overcame and destroyed the ducal fortress of Weyhe south of Bassum on the lower Weser. The citizens welcomed the Count in the hope of shaking off Henry's rule, which they found burdensome, and sealed the alliance by taking an oath of fealty to him.

In the early summer, after the truce of Haldensleben, Henry turned his forces against Count Christian. The two armies faced each other for days across the narrow Gete river east of Bremen, without an open struggle; then Henry brought up reinforcements, and Christian withdrew to his fastness of Oldenburg.

The duke next turned against Bremen, which he captured and sacked. The citizens, many of whom had fled to the marshy lands round about, were declared outlaws and violators of the *Landfrieden*. At the entreaty of Archbishop Hartwig Henry later made peace with them in return for a heavy fine of over 1,000 marks in silver.

Henry then laid siege to Oldenburg. Count Christian died a few days afterwards, but his forces resisted for some time longer. Finally Henry captured this stronghold also, and added it to his domain.

Meanwhile the situation in eastern Saxony had once more become acute, as Henry had not kept the terms of the truce or yielded Haldensleben to the archbishop of Magdeburg. In summer 1167 his opponents entered into a formal compact against him and made preparations for a joint attack in which Reinald of Dassel, the archbishop of Cologne, was to join. After written consultation with Reinald, who was then in Italy, at the beginning of July representatives of the archbishopric and of its vassals and *ministeriales*, including Count Henry of Arnsberg, came to Magdeburg to sign a formal offensive and defensive alliance, to be ratified by Reinald after his return to Germany. The alliance, dated 12 July, was signed for the conspirators by Archbishop Wichmann, Albert the Bear and his son the Margrave Otto of Meissen, Ludwig of Thuringia, and other Saxon lords. The parties undertook to give each other full support against Henry and not to conclude a separate peace. If, after a joint peace with Henry, he were to attempt revenge on either of the parties, the other would come to its aid. Two days later a diet was held, attended by numerous princes, at Santersleben south of Haldensleben: here the alliance was joined by the Count Palatine Adalbert, three more sons of Albert the Bear, the son of Ludwig II of Thuringia (also named Ludwig), and other Saxon nobles. However, as Reinald of Dassel died soon after, the treaty with the Cologne archbishopric had no practical effect: the new archbishop, Philip of Heinsberg, thought it wiser not to take part in the contest with the duke.

On the other hand, Henry's adversaries were now able to get Archbishop Hartwig of Bremen on to their side. After his early reverses at the duke's hands Hartwig had remained neutral at the time of the initial fighting in Saxony in 1166; after Henry's capture of Bremen he had withdrawn to Hamburg to await developments, while fortifying the strongholds of Freiburg and Harburg and reinforcing their garrisons. Reinald of Dassel had previously advised him by letter to join the duke's opponents, as only so could he recover the countship of Stade. Bishop Conrad of Lübeck, who had had to leave his see as he refused to do homage to Henry, urged the archbishop in the same sense. Hartwig now joined Archbishop Wichmann in Magdeburg, thus clearly associating himself with the opposition to Henry the Lion.

In the late summer of 1167 the fight against Henry broke out again on all sides. Hartwig's followers, based on Freiburg and Harburg, plundered Henry's territory in the neighbourhood. The duke counter-attacked, capturing and destroying Freiburg; Harburg, protected by swamps, managed to resist. Henry occupied the whole of the diocese and appropriated its revenues.

Again the main scene of hostilities was in eastern Saxony. The troops of the archbishop of Magdeburg captured Althaldensleben and the nearby fortress of Niendorf on the Ohre, which they dismantled. The Saxon princes then turned against Goslar, capturing some nearby fortifications and finally the town itself. From Helmold's brief statement it might appear that the citizens themselves opened the gates: at this time Henry had lost much of the influence he had formerly enjoyed in the city and its surroundings. He placed a watch on the roads leading to Goslar so as to cut off its supplies, but was unable to subdue the city. At this time he also laid waste the diocese of Hildesheim.

The severe battles raging over large parts of Saxony prompted the Emperor to attempt mediation from Italy. As we shall see in the context of imperial policy, Frederick I had suffered a severe setback in the course of his fourth expedition. After a victorious advance through northern and central Italy and a successful battle at the gates of Rome, at the beginning of August 1167 the imperial army was devastated by malaria, which struck down over 2,000 knights and churchmen. Only with great difficulty could Frederick bring the remnants of his army back to Upper Italy, where the Lombard cities formed a league against him.

The threatening situation in Italy made it essential to pacify Germany. Accordingly, towards the end of the year Frederick sent Archbishop Christian of Mainz and Duke Berthold of Zähringen, who were able to bring about a truce between the parties in Saxony pending the Emperor's return.

Despite these arrangements, at the beginning of 1168 Henry's opponents renewed their alliance at a meeting in Merseburg and began to raid his territories. The statement by an English source that he suffered a severe defeat is not true, however. The Emperor, back in Germany, summoned a diet at Würzburg on 5 May to bring about a peace; but the princes stayed away and continued their hostilities against the duke. They also ignored the summons to a second diet at Whitsun (19 May). Finally the duke and a number of his opponents appeared at a third diet at Würzburg at the end of June. The Emperor was firmly on Henry's side and regarded the princes as in breach of the peace, but refrained from severe measures in the hope of a peaceful solution. All he could achieve at this stage was a promise by both sides to observe a truce until the next imperial diet.

A fresh upheaval was caused in Saxony by Archbishop Hartwig's death on 11 October 1168, after a chequered pontificate which had lasted 20 years. The ensuing election in Bremen was disputed. The anti-Welf electors, led by Provost Otto, voted for Albert the Bear's third son Siegfried, who was a canon at Magdeburg, while the opposing party's choice fell on Dean Otbert of Bremen.

The proposal to elevate an Ascanian to the archbishopric was an overt challenge to Henry the Lion. When disturbances broke out as a result of the contested election, Count Gunzelin of Schwerin intervened by force on behalf of Henry, who was at that time on an imperial embassy to the kings of England and France, accompanied by the archbishops of Mainz and Cologne. Siegfried, who was already in Bremen, had to flee with Provost Otto to Oldenburg, while his other adherents sought refuge in Harburg. What became of Otbert is not known. Further fighting now broke out in Saxony. At a diet at the beginning of November, the location of which is not recorded, the Emperor again enjoined the parties to keep the peace, but without success.

Accordingly Frederick himself went to Saxony at the beginning of 1169. At a diet on Candlemas day (2 February) in his palace of Wallhausen in the southern part of the Harz district, he renewed his injunction to keep the peace and took away some Saxon princes as hostages. A further diet in Bamberg at the beginning of April was again inconclusive.

A settlement was reached for the time being at a large diet at Bamberg in June. The Emperor—whose three-year-old son Henry was elected king on this occasion—took decisions with regard to keeping the peace in Saxony, the details of which are unknown to us. However, to all appearances Henry the Lion's power was left virtually intact.

The settlement concerning the filling of the Bremen archbishopric was also a success for Henry. The Emperor declared the two elections that had taken place after Hartwig's death to be invalid and—no doubt in agreement with Henry the Lion—appointed Baldwin, the aged provost of Halberstadt, to the vacant see, without any process of election in Bremen. Although a member of the Halberstadt chapter, Baldwin was close to the duke. It is questionable whether he was Henry's chaplain, as suggested by fourteenth-century annals, but he was a faithful instrument of Henry's during his nine years' pontificate, and made over many church lands to the duke and his followers. During these years Henry was the real master of the archbishopric and the city of Bremen. As an instance, in 1171 he instructed a nobleman, Frederick of Mackenstedt, to organize the settlement of some marshland on church property south-west of Bremen, and in so doing made only an incidental reference to the archbishop's consent.

The Ascanian Siegfried never gave up his claim to the archbishopric. However, he soon abandoned the idea of achieving his aim
by joining the supporters of Alexander III, and instead tried to
establish good relations with Frederick I. In 1173 he became bishop
of Brandenburg.

Despite the Emperor's efforts, the diet of 1169 at Bamberg failed to
bring lasting peace to Saxony. Widukind of Schwalenberg, despite his
undertakings, continued hostilities against the duke, who besieged
Widukind's castle of Desenberg. However, the citadel was at the top
of a mountain, with precipitous slopes on all sides, and Henry's siege
engines were of no effect. Accordingly the duke called in miners from
the Rammelsberg near Goslar, who drove a shaft into the mountain
and in so doing came across the spring which provided the castle's
water supply. Henry had it stopped up and thus compelled
Widukind and his men to surrender. The count was imprisoned and
subsequently released: at the beginning of the 1170s we find him in
the entourage of Bishop Evergisus of Paderborn. The fact that in 1169
Henry was able to call on the Rammelsberg miners for help shows
that he still had some influence in the Goslar area, even though the
town itself was no longer in his possession.

Fighting in Saxony broke out again early in 1170. This time Henry
was the aggressor: at the end of February he invaded and plundered
the territory of the archbishop of Magdeburg. He also captured and
destroyed the fortress of Harburg, where the Ascanian Siegfried's
supporters in Bremen had taken refuge. Other Saxon princes were
also involved in this fighting. The Emperor summoned the disputants
to a diet at Erfurt at the end of June, where he was at last able to bring
about a peace between Henry and his opponents. In November 1170
Albert the Bear died, relieving Henry of his chief adversary in eastern
Saxony.

The Erfurt settlement brought an end to the fighting that had been
going on in Saxony since 1166. Modern accounts frequently speak of
it as a 'rebellion of the princes', but this gives a false impression. It
was not a question of princes rebelling against a ruler to whom they
owed allegiance, but rather a struggle for power between the duke
and other spiritual and temporal magnates, who considered their
position as direct vassals of the Empire to be threatened by Henry's
expansionist ambitions. Despite his enemies' numerical superiority,
Henry was able to maintain his position in Saxony without any major
loss, thanks to the fact that the Emperor throughout his mediation

efforts remained firmly on Henry's side. Here again the close understanding between Hohenstaufen and Welf paid rich dividends for Henry.

The peace of 1170 did not put a stop to Henry's expansionist aims. On the death of Count Otto of Assel, the last male Winzenburger, he laid claim to the inheritance. We do not know the exact time or circumstances of this, as the date of the count's death is not known either: he is last mentioned in documents in 1170. However, Henry's acquisition of the Assel inheritance, including the stronghold of Lichtenberg, can reasonably be dated between 1170 and 1177. The location of this complex of estates to the east of Hildesheim reinforced the duke's already strong position in the Hildesheim diocese. We do not know on what grounds he based his claim, which led to friction with Archbishop Philip of Cologne. The latter's sister, Salome of Heinsberg, was Count Otto's widow, and the archbishop subsequently laid claim to the inheritance on her behalf.

Henry the Lion's last attempt to enlarge his territorial base in Saxony belongs to the period of conflict connected with the legal process against the duke. The Count Palatine Adalbert of Sommerschenburg died in 1179, and Henry saw the opportunity to improve his position in the eastern foreland of the Harz mountains. Adalbert's heir was his sister Adelheid, abbess of Quedlinburg. Being hard put to it to defend her rights against the powerful duke, she sold them to the archbishopric of Magdeburg. Henry for his part laid claim especially to the Sommerschenburgers' allodial property; part of this he was able to acquire towards the end of 1179, but lost it again when he was deposed in the following year. Once more we do not know what legal grounds he had for his claim, if any. After his fall Archbishop Wichmann asserted his own title to the estates; however, in the thirteenth century the Welfs recovered some of the Sommerschenburg possessions.

Looking back in 1170 at the results of his territorial policy in the two decades since the accession of Frederick I, Henry had good reason to be satisfied. Despite various setbacks he had come a good way closer to his objective of building up a consolidated domain in Saxony. At the same time relations with his rivals were increasingly tense, and it was likely that they would again come to a head sooner or later.

6

The Administration of the Duchy of Saxony; Policy towards Cities and the Church

THE administration of such an extensive area with its many variations of local structure presented Henry with a difficult task. True, he had in his immediate entourage some court officials and other dignitaries; but, like the German king and the other German princes of his time, he lacked a body of administrators in the proper sense, with whose help he could exercise steady and uniform control over his large territory. He therefore had to make use of institutions as he found them. However, by developing them he made important progress towards building up an administration in the Low German area, of the type that was to characterize the German territorial state of the late Middle Ages.

The Billung dukes had been unable themselves to exercise their numerous rights of countship and advocacy. Instead they appointed members of the free-born nobility to be viscounts and vice-advocates (*Vizevögte*); these rights were granted as a hereditary fief, and the holders were able, thanks to them and to their allodial possessions, gradually to build up a domain of their own. These vassal counts and advocates first appear in the region along the middle and upper Weser, being furthest away from the Billungs' residence at Lüneburg. Thus in the second half of the eleventh century the Schwalenbergers, whose ancestral castle was situated west of the middle Weser near present-day Schwalenberg, exercised county rights for the Billungs in that area. Later they acquired from the Northeimers the important vice-advocacy over the monastery of Corvey. At the beginning of the twelfth century we meet the lords of Everstein, resident in the area north of Holzminden, and those of Roden, who originated in the Weser mountain area but later became the duke's vassal counts in the region of Hanover.

Lothair of Supplinburg, both as duke and as king, continued this policy by creating new countships. Among the new families with county rights that arose while he was duke of Saxony the most prominent are the Schauenburgers, whom he invested with the countship of Holstein-Stormarn in Nordalbingia, and who in course of time managed to build up a self-contained territory in their ancestral region between the Weser, the Steinhuder Meer, and the Deister. In the Loingau and the Grindergau, the northern part of the Minden diocese east of the Weser, the lords of Wölpe, whose home was near Nienburg, exercised county rights under Lothair; like the Schauenburgers, they were subsequently loyal supporters of the Welfs.

Lothair created new countships especially in the Harz region. North of the mountains, in his time as duke he made the lords of Blankenburg his viscounts in part of the large Harzgau. In the north-western foreland of the Harz, when already king, he created a countship on both banks of the Oker which he conferred on the lords of Wöltingerode. The beginnings of the countship of Wernigerode also probably go back to Lothair. South of the Harz he created the countships of Scharzfels, Ilfeld-Honstein, and perhaps also Rothenburg. Although these countships, except that of the Blankenburgers, were fiefs of the Empire, their holders as a rule supported the Welfs in later times, as did members of their families.

Lothair chose quite a different form of administration in his own immediate domain, whether the Supplinburg patrimony or the lands he acquired later through his mother-in-law Gertrude as heir of the Brunonians. Here for the most part he allowed his various seigniorial rights to be exercised by his own household officers or *ministeriales*. Thus began in Saxony the role of the class who were to be the dukes' chief assistants in the administration of the duchy during the following decades. In Lothair's entourage we already find members of the families which were later to provide the Welfs with their chief *ministeriales*. These were: the lords of Blankenburg, with a civil status clearly distinct from that of the counts of the same name; those of Heimburg, Dahlum (near Schöningen), Peine, and Wolfenbüttel; and those of Weida, whose oldest family seat (no longer extant) lay to the north-east of Mühlhausen, but who subsequently took root in the region south of Gera.

Henry the Lion took over and developed this administrative structure as it had been shaped by his grandfather. The institution of a hereditary viscountcy was widespread not only in the domains that had descended to him from Lothair and Henry the Proud, but also in the extensive lands that he acquired from the Stade, Northeim, and Winzenburg inheritances. Hence the number of countships of which Henry could dispose freely was very small.

The importance he still attached, however, to this traditional form of county organization is seen in the fact that he created the county of Ratzeburg in 1143, and in 1167 that of Schwerin for Gunzelin of Hagen, after his reconciliation with the Obodrite prince Pribislav. Around the middle of the century the new counties of Lüchow and Dannenberg were created in the Hannoversches Wendland ('Hanover Wendish territory') on the left bank of the Elbe. The holders of county rights in both of these appear time and again in the duke's entourage; however, the view often repeated that they were created by Henry as counties of colonization remains uncertain. There is good reason to think that both were independent domains established by members of the nobility from the Altmark who took part in the Wendish crusade of 1147. It is true, however, that Henry the Lion and the later Saxon dukes regarded these two counties as part of their duchy.

We know little of Henry's relations with the numerous feudal counts in Saxony proper. For the most part we only encounter them as witnesses to ducal charters, along with other free-born nobles who were not his vassals. Henry was obliged to respect the hereditary character that by now attached to the office, and could only withdraw comital rights if a family died out or if the holder committed a serious violation of his feudal duties. Consequently it was Henry's aim to suppress the efforts towards independence that manifested themselves again and again in these families, particularly the older ones, and to assert his authority over them by every possible means. For this reason he was strict in enforcing their feudal obligations, including the payment of dues. Again and again he summoned his vassals to attend his many courts and diets in Saxony proper and in Nordalbingia, and to assist in the administration of justice. He also invariably summoned them to provide military aid, for the Emperor's first Italian expedition and other imperial enterprises, and for his own campaigns in Nordalbingia and Saxony.

As time went on, Henry's harsh regime excited opposition among the vassal counts, as well as among the Saxon nobles who owed fealty to the king alone. This can be seen in the behaviour of the Schwalenbergs. Although, as we saw, Widukind of Schwalenberg regained the duke's favour after being condemned for his grave breach of the peace in attacking the monastery of Corvey, he joined the coalition of princes against Henry in 1166 and continued fighting in Saxony even after the Emperor's first attempt at a settlement. Again, Count Christian of Oldenburg, who also joined the conspiracy against Henry, was his vassal for some territory in Frisia. The opposition of the feudal counts reached a peak at the end of the 1170s, when the fighting in Saxony erupted once again. Before the duke's condemnation by the Emperor, many of his vassals sided with his enemies; and relatively few—such as Gunzelin of Schwerin, Bernard of Lippe, and Conrad of Roden—remained loyal after his fall. The tension between feudal loyalty on the one hand and sense of status on the other, which became very clear at this time, shows that the institution of vassal counts did not provide a basis for the establishment of a strong ducal power.

This explains the increasing importance of the ministerial class in the ducal administration. As with other contemporary rulers of the time, whether spiritual or temporal, the *ministeriales* in Saxony formed the executive organ for the administration of the developing territorial state. In numbers alone, the size of this class under the Welfs increased dramatically around the middle of the twelfth century. The families which had provided officers to Lothair of Supplinburg were joined under Henry the Lion by *ministeriales* resident in the extensive allodial lands of the Billung family that had been inherited by his father Henry the Proud. Further *ministeriales* came into Henry's ownership with the Stade, Northeim, and Winzenburg estates acquired in the first decade of his rule.

We have no exact knowledge as to the total number of *ministeriales* who were eventually at Henry's disposal. Only a small proportion are mentioned by name as witnesses to ducal charters or in other sources. The estimate of 300 families that has been suggested is certainly too low. The list of allodial estates of the last Northeimer, Count Siegfried IV of Boyneburg, which was presumably drawn up soon after his death in 1144, mentions about 100 *ministeriales* for those lands alone. In 1219, when the Count Palatine Henry, the eldest son of Henry the Lion, made an agreement with Archbishop Gerhard II of Bremen returning the Stade estates to the Bremen church, at his command over seventy *ministeriales* swore fealty to the archbishop as their new overlord. In 1158, at the time of Henry the Lion's great exchange of property with the Emperor, as many as 100 *ministeriales* were attached to the lands in and around Badenweiler that had been the Duchess Clementia's dowry. This indicates how widespread was the use of *ministeriales* by German princes at that time, over and above those in the service of the Empire. On this basis we may perhaps reckon the number of Welf *ministeriales* in Saxony in Henry the Lion's time at 400 families or more.

All the members of this class in Saxony possessed a uniform legal status. We only know it in broad lines, since Henry the Lion, unlike some other dynasts of the time, did not record it in detail. A basic principle was that the *ministeriales* were unfree; at the same time they possessed legal capacity under customary law (*Landrecht*), were allowed to possess allodial property and could dispose of it within certain narrow limits. Already at this period it can be observed that the Welf *ministeriales* sought to be liberated from their unfree status.

As can be seen with especial clarity from the exchange of 1158, that status allowed the duke to dispose of his *ministeriales* or barter them at will, together with their personal property and fiefs; he could also move them at pleasure within his dominions. On the other hand he owed them a duty of protection and had to reward them suitably for their various services. This he generally did by granting a 'service fief' from his extensive allodial estates. In this way he was able to use them to administer large areas and assert his authority in distant parts of his realm. Thus we find that on acquiring the Stade inheritance he appointed a number of *ministeriales* to that area.

The military obligations of the ministerial class were closely bound up with their other duties. Entrusted with the command of ducal castles, they not only administered the surrounding territory but also defended it. They provided the main contingent of the ducal levy, in which they had to serve as mounted knights.

Although the *ministeriales* had a common legal status, there were wide social differences between them. Amid the mass who are often known to us by personal name alone and can seldom be assigned to a particular family, there stands out a group of some size which performed a multiplicity of functions. The most important offices were reserved for a few families who formed an élite among the *ministeriales* and who, in wealth and prestige, sometimes outranked even the lesser nobility. These were chiefly families that had already served Duke Lothair: the lords of Blankenburg, Dahlum, Heimburg, Peine, Weida, and Wolfenbüttel. The lords of Volkmarode near

Brunswick also belong to this category, though we first meet them as servants of Henry the Lion.

The best-known of the Welf *ministeriales* is Jordan of Blankenburg. He is mentioned for the first time in the duke's entourage in 1161, and a year later is heard of as 'steward' (*dapifer*), or manager of the ducal household. He held this office under Henry the Lion, to whom he remained faithful after his fall, and subsequently under Henry's son the count palatine, till he died in extreme old age, probably as late as 1221. He was apparently the duke's chief adviser and nearly always accompanied him on journeys, including the pilgrimage to Jerusalem. The chronicler Arnold of Lübeck describes him as a rich man. It is noteworthy that when, in 1190, Jordan was taken prisoner by enemies of the duke in Nordalbingia they demanded a ransom of 500 marks in silver, whereas Count Helmold of Schwerin on the same occasion was rated at only 300 marks. Some other *ministeriales* who are also described as 'stewards' were no doubt assistants to Jordan.

The most important court official next to the steward was the treasurer, in charge of valuables and finance. Anno of Heimburg, whom we have met as a temporary advocate (*Vogt*) in Goslar, was treasurer under Lothair III with the title of *cubicularius*, and served Henry in the same capacity till about 1170; he seems to have died soon after. The office of cup-bearer does not seem to have played a great part at the ducal court; the two *ministeriales* who are recorded as having filled it at one time or another cannot be assigned to any family. On the other hand feudalization of the army lent importance to the 'marshal', the officer in charge of stables. This position was filled under Henry the Lion and his successors by, among other *ministeriales*, the lords of Volkmarode.

The ministerial class also provided the duke with *Vögte* (bailiffs and/or justiciars) in castles, towns, and toll stations. We have already mentioned Reinold, who for a time was *Stadtvogt* of Lübeck. From the time of Lothair III onwards the lords of Dahlum filled the office of *Vogt* for Brunswick. Their counterparts in Lüneburg, Stade, Einbeck, Hitzacker, and the Ertheneburg were also Welf *ministeriales*, as was Gerhard, mayor of Bardowick, who acted as *Vogt* there. On the other hand it was exceptional for *ministeriales* to be entrusted with a countship. However, Lothair III appointed his *ministerialis* Berthold of Peine to administer that county; he and his son Liudolf also did so under Henry the Lion, and Liudolf's son of the same name held the fief until he died childless in about 1200. The only other instance known to us is Berthold of Wolbrechtshausen north of Göttingen, who was count of the Leinegau around 1170.

As we have seen, after the campaign against the Obodrites and the death of Prince Niklot in 1160, Henry attempted to take the conquered territory under his own administration. Among those whom he then entrusted with the command of fortresses and the accompanying political responsibilities were two of his chief *ministeriales*. Liudolf of Dahlum, at that time *Vogt* of Brunswick, was appointed to Quetzin on the Plauer See, and Liudolf of Peine to Malchow in the Müritzgau; both also retained their existing offices. We have no details of their activity in that area, which came to an end a few years later when Henry reinstated Pribislav as chief of the Obodrites.

Within the large sphere of power that Henry had created by his expansionist policy in Saxony, the towns were of great importance in many respects. Henry ranks as one of the German princes who did most to foster the independence of the burgher class in the twelfth century. He has indeed been regarded, though wrongly, as the originator of the German system of government by municipal council.

A number of towns in Lower Saxony claim Henry as their founder, though in a few cases this rests only on a later oral tradition. It is often hard to determine whether the claim is justified, owing to the poverty of sources for twelfth-century municipal history in the Low German area. We possess no charter granted by Henry to a town under his suzerainty. Only later thirteenth-century municipal records refer to the grant of rights by the duke and purport to confirm these. Contemporary chronicles also have as a rule little to say about Henry's attitude towards the civic movement in the twelfth century. Helmold of Bosau gives a full account of the beginnings of Lübeck under Count Adolf II and Duke Henry, but we have nothing similar for any other Saxon town. Consequently we have to reconstruct Henry's actions from uncommunicative sources, partly by way of hypothesis. In recent decades, however, important new light has been thrown on the origins of many places by urban topographical research, frequently supported by archaeological investigations.

We have already described the first beginnings of Lübeck and Schwerin, the two towns in the area of east German settlement in the development of which Henry the Lion played a decisive part.

Although the rudiments of a city can be seen to have existed in both cases, the layout as we see it today affords clear evidence of planning. By contrast, the localities in the interior of Saxony which developed into cities around the middle of the twelfth century, thanks primarily to Henry's policy, for the most part bear evidence of gradual evolution.

This is especially true of Brunswick, which became the political and cultural centre of the Saxon duchy during the period of Henry's rule. When he became duke in 1142 there were in the area five settlements, separated geographically and with different codes of law. There were in the first place the fortress of the Brunonians on an island formed by the river Oker; the 'old city' (Altstadt) on the left bank, which had for some time flourished as a trading settlement; and on the right bank, with St Magnus's church as its centre, the village of Brunswik, also on former Brunonian ground, from whose farms the inhabitants of the fortress were supplied with provisions. In addition there was the monastery of St Giles (Ägidius) and St Cyriac's church, both enjoying independent legal status. The Oker became navigable at Brunswik, which was also the place where the old trade route from Cologne to Magdeburg crossed the lines of communication from south-western Germany and the northern foreland of the Harz to the lower Elbe, so that since the end of the ninth century Brunswick had been a major centre of trade in eastern Saxony. Later it also became important as an emporium for the ores mined near Goslar. It is probable that civic privileges were already granted to the Altstadt by Lothair III.

Henry left his mark on Brunswick in three important ways. Firstly he created a new settlement, the Hagensiedlung. Secondly, he constructed fortifications which bound the settlements together, physically if not as yet legally, with the exception of Brunswik, which was somewhat further off. Finally, he developed the old Brunonian fortress, henceforth more often referred to as Dankwarderode, into a princely residence unique in Germany at that time.

Contemporary sources tell us nothing of the beginnings of the Hagen district, but in somewhat later tradition the duke is expressly mentioned as its founder. It came into existence not by a single act but by a development which probably began in the early 1150s. It was necessary first to drain and clear the marshy area on the right bank of the Oker, which was probably an allodial Welf possession. For this purpose the duke brought in Flemish settlers who were especially skilled at such work. Originally the settlement occupied a narrow area, its only thoroughfare from north to south being the later *Bohlweg* (corduroy road). The Flemings also brought with them the art of wool-weaving, which they made a local speciality. Thus Hagen became a kind of industrial quarter, the development of which may have been assisted by merchants from the Altstadt.

The legal status of the new quarter was embodied by Henry in a charter of rights. The *Iura Indaginis*, a compendium of the 'Hagen code' dating from the beginning of the thirteenth century, purports to be a record of rights granted by the duke, but it is not clear which of these go back to the middle of the twelfth century. Certainly Henry allowed the Flemish settlers to keep the code of laws they had brought with them; he also permitted them to trade freely on the Oker and the Aller as far as Celle and Bremen. Provisions concerning the acquisition of personal freedom within 'a year and a day', and for the settlement of intestacies, also belong to the earliest features of the code. The Hagen settlers probably possessed from the outset the right to elect a *Bürgervogt* for purposes of 'low justice' and policing the market. Here as in his other cities, the duke reserved to himself jurisdiction over serious crimes, especially those against life and limb, and appointed a *Stadtvogt* (bailiff) to exercise it on his behalf in Hagen and the other quarters of the municipality. He certainly encouraged the development of the Altstadt also, though it is very doubtful whether he granted it a charter as has been supposed.

Today Henry's mark is most clearly seen in the fortress quarter. Here he had the old Brunonian church pulled down and, in 1173, founded a new basilica on a cruciform plan, dedicated to St Blaise and St John the Baptist. This building, which was essentially completed by the time of the duke's death in 1195, is a landmark in the architectural history of Lower Saxony, the first vault construction to have been executed as a unity. The old Brunonian citadel was replaced by a palace (*Pfalz*) modelled on the one constructed by the Salian emperors at Goslar, as indicated not only by its proximity to the collegiate church but also by the two-storied chapel. Above all, Brunswick was increasingly favoured by the duke as a permanent capital, something the German kings as yet did not possess. The fortifications constructed by him, probably during the hostilities in the 1160s, had the effect of combining the ducal seat and the urban settlements into a single unit, which was also a rare phenomenon at the time.

On the lower Elbe, Stade had developed since the eighth century into the principal centre of trade and communications, a position it yielded to Hamburg only in the mid-thirteenth century. In 1144–5, when Henry the Lion gained possession of the Stade inheritance and the locality itself, there were on the lower course of the Schwinge five embryonic settlements, dependent either on the count or on the archbishopric of Bremen. As the duke was supreme advocate over the archbishopric he was able to assert his authority in both the secular and the ecclesiastical spheres, though initially Archbishop Hartwig, who was frequently in Stade, could claim a voice in its affairs also.

Henry enclosed the whole of Stade, except for the more distant fishing settlement, with a ring of strong fortifications and thus made it a topographical unity, on which he conferred civic rights. This probably took place in the 1160s, when the duke was particularly active in the affairs of Saxony.

Henry's son, King Otto IV, issued a *privilegium majus* to the citizens of Stade in 1209, in which he referred expressly to the rights granted by his father, confirming and extending them. Among the rights mentioned in this diploma, those concerning judicial matters and the amount of certain fines belong to the oldest core of municipal law. The provisions for the acquisition of personal freedom after a year and a day, and for dealing with intestacy, reflect those found at Lübeck and at Hagen in Brunswick, and probably therefore date from Henry the Lion's time.

The duke's advocacy over the archbishopric of Bremen enabled him to intervene in the city's judicial system. To all appearances, however, he did not exercise this right personally after November 1155, when he administered justice in the city after his return from Italy. In 1159 a *Stadtvogt* was for the first time appointed for Bremen in the person of Adolf of Nienkerken (probably Neuenkirchen on the Weser below Bremen). He was a vassal of Henry's, much in attendance on the duke in the 1150s and 1160s, and we may therefore suppose that Henry appointed him. There is also mention of an *Untervogt* named Bernhard, but we do not know if his authority extended to the city; nor have we any information on Adolf of Nienkerken's activity as *Stadtvogt*.

Around the middle of the century the civic community of Bremen developed steadily into an independent body which frequently took action on its own account, separately from the archbishop who was lord of the city. It is sometimes suggested that the duke materially assisted this process by a charter (now lost) granting the citizens of Bremen the same rights as those of Stade. This is not correct: we know nothing of any privilege granted to Bremen by Henry the Lion. On the contrary, there is evidence suggesting that his relations with the town in the 1160s were rather strained; as we saw, the citizens sided with his opponents during the fighting in Saxony in 1167.

In north-eastern Saxony the neighbouring localities of Bardowick and Lüneburg on the Ilmenau were an important buttress of Henry's rule. They were for a long time closely connected economically. Lüneburg was the centre for the production of salt, which was transported via Bardowick especially to the north and east. Bardowick was a major trading centre in the Saxon–Slav borderland from as far back as the eighth century, and had since developed into a considerable market. It has been supposed, but is not certain, that Charlemagne created a missionary bishopric in this part of Saxony, which was soon afterwards transferred to Verden. Originally the township with its market, mint, and toll belonged to the crown; it was probably granted as a fief to the Welfs by Lothair III. Although we hear nothing of a grant of civic rights, by the middle of the twelfth century Bardowick was a city from the topographic point of view and perhaps legally as well. In the early 1160s it had as its mayor (*Schultheiss*) a *ministerialis* of Henry the Lion, and at the beginning of the next century Henry's son William of Lüneburg granted to the town of Bleckede, which he founded, the rights that had been customary in Bardowick.

The foundation of Lübeck by Count Adolf II soon did considerable harm to Bardowick's trade. The duke sought to eliminate this competition by placing a market ban on Lübeck; but after himself becoming lord of Lübeck in 1159, he no longer had an interest in fostering Bardowick, which accordingly declined in the second half of the century. The resulting tension between the townsfolk and the duke flared into an open breach after his fall, when Bardowick reverted to the Empire. Even in 1182—according to what is admittedly a later source—the townsfolk greeted Henry with mockery and barred their gates when he passed by the city on his way into exile. They also opposed him with force in the autumn of 1189, when, returning ahead of time from his second exile, he attempted to reassert his authority in eastern Saxony. This time the duke took a ferocious revenge: he captured the town and destroyed it so completely that it was thereafter no more than an insignificant village.

The churches went up in flames; only the subsequently rebuilt 'cathedral' bears witness to the town's former greatness. It is, however, a legend of later date that the duke caused the ruined building to be inscribed with the words *Vestigia Leonis*.

In the case of Lüneburg also, the beginnings of the city probably go back to Carolingian times. The settlement by the salt-works probably originated in the ninth century. Somewhat more recent is the settlement below the castle on the Kalkberg, which was no doubt erected as a refuge. From the tenth century onwards this stronghold was the chief residence of the Billung family, to whose allodial estates the district belonged. Under its protection they founded a monastery in honour of St Michael, the church of which became their family burial-place. Gradually a settlement grew up at the foot of the mountain. Henry the Lion and Clementia frequently resided in the castle at the beginning of his rule; it was probably the birthplace of their son Henry, who died in an accident in early childhood and was buried in the monastery church. In later years too, Henry often held court at Lüneburg.

Besides the citadel and the salt-workers' settlement, there is record in the tenth century of a market on what came to be the street called 'Auf der Altstadt'. By the middle of the twelfth century Lüneburg already presented the appearance of a city. The destruction of Bardowick operated to its advantage. It cannot be confirmed, however, as is occasionally suggested, that in the last decade of his rule Henry the Lion, by creating the so-called Neustadt, enlarged the area of Lüneburg and conferred municipal rights on it. It was probably not until the first decades of the thirteenth century that Lüneburg finally became a city. As before, Henry's role in the process should not be exaggerated.

The beginnings of Hanover in the twelfth century must also remain uncertain, given the state of our sources. When the Billungs died out in 1106 their county rights in this area, the Marstemgau, passed to the counts of Roden, who, around 1125, founded St George's church and its adjacent market. There was also an independent settlement attached to St Giles's church. Henry the Lion, as duke, once more asserted his suzerainty over the counts of Roden. In 1163 he held a much-attended court in Hanover, where he possessed a manor. It was probably on this occasion that his new building of St Giles's was consecrated by the bishop of Minden. He enlarged the settled area round the church, built fortifications and established a mint; he may also have granted Hanover its first municipal charter. When King Henry VI sacked Hanover in 1189 in the course of the fighting with Henry the Lion, it was described as a *civitas*; but it does not follow that it was already legally a city, which can only be stated with certainty for the early part of the thirteenth century.

In the south of Saxony, Münden (or Hannoversch-Münden) and Göttingen were Welf strongholds from the thirteenth century onwards, and their origin as cities has therefore also been ascribed to Henry the Lion. This is especially true of Münden. The fact that the Welfs owned estates in the upper Weser area has until very recently been regarded as proof that Münden, which first appears as a city in the 1180s, was founded by Henry. Its ground-plan was also thought to bear this out. However, a close study of ownership conditions in the triangle at the confluence of the Werra and Fulda, on which the city is situated, has clearly shown that it was a crown property of ancient date, enfeoffed to the landgraves of Thuringia of the Ludolfinger (Ludowinger) dynasty. Münden was therefore a Thuringian foundation; the Landgrave Ludwig II or his sons probably established it between about 1155 and 1180. It did not become Welf property until the Ludolfingers died out in 1247.

We can likewise only speculate as to when Göttingen became a city, as there are no written sources for its history in the twelfth century. Next to the old village of Gutingi, around the middle of the century there may already have been, on the site of the present city, a market settlement by St John's church and probably a Welf trading centre (*Wirtschaftshof*) where the ducal castle was subsequently built. Henry the Lion is not recorded as having been in the Göttingen area at any time. After a long interval the town is mentioned in the partition of 1202 among his three surviving sons. Göttingen was allotted to the eldest son, the Count Palatine Henry, and, with the rest of the latter's possessions, went after his death to his nephew, Duke Otto the Child. The count palatine probably made Göttingen a city soon after the partition. In 1232 Duke Otto confirmed to the citizens the rights they had enjoyed under the count palatine and the Emperor Otto IV. It is very unlikely that it was Henry the Lion who conferred municipal rights, as is occasionally suggested.

In the case of Haldensleben, the chief stronghold of ducal power in eastern Saxony, it has likewise often been supposed that Henry the Lion founded the place and conferred extensive municipal rights on it. The settlement in this area originated in the county fortress of Althaldensleben, which, after the extinction of the family then resident, passed to Lothair III and then to the Welfs. As we have seen, although strongly fortified it was sacked and destroyed by Archbishop Wichmann of Magdeburg and his allies during the fighting in Saxony in 1167. Somewhat further north, at the intersection of important trade routes on the river Ohre there arose, about the middle of the century, the trading settlement of Neuhaldensleben, which presented a certain competition to Magdeburg. Henry the Lion no doubt played a part in its foundation, as it was situated on his territory. It is soon mentioned as a *civitas* and there are references to its citizens and its strong fortifications. At the beginning of the thirteenth century the archbishop of Magdeburg confirmed the rights granted to the inhabitants by Henry the Lion. These indications suggest that the duke conferred municipal rights on Neuhaldensleben, but it cannot be definitely proved. In the fighting that again broke out in Saxony towards the end of 1177 and to which we shall revert in more detail, Archbishop Wichmann captured Neuhaldensleben in the summer of 1181 after several vain attempts, and gave it over to the citizens of Magdeburg to be destroyed. At the beginning of the next century the archbishops of Magdeburg finally came into possession of the town, after which they set about rebuilding it.

Reviewing the duke's attitude towards the Low German municipal movement in his time, it can be said that he did much to promote the development of several important localities, on some of which he conferred a charter to complete the process. This activity reached its height between the late 1150s and about 1170, when his territorial ambitions were also most in evidence. We cannot, however, speak, as is occasionally done, of his having pursued a municipal policy on a grand scale. Moreover, it is noteworthy that the measures in question were confined to his immediate dominions in eastern Saxony and to Nordalbingia. West of the Weser he did not create any new towns; in Westphalia he retarded rather than encouraged the process, and a period of new foundations set in only after his fall from power.

This leads to the question as to the aims of his policy. Without doubt they were chiefly economic. He principally favoured places that had already proved valuable as trading centres or were likely to do so on account of their location. However, it is wrong to speak as if he consciously set about creating a self-contained economic area. For this the main condition was lacking, namely a rounded-off territory.

However, Henry's attitude was determined above all by questions of revenue. The growth of trade and the increasing population of the towns swelled the income deriving from market dues, mint and customs receipts, and the administration of justice. In this way he acquired resources which, as barter steadily gave place to a money economy, could be used to further political aims as well.

The growing use of money was also reflected in the rapidly increasing scale on which coins were minted during the duke's rule. From the outset he possessed the long-established mints of Brunswick, Bardowick, Lüneburg, and Stade. For a time he gained control of the Bremen mint. In 1158, together with county rights in the Lisgau, he acquired the mint at Gittelde south of Gandersheim. Soon afterwards he established a mint at Lübeck, which rapidly became important for the whole Baltic area, and another at Hanover.

At the same time the form of coins underwent an important change. The pfennige (denarii), stamped on both sides, were replaced by bracteates, coins of thin silver foil, stamped on one side only and hence in higher relief. The heyday of this process was in the second half of the twelfth century, especially in southern and eastern Saxony. Almost all Henry the Lion's coins are bracteates. They seldom bear the duke's effigy, but usually a lion in various forms. The variety of impressions is due to the medieval custom of minting new coins each year so as to increase the gain from seigniorage. On special occasions, such as Henry the Lion's marriage to Clementia and subsequently to Matilda of England, especially fine commemorative medals were struck and distributed. Such a medal was also struck in 1166 to celebrate the erection of the lion monument in Brunswick. From the artistic point of view Henry the Lion's bracteates are certainly the finest specimens struck in Saxony.

The duke and the citizens were drawn together by their shared interest in economic growth, and there is therefore no point in asking which of them deserved more credit for the towns' prosperity. The duke reserved governmental powers to himself, especially those of jurisdiction in major cases, and exercised them through representatives known as burgraves (*Burggrafen*), bailiffs (*Stadtgrafen*), or governors (*Vögte*).

Like other contemporary rulers Henry was at pains to attract new townsfolk by means of privileges. An opportunity was afforded by the civic customary law that had developed since the end of the eleventh century in the districts on the lower Rhine, and was brought to Saxony by merchants from those parts. Apart from economic advantages such as exemption from ground rent, these related to the acquisition of personal freedom and the right to make regulations for law and order in the civic community while respecting local custom. The principle that 'city air makes a man free', i.e. that a townsman could cease to be dependent on a territorial lord and become a free man, attracted valuable elements from the surrounding countryside. The citizens, formed into a sworn confederation, were allowed to regulate internal affairs such as the supervision of markets and jurisdiction over them. In the governing body of these civic corporations they created the beginnings of an administrative system which by the end of the century had evolved into the town council as the embodiment of municipal self-government.

However, Henry's interest in the cities was not confined to economics and finance: it was also related to political and military aims. The towns, usually protected by a ducal castle, served to defend the surrounding territory. This was true not only of the two new foundations east of the lower Elbe, but also of the cities in Saxony proper. During the heavy fighting of the 1160s the towns in eastern Saxony were important bastions of ducal power. Apart from their military function they also played a special part in government. It was Henry's aim to consolidate his territorial base as much as possible in the Welf heartland, and the towns were to be centres and points of radiation for the administration of the periphery. The energies of the rising bourgeoisie were to be harnessed to the developing territorial state.

In any political formation in the Middle Ages, the church occupied a place of special importance. Given the close interrelation of spiritual and temporal affairs, it could be a valuable aid to any ruler in building up a position of power. Henry the Lion made extensive use of this opportunity. At a time when the German monarchy, since the Concordat of Worms, had lost much of its previously dominant influence over the church, the duke was more successful than any other twelfth-century German territorial prince in making the church and its institutions serviceable to his own domestic ends.

As we have seen, this was especially so in Nordalbingia, where Henry was able to assert rights over the bishoprics of Oldenburg-Lübeck, Ratzeburg, and Schwerin that went considerably beyond the terms of the investiture privilege granted him by Frederick I in

1154. The duke not only invested the bishops but as a rule decided who should be appointed to a vacant see, and was also able to use the bishops for political tasks. In the regions of episcopal immunity he still maintained the ancient rights of a margrave and reserved to himself supreme jurisdiction over ecclesiastical rear-vassals.

In the other bishoprics and imperial abbeys in Saxony the right of investiture was exercised by the Emperor. In some of them, however, the duke was able to exert strong influence thanks to the privilege of advocacy. This also enabled him to control the church to a considerable degree in other ways. He probably held about fifty advocacies altogether; the exact number cannot be stated, as we do not possess full information with regard to several monasteries and other foundations in Saxony in the mid-eleventh century. As Henry's adversary Albert the Bear possessed only about twenty advocacies, it can be seen how strong the duke's position was in church matters also.

As we saw in connection with the affairs of the archbishopric and city of Bremen, these rights of advocacy offered wide opportunities. Certainly Henry gained a stronger position *vis-à-vis* the church and city than was due to such rights alone, but at the outset of his rule they served him well as a basis for intervention. Verden and Osnabrück were the other two Saxon bishoprics in which the Welfs were advocates over the cathedral chapter. We have no specific information as to Henry's relations with them, but he no doubt asserted his influence in important matters such as the election to the Verden see, in 1148, of Bishop Herman, who belonged to a family of Welf *ministeriales*.

The legal basis of church advocacies varied considerably. In the case of monasteries that Henry had inherited from his forebears or acquired as part of his new possessions, he exercised these rights as the owner of a proprietary church. Then there was a considerable number over which the advocacy was held as a fief from the Empire or a particular bishop. As the hereditary principle had come largely to apply to church advocacies, almost all of the many such fiefs granted to the counts of Stade, Northeim, and Winzenburg fell into Henry's hands. They included the two great imperial monasteries on the Weser, Corvey and Helmarshausen; the proprietary monastery of Heiligenstadt in the Eichsfeld, belonging to the see of Mainz; and the monastery of Flechtdorf in the Waldeck region, a dependency of Cologne. These four advocacies originally belonged to the counts of

Northeim and were inherited by the Winzenburgers and sub-sequently by Henry the Lion.

The practice of bequeathing advocacies was often very injurious to churches and monasteries, as the advocates grossly neglected their duty of protection and used the office purely to their own advantage. They were in fact destroyers and not protectors of the churches, to use the language of a charter of 1144—the earliest of Henry's that has survived in original form—addressed to Bursfelde on the Weser, originally a proprietary monastery of the Northeim family. Under the great dynasties the custom had developed whereby advocates appointed their own deputies, and these vice-advocates managed to convert the office into a hereditary fief for their families' benefit.

As a result of these abuses the church reform movement from the eleventh century onwards increasingly held out for the free election of advocates (*freie Vogtwahl*): instead of the office being hereditary, it should be filled by an agent of the abbot and community, whom they would appoint for life. The Cistercians even sought to have their foundations exempt from the system, relying solely on the king's general obligation of protection. All these endeavours were at the same time an expression of the determination of the church reform movement to fight against the old system of proprietary churches.

Such was the mid-century background to Henry the Lion's policy towards the monasteries. He succeeded in maintaining, and in some cases strengthening, his position as the owner of proprietary churches and the holder of rights of advocacy in the areas of church immunity that were subject to him. Thus he obtained the advocacy over the monastery of Northeim by purchase from Count Poppo of Blankenburg and his brothers. In the case of Reinhausen and of Homburg he expressly reserved the right of patronage to himself. However, as with the counties, so with the advocacies he was unable himself to administer these rights to their full extent, and the system of vice-advocacy remained in being, often as a fief belonging to free noble families: thus the Schwalenbergers held the vice-advocacy over Corvey and Flechtdorf, already in Siegfried of Boyneburg's time. Lothair III occasionally entrusted this office to a *ministerialis*, as in the family monasteries of St Michael in Lüneburg, Königslutter, and Supplinburg. His grandson did not extend the practice of using *ministeriales* as advocates.

The duke took account of reformist ideas inasmuch as he occasion-ally granted the right of free election. However, the right as it was conceded to the monastery of Bursfelde in 1144 related to the vice-advocacy only. In the case of Northeim it was provided that the advocacy should not be granted as a fief: an advocate appointed by the duke or his successors was to be deprived of the post if he proved unworthy.

Apart from this, in the comparatively few cases in which Henry was free to dispose of a vice-advocacy, his principle was to regrant it as a fief and so prevent its becoming hereditary. It would seem that in case of need he laid on individual vassals the task of exercising advocate's rights: this was the case at Osnabrück, and at Helmarshausen we find under his rule several vice-advocates belonging to different families. Apart from these exceptions, the duke administered the areas of church immunity on customary lines and did not make any innovations.

Another feature of Henry's church policy is that in all his vast dominions he did not create a single new religious foundation. Admittedly the large number of new monastery foundations in the eleventh century, due to the church reform movement, declined during the first half of the twelfth, in Saxony as elsewhere in the Empire; but nevertheless there were some new foundations by lay magnates or bishops. The duke, however, took no part in any of these, showing that the monastic movement was quite alien to him. Even the Cistercian monastery of Riddagshausen just outside Brunswick was not founded by him but by his *ministerialis* Liudolf of Dahlum, though Henry afterwards endowed it generously.

In general Henry did not provide so lavishly for churches and monasteries as might be supposed from the conventional prefatory words of his charters. If we examine these documents, the great majority of which are addressed to ecclesiastics, we find that he made large donations only to his family monasteries in and around Brunswick or in Lüneburg; other churches and monasteries received only smaller benefits from him. In several cases he only confirmed donations and rights granted by his forebears. Apart from this there are a fair number of charters in which he confirmed or gave his consent to legal transactions such as the sale, purchase, or exchange of possessions among individual churches and monasteries, or between them and secular lords.

The duke was able to assert his influence in church matters not only in Nordalbingia but to a large extent in Saxony proper, thanks to the aid of a large group of ecclesiastics, mostly from the Brunswick area, who have been termed his 'clerical administrators'. They belonged to the collegiate churches of St Blaise or St Cyriac, to St Giles's monastery in Brunswick, or to Riddagshausen, but Henry also brought churchmen to his court from other localities. As a rule they served for a time as court chaplains; later they were often transferred to important posts in the church.

Besides ministering to the court, some of these clergy regularly accompanied Henry on campaigns and journeys. Their duties were not purely spiritual: like other rulers of the time, Henry also employed his chaplains to carry out political tasks, including embassies.

The duke's notaries also came mainly from the chaplains' ranks. Henry the Lion was the first Saxon duke to issue charters relating to legal transactions. No such documents have come down to us from the ducal reign of his grandfather Lothair or the short period of his father's rule. Those of Henry the Lion's time enable us to trace the gradual development of a system of registration that may, with due reserve, be described as a chancery, though it was not yet an organized administrative institution.

Of Henry's seven notaries that we know of, as a rule only one functioned at any given time. The first was Gerold, whose career was in many ways typical of that of the other chaplains. Of a noble Swabian family, he came to Brunswick probably as a youth and became canon of St Blaise's (where, owing to his learning, he was put in charge of the monastery school) and chaplain to the duke. We only meet him as a notary on one occasion; in 1155, on Vizelin's death, he became bishop of Oldenburg. The most brilliant of those clerics who became notaries was undoubtedly Hartwig, who belonged to a Bremen family of *ministeriales* from Uthlede on the lower Weser. He became a chaplain of the duke's, who procured for him a canonry in Bremen. Serving as a notary from about 1158 to the early 1170s, he left his mark on the system to such purpose that he is once referred to as 'magister cartularii'. Elected archbishop of Bremen in 1185, he died in 1207 after a pontificate of many vicissitudes.

The preparation of charters, for which a considerable fee was charged, was entrusted to the clerical beneficiaries in cases where they possessed a writing-school of their own. However, the documents were finally supervised by the duke's notaries and their validity confirmed by the ducal seal. As with the German Emperors and kings and other rulers, the impression was changed after a period of years, no doubt to make forgery more difficult. Up to the time of his downfall Henry used seven slightly different seals with his effigy on horseback; after the loss of his duchies these were replaced by a smaller seal representing a lion.

Having surveyed the rule of Henry the Lion in Saxony, we may consider the question of his objectives. For a long time it was incorrectly supposed that he intended to re-create a 'stem duchy' in Saxony. He could not have done so, if only because there never was a duchy embracing the whole Saxon tribe. Nor can it be said that, after the pattern of the Norman monarchies in Sicily and England, he set to work to create a firm political structure in which the feudal system was largely replaced by a more modern type of state administration. Feudalism reached its zenith in Western Europe in the twelfth century, and it determined the predominant character of the Welf duchy in Saxony. In this respect Henry's policy in no way differed from that of other contemporary dynasts.

In large parts of his dominions his ducal power depended on his vast allodial possessions, countships, advocacies, and other connected privileges; but it was not only a conglomeration of these various rights. Certainly he seldom expressly based his actions on his ducal authority, but his legal status was superior to that of a count or advocate, as was especially clear in the important sphere of the public peace. The right to take steps to maintain the peace became an important factor in the establishment of ducal supremacy, enabling him to assert his rule in regions where he had no other legal basis of action. His authority throughout Saxony was also attested by the provincial diets (*Landtage*), attendance at which was not confined to his vassals and *ministeriales*. Such diets were held especially for the old border territory in Nordalbingia, but also in Saxony proper. Thus in 1163 a diet at Hanover was attended by Westphalian dynasts, and in 1173 we hear of a grand assembly at Paderborn. Saxony under Henry has been well described as a 'duchy on a tribal basis' (*stammesbezogenes Herzogtum*).

Throughout twelfth-century Germany a decisive constitutional change was taking place: the transition from loosely organized complexes of domains, based on authority over persons and associations, to compact, self-contained territorial units, the precursors of the modern administrative state. In the time of transition it was Henry's aim to combine his various seigniorial rights in Saxony into a unified territorial duchy and to establish his rule over a wide area.

For this purpose he made use of every opportunity offered him by the legal system of the time, especially customary and feudal law; but he was also prepared to override such laws when they were contrary to his interests. His often ruthless pursuit of power increasingly provoked resistance on the part of those whose rights he violated. Thus there loomed with increasing clarity the conflict between power and legality which was to be the decisive issue in the latter years of his rule.

7

Henry as Duke of Bavaria

AT the diet of Regensburg in September 1156, as we have seen, Henry the Lion succeeded after a hard struggle in obtaining the restoration of the Welf title to Bavaria, diminished though it was by the creation of a separate duchy of Austria. The legal situation in his new duchy was in many ways substantially different from that in Saxony.

Despite the frequent replacement of one dynasty by another, Bavaria in the twelfth century was still the most self-contained duchy of the Empire. This was chiefly because the German kings since the middle of the tenth century had repeatedly appointed kinsmen of theirs as dukes, and for a time in the eleventh century administered the duchy themselves, so that Bavaria was almost in the position of a crown territory. The extensive delegation of royal rights to the dukes did much to increase their prestige among the other stem duchies.

The duke of Bavaria was the commander of the tribal levy. Even the troops that the Bavarian bishops supplied to the king in their capacity of princes of the Empire often appeared as part of the ducal forces. The dukes' position was also especially strong in jurisdictional matters. To all appearances, by virtue of the royal authority (*Bannleihe*) they exercised supreme judicial power in the duchy from an early date, and Henry the Lion is expressly referred to as 'iudex provinciae'. One of his chief responsibilities was to maintain the public peace in accordance with imperial legislation and ducal ordinances. Unlike the position in Saxony, in Bavaria the margraviates were subordinate to the duke. After the march of Austria was made into a separate duchy in 1156, the duke was still suzerain of the Bavarian Nordgau under the lords of Vohburg and of Styria under the Ottokars. The more distant march of Istria was already almost independent by Henry the Lion's time. Above all, however, the dukes of Bavaria were able in course of time to acquire a large measure of control over the counties, which thus became fiefs of theirs and not of the king. There is no record in the twelfth century of a count being appointed by the crown.

From the twelfth century onwards the dukes claimed a reversionary right to the estates of families that became extinct. They were frequently successful in this, as a matter of power politics, though the king never granted them a general right of escheatage.

The dukes' strong position was also seen in the numerous diets they held at Regensburg and elsewhere. Besides the dukes' vassals these were attended by numerous spiritual and temporal lords who were not their feudal dependants.

Bavaria was also the only German duchy in which there was an express provision for the ducal household. This probably originated in confiscations of church property in the tenth century. It was afterwards somewhat diminished by grants to ecclesiastical and lay recipients, but around the middle of the twelfth century some estates devoted to this purpose (*Kammergüter*) can still be traced in the vicinity of Regensburg and Munich and on both banks of the Salzach and the Inn.

In addition, from the beginning of the twelfth century onwards the Welfs received imperial lands from the kings as fiefs: this was the case with Welf V, his brother Henry the Black, and the latter's son Henry the Proud. After the latter's deposition Conrad III retained these lands, but when Frederick I invested Henry the Lion with the dukedom he also enfeoffed him with crown lands on a large scale. Henry in his legal dispositions frequently speaks of them as being his by hereditary right. The fact that some Welf *ministeriales*, for instance in the neighbourhood of Ranshofen on the Inn, are also referred to as the king's servants can only signify that Henry was invested with imperial lands.

The Welf patrimony in Bavaria, on the other hand, was not very large, and was not increased to any great extent in the late eleventh and the twelfth century. It was situated chiefly in the border area with Swabia on the right bank of the Lech and, together with the lands on the left bank, formed a fairly compact territory extending from the Gunzenlee to Füssen. In addition there were Welf allodial states in the Tyrol, especially in the upper Inn valley and the Vintschgau. The church foundation of Wilten near Innsbruck was an important base on the road leading to the Brenner. In the north and east of the duchy the Welfs had only scattered possessions; none, it is to be noted, in the area around Regensburg.

It is not known for certain how the extensive Welf patrimony in Swabia and Bavaria was divided between Welf VI and Henry the Lion. In the heartland north of Lake Constance Welf VI possessed most of the estates, but his nephew had a substantial part of the allodial lands in that area. Of the numerous Welf *ministeriales* in Swabia, many were in the service of both lords. Henry was determined to hold on to his rights and possessions in Swabia, but did not intervene in the dissensions that took place in the 1160s between Duke Frederick IV on the one hand and Welf VI and his son on the other. In the border area between Swabia and Bavaria there seems to have been a detailed partition, while the other possessions in Bavaria mostly went to Henry the Lion.

Compared to the Welf patrimonial lands, some other Bavarian noble families were considerably better off. This was especially true of the Wittelsbachs, who at an early date built up a fairly compact domain between the Lech and the Isar, based on their ancestral seat at Scheyern on the Inn and later their castle of Wittelsbach further westward. From the beginning of the twelfth century onwards they were hereditary counts palatine of Bavaria. Next to them the richest Bavarian family were the counts of Andechs, whose possessions and rights originally lay in the area between the upper Lech and the upper Isar. To these they added lands in Franconia, Tyrol, Carinthia, and Istria, thanks to which they rose to the status of a titular duchy.

As in Saxony, so in Bavaria it is thus not possible to define the exact area under Henry the Lion's control, and the question of its extension eastward is especially controversial. Two sources—the *Chronicle* of the abbey of Melk and that of Abbot Herman of Niederaltaich—state that in 1156 Henry Jasomirgott was granted, along with the duchy of Austria, the Attergau and jurisdictional rights to the west of the lower Enns as far as Passau, i.e. in the Traungau. This, however, is contradicted by the fact that as late as 1176 Henry the Lion held a court session on the Enns and, accompanied by a large retinue, held a meeting on that occasion with Henry Jasomirgott. The Traungau, which by then was already to a great extent under the control of the margraves of Steyr, was subject to Bavaria until 1180 for the purpose of customary law. Only after Henry the Lion's fall did this area become part of the newly created duchy of Styria, which fell to Austria in 1192.

Owing to the profusion of tasks that faced Henry in Nordalbingia and the rest of Saxony between 1155 and 1170, and his frequent involvement in the Emperor's affairs in Germany and Italy during those years, he had less time to spare for Bavaria; the 1170s brought a change in this respect. This can be seen from the record of his travels: before 1170 he visited Bavaria seldom and for short periods. He held his first diet in Bavaria at Regensburg in 1157. During the Emperor's second Italian expedition he furnished military help on two occasions, and in 1159–61 he crossed Bavaria several times on the march to Upper Italy and back to Saxony. In 1162 he was in Bavaria before and after the diet of Saint-Jean-de-Losne, and in the autumn of that year he held a great diet at Karpfham an der Rott.

His next certainly known visit to Bavaria was in 1166, when, together with Frederick I, he settled the difficult problem of filling the vacant archbishopric of Salzburg during the Papal schism. In the same year heavy fighting broke out in Saxony, which prevented Henry from visiting his south German duchy again till the beginning of 1171. On his pilgrimage in 1172 he stopped briefly in Bavaria on the outward and return journeys. His longest stay in the duchy was not until 1174. This time he stayed almost six months, once more engaged with the Emperor in settling the affairs of the Salzburg archbishopric. At the beginning of 1176 he again spent some weeks in Bavaria; this was his last visit.

Henry's relatively short stays in Bavaria show that although the duchy had been under Welf rule for so long, he regarded it as of secondary importance to Saxony. This can also be seen from his administrative activity: only about a sixth of the transactions by him of which we have evidence in the form of charters or legal records are concerned with Bavaria.

Numerous disputes concerning property matters were brought before his jurisdiction. He also confirmed grants made to churches and monasteries in his territory by third parties such as his *ministeriales*, and ratified exchanges of property among such establishments or between them and secular lords. He very seldom himself made grants to religious foundations in Bavaria, one reason being the relatively small extent of Welf possessions in the duchy.

More important than these decisions, which for the most part belonged to county jurisdiction and were of local interest, were measures indicating the duke's economic and financial objectives. Unfortunately the sources often do not tell us enough about these, and many questions have to remain open.

The most important of such matters is the foundation of Munich in

1157–8. Previously the salt-trading route from Salzburg to Swabia crossed the Isar at Föhring, a village belonging to the Freising bishopric. Presumably during his stay in Bavaria in the autumn of 1157, Henry had the bridge at Föhring destroyed and closed down the market, mint, and toll station established by the bishops of Freising. These he transferred about a mile upstream to Munichen, a monastic settlement which may have been founded by the abbey of Tegernsee and which possessed a church or chapel dedicated to St Peter. A new bridge was built across the Isar, and the salt supplies were diverted to this route. It is not certain to whom the area in question belonged in the middle of the twelfth century. We have no evidence of Welf ownership; it would seem more likely to have been a ducal *Kammergut* of long standing. It has also been suggested that it was originally ownerless gravel-land on the Isar, or else imperial territory enfeoffed to the counts of Wolfratshausen and reclaimed by Henry after the line died out in 1157. But all these are mere suppositions.

As we have seen earlier, Bishop Otto of Freising protested against Henry's action, and Frederick I delivered judgment on his complaint at the diet of Augsburg at Whitsun 1158, before setting out on his second expedition to Italy. In a diploma of 14 June the Emperor gave his approval to Henry's diversion of the trade route and removal of the market from Föhring to Munich; however, as a compromise the bishop was to receive one third of the customs receipts and the income from the mint. He was also permitted to share in the administration of these regalia. The toll station was to be administered by an official on the duke's behalf and one on the bishop's, or by a single official representing both. Henry, on the other hand, was to receive a third of the mint receipts as a fief from the bishop.

Apart from these events in 1157 and 1158 we hear nothing of any subsequent measures by the duke in aid of his new foundation. As far as we know he did not revisit Munich. It is occasionally suggested that he built a castle there, but there is no evidence for this. Munich was not created as a princely residence but as a market and trading centre. It was fortified before the end of Henry's rule, but he appears not to have granted it a charter, leaving judicial matters in the hands of a ducal representative. Altogether we only find ducal officials in Munich at this time, with no trace of civic self-government.

After the duke's fall in 1180 his foundation seemed to be doomed, as in the same year Frederick I, acceding to a request by Bishop

Albert of Freising, revoked his consent to the transfer of the market and bridge from Föhring to Munich and confirmed the bishopric in its original rights. However, this judgment was never carried out. The market was not re-established at Föhring; but the fortifications of Munich were probably razed for a time. The new Wittelsbach dukes struggled hard and successfully with the bishops of Freising for control over Munich; it prospered, and probably acquired a municipal charter by the end of the twelfth century.

Henry the Lion took another measure designed to bring under his control, and to draw financial gain from, the salt-trading route that led from Salzburg and Reichenhall via Wasserburg and Munich to Memmingen in Swabia. At the beginning of the 1160s he built a castle on the east bank of the middle Lech near the village of Pfetten, which was the abode of a family of Welf *ministeriales*. This castle, which soon came to be known as Landsberg, enclosed the smaller fortress of the lords of Pfetten. It was intended to protect the salt route, which crossed the Lech by a bridge at that point, and also to be an administrative centre for the many Welf possessions in the area. A trading settlement grew up beside the bridge in the twelfth century, and in the thirteenth century this settlement and the village of Pfetten combined to form the town of Landsberg.

Reichenhall, then the principal salt mine in South Germany, belonged to the archbishops of Salzburg; but the Welfs had some property in the area, as did other local dynasts and several monasteries. In 1172 Henry granted a share in the salt-works to St Zeno's at Reichenhall.

Above all, Henry was able to gain possession of the so-called 'Hall countship', though we do not know at what date or in what exact circumstances. The fact that he owned it for a time is expressly stated in the thirteenth century. In 1169 the then *Hallgraf* entered the community of Augustinian canons at Reichersberg, after attending a diet held by Frederick I at Bamberg. As Henry the Lion, who was also at Bamberg, is subsequently referred to several times as *Hallgraf*, it seems likely that he took over the countship in 1169, perhaps with the Emperor's approval. The rights of a younger brother of the previous *Hallgraf* were overridden. The area involved was not large, only Reichenhall and its immediate surroundings; with it went a toll station and a share in the dues paid to the Salzburg mint.

A few years before, probably in 1165, Henry inherited the count-ship of a kinsman of his, Gebhard of Burghausen, who left only minor children. Here again we do not know the details, or whether it was a matter of reversionary right. The countship included not only a castle on the Salzach and the toll station there, but also fairly large estates on both sides of the river. The duke thus gained an important base on the trade route leading from Reichenhall northwards to the Danube by way of the Salzach and the Inn.

Regensburg, with its ducal manor, had always been the residence of the dukes of Bavaria. The city was largely under the overlordship of the crown, until it became an imperial free city in the thirteenth century. The bishops in Regensburg also enjoyed a large area of immunity. From early times the city was of great importance as a base for trade with the south-east. In 1161 hostilities broke out between Henry and Bishop Hartwig II. The duke, with superior forces, captured a stronghold of the bishop's; we are not told its name, but it must have been Donaustauf east of the city, which had for a time been in the possession of Henry's father, Henry the Proud. Thus the duke was able to control the Danube trade to the east of Regensburg. The bishop was obliged to yield, but Archbishop Eberhard of Salzburg was able to persuade Henry to release the prisoners he had taken.

The duke's object in all these proceedings was not only to gain command of important trade routes and increase his revenues, but also to strengthen his power base in Bavaria, while avoiding conflict with the other local magnates. When the schism broke out in Rome he did not endorse the tough line advocated by Otto of Wittelsbach, the count palatine and one of the Emperor's closest counsellors and supporters in matters of church policy; but, as far as can be seen, this did not give rise to friction in Bavaria between the duke and the Wittelsbachs.

The fact that Henry was seldom in Bavaria was one reason why his rule was felt to be less oppressive there than in Saxony, and practically no opposition stirred against him. The rising of the Saxon princes in 1166 and the heavy fighting of the following years had no repercussions in Bavaria, nor are they mentioned at the time by any Bavarian chronicler. This freedom from opposition in South Germany was a great advantage to the duke.

In church matters Henry's influence in Bavaria was also a good deal less strong than in Saxony. He possessed few church advocacies in the former duchy. Before becoming duke of Bavaria he exercised advocate's jurisdiction in the Welf foundation of Wilten near Innsbruck and the monastery of Wessobrunn south of the Ammersee, where the Welf authority was of even earlier date. In the autumn of 1155 Frederick I, on return from his first Italian expedition, assured the monks that no sub-advocates could be appointed under Henry and that they might elect their own advocate in the event of Henry's death.

After his investment with Bavaria Henry, as duke, assumed the advocacy of Ranshofen on the Inn, which his grandfather Henry the Black had converted from a monastery into a foundation of Augustinian canons. Ranshofen was an imperial estate that had been granted to the dukes as a fief. In an important charter, as early as 1157, Henry confirmed and increased the grants made by his ancestors; at the same time he defined the powers of his sub-advocate, who was made responsible for defending the community and its possessions and was forbidden to levy unjustified imposts.

In 1160 Henry obtained as a fief from the bishop of Brixen the advocacy of Polling near the Ammersee, which had been presented to the bishopric by the Emperor Henry IV. This was a new important base in an area where Henry already held estates. He undertook not to appoint sub-advocates and to levy only the customary dues; accordingly he himself exercised the advocate's functions at all time thereafter.

In his last years as duke, perhaps in 1174, he also obtained as a hereditary fief from Bishop Albert of Freising the advocacy of Innichen in the Pustertal in south Tyrol. Innichen, one of the oldest monasteries in the eastern Alps, had been assigned to the Freising bishopric soon after its foundation. With the advocacy, which extended to the other Freising estates in the area, Henry gained appreciable influence over the various routes traversing the Pustertal. He undertook to seek the bishop's consent before appointing a sub-advocate or building a castle in the area covered by the advocacy.

Finally, Henry exercised rights of advocacy over the important foundation of Reichersberg on the Inn. These, however, did not apply to the foundation as a whole but only to the nearby village of Münsteuer, for the possession of which the clergy had to litigate for more than two decades. The sources in this case enable us to follow events closely, and the question of advocate's jurisdiction over a small village thus occupies a comparatively large place in the story of Henry the Lion's transactions in Bavaria.

In the early 1150s the chapter acquired Münsteuer, in exchange for a more distant possession of theirs, from a nobleman, Werner of

Stein, who had a castle in the Reichersberg area. The transfer of ownership was a long and complicated process because the lords of Stein held Münsteuer not as an allodium but as a fief from the margraves of Steyr, who themselves held it from the church of Bamberg. The solemn transfer of the village to the chapter and its provost, the noted theologian Gerhoch, finally took place in 1162 at the diet held by Henry the Lion at Karpfham. At the request of Archbishop Eberhard I of Salzburg—the establishment being his proprietary church—Henry took over the advocacy of Münsteuer on terms which he agreed with Gerhoch.

Shortly afterwards, in the summer of 1165, Henry of Stein—a son of Werner's who, after the loss of his ancestral fastness, also styled himself after the castle of Baumgarten—contested the validity of his father's action on the ground that it infringed his rights as an heir. The legal proceedings that followed lasted for more than ten years. However, in 1166 Henry of Baumgarten took possession of Münsteuer by force, taking advantage of the fact that Frederick I in that year pronounced a ban on the archdiocese and all its possessions for continuing to support Pope Alexander III.

The chapter appealed for help to Henry as the supreme keeper of the public peace and advocate of the property in dispute. The duke sent a temporizing reply from Saxony, where he was about to do battle with the coalition of nobles. He told the clergy that he could not for the present help to reconcile them with the Emperor, as he was not in the latter's vicinity; he had, however, requested the count palatine, Otto of Wittelsbach, to settle the dispute, and would intervene if the count was unsuccessful. This was cold comfort, as Otto was a sworn enemy of the archbishopric. As Henry of Baumgarten continued his incursions the clergy even had to flee from Reichersberg for a time, and were only able to return in the summer of 1167 with the help of some well-disposed nobles.

After Gerhoch's death in 1169 the lawsuit was continued by his brother and successor Arno, but in the next few years we hear nothing of any intervention by the duke. The chapter again appealed to him as advocate in 1174. He was then in Bavaria, but about to return to Saxony, and referred the dispute for arbitration to a court of three nobles in the Inn valley; this, however, brought no solution.

Only when Henry returned to Bavaria at the beginning of 1176 was he able to settle the long-standing quarrel. Henry of Baumgarten having disobeyed his first summons to a court hearing, the duke pronounced final sentence at a solemn diet at Enns on 14 March. We have a full and instructive account of the proceedings. The chapter produced a document in which the bishop of Bamberg had endorsed the exchange of property; Henry of Baumgarten invoked a promise by Provost Arno, who had died the year before, to add two hides to the estate given in exchange. The chapter finally agreed to this, and Henry of Baumgarten waived his claim to Münsteuer. The duke and his retinue crossed the bridge over the Enns and met with Henry Jasomirgott of Austria on the east bank; then Henry of Baumgarten confirmed the waiver of his claim after Philip, the new provost of Reichersberg, had formally ceded the two hides of land. This judicial procedure at Enns, which throws light on a particularly complicated case of the transfer of feudal property, was, as far as our knowledge goes, the last official transaction by Henry the Lion in Bavaria.

The lengthy dispute over the small village of Münsteuer illustrates clearly enough how the schism in the Western church could affect a particular religious establishment. It may also be taken as an example of conditions affecting the whole of the Bavarian church during the eighteen years of the schism, from 1159 to 1177. Henry the Lion, who consistently supported the Emperor and his anti-Pope, was in difficulties owing to the fact that the Bavarian church, headed by the Salzburg archbishopric, was the mainstay of Alexander III's cause in Germany. While it was the Emperor himself who took the decisive steps to compel the Bavarian bishops, as princes of the Empire, to recognize 'his' Popes, these measures also determined the duke's attitude towards the Bavarian clergy.

Archbishop Eberhard I of Salzburg, a prince of the church who was widely respected beyond his own archdiocese, had decided for Alexander III soon after the disputed election of 1159. On the pretext of illness he did not attend the Emperor's summons to the Council of Pavia at the beginning of 1160; he sent as his deputy Provost Henry of Berchtesgaden, who refrained from committing himself. Two suffragans of Salzburg, Hartmann of Brixen and Albert of Freising, also failed to appear. The attitude of the former, who died a few years later, is not quite clear. Albert of Freising endeavoured during his long pontificate to remain neutral between the claimants. The other two suffragans—Conrad of Passau, a brother of Duke Henry Jasomirgott of Austria, and Hartwig of Regensburg—attended the Council and recognized Victor IV, but, like some other bishops, made their recognition conditional on a review of the disputed election.

The Emperor, hoping at first for a peaceful solution, refrained from taking action against the aged archbishop and his clergy; and accordingly Henry the Lion took no steps against Alexander III's adherents in Bavaria. Eberhard I died in the summer of 1164, whereupon the Salzburg clergy and *ministeriales* elected the bishop of Passau to be their new metropolitan; they made the condition, however, that Conrad, who was believed to be a supporter of Alexander III, should defend his cause with the utmost energy.

Soon afterwards Conrad made his way to the Emperor's camp at Pavia to be invested with the regalia of his see. The Emperor refused, however, as Conrad would not recognize the new anti-Pope Pascal III. Conrad's later attempts to obtain investment from the Emperor were likewise in vain.

In 1165 the tension in Bavaria increased. In May, at a great diet at Würzburg, the importance of which for Frederick's imperial policy will be seen in another context, the Emperor, despite strong opposition, decreed that all lay and ecclesiastical princes in the Empire must take an oath never to recognize Alexander III or any Pope elected by his supporters. Anyone who refused to take the oath was to be deprived of his offices, fiefs, and personal possessions.

Following the diet, the Emperor proceeded to visit Bavaria and Austria, where he was able to compel the Salzburg suffragans to recognize the Würzburg decisions. Bishop Albert of Freising took the oath, though with reservations. Archbishop Conrad refused to do so, and in the following September the Emperor, holding court at Worms, solemnly initiated proceedings to deprive him of his feudal rights. Conrad ignored the first two summonses but finally presented himself at a diet at Nuremberg in February 1166, which Henry the Lion also attended. In reply to the charge that he had taken possession of his archbishopric illegally, since he had neither received the regalia nor recognized Pascal as Pope, the archbishop stated through Henry the Lion, whom he chose as his spokesman (*prolocutor*), that he had been duly elected to his office by the clergy, *ministeriales*, and people of the archbishopric, and that he had thrice within a year applied in vain to the Emperor for investment with the regalia.

Although Henry the Lion acted as spokesman for the archbishop, this did not mean that he endorsed his attitude. According to medieval custom no one might refuse a request to act in that capacity, it being understood that he stated a case with which he did not necessarily agree. No doubt Conrad of Salzburg thought he had done well to entrust his plea to the duke, as the Emperor's trusted supporter and adviser.

We do not know whether sentence was finally pronounced on this occasion. The archbishop was given a last extension of time. An imperial diet was held on 29 March 1166 in the territory of the archdiocese at Laufen on the Salzach, attended by the dukes of Bavaria and Austria. Conrad stayed away, however, appointing his brother, Henry Jasomirgott of Austria, to speak for him. Despite the latter's efforts, Conrad and the Salzburg clergy were put to the ban of the Empire; the fiefs and possession of the Salzburg church were confiscated and regranted to nobles loyal to the Emperor, who were also commanded to take military measures against the archbishopric. Henry the Lion concurred in this severe judgment.

There now began a time of confusion and conflict in the archdiocese, in which, as we have seen, Reichersberg was also involved. Archbishop Conrad, supported by many of his clergy and ministeriales, took up the challenge and excommunicated his adversary. Salzburg became a place of refuge for all clergy in Bavaria who refused to recognize Pascal as Pope. In September 1166 Conrad is said to have consecrated about 500 clergy in Salzburg. At the beginning of the next year, however, he had to withdraw to Friesach castle near Klagenfurt, whence he tried to carry on official business. In April Salzburg was badly damaged by fire, the outbreak of which was blamed—probably unjustly—on Conrad's opponents.

After Conrad's death in 1168 the election at Salzburg fell on Adalbert, a son of King Vladislav II of Bohemia. Adalbert was also a supporter of Alexander III, who sent him the pallium; but, unlike his predecessor, he did not take up the fight when the Emperor, at a diet at Bamberg in June 1169, refused to confirm his appointment. Hoping to save at least his spiritual office, Adalbert waived his title to the temporalities of the archdiocese, which the Emperor himself set about administering. Henry the Lion was present at Bamberg, but we do not know what his attitude was. He would no doubt have supported the Emperor's measures, since he needed the latter's help at that time against his opponents in Saxony.

The Emperor's policy in the next few years was to get a new occupant for the Salzburg see and thus put an end to the troubles within the archdiocese. After an unsuccessful attempt in 1172 he achieved his aim at a diet in Regensburg at the end of June 1174, when Adalbert was deposed with the assent of a large number of lay and ecclesiastical magnates, including Henry the Lion. Only his uncle, Henry Jasomirgott of Austria, raised objection. A group of Salzburg clergy then elected as their metropolitan Provost Henry of Berchtesgaden, who had represented Eberhard of Salzburg at the Council of Pavia in 1160. Although he was close to the adherents of Alexander III, the Emperor invested him with the regalia and returned to him the Salzburg possessions he had confiscated in 1169. The temporal princes who were present consented to be reinvested with the fiefs they held of the Salzburg church and did homage to the archbishop for them; Henry the Lion was one of the first to do so.

Adalbert, however, refused to be deprived of his dignity, and the troubles went on, with Henry the Lion actively supporting the new archbishop. Thus, before returning to Saxony in the autumn, he summoned to judgment the clergy of St Peter's abbey in Salzburg, who had opposed Archbishop Henry. We do not have details of this action, however. Archbishop Henry finally prevailed over Adalbert thanks to decisive help from the Wittelsbachs.

The central event of Henry the Lion's last stay in Bavaria in the early months of 1176 was the meeting with his stepfather, Duke Henry Jasomirgott of Austria, with whom he had long been reconciled. We have no details of what took place at the meeting on the Enns in March, which is only known to us from the record of Henry the Lion's award in the Münsteuer affair. He may have promised help over frontier disputes with the new King Soběslav of Bohemia; but any such agreement would have had no effect, as Henry Jasomirgott died in the following year.

Events in Bavaria following the schism of 1159 show how closely Henry's activity as duke was bound up with the great political issues of the Western world, to which we must now again turn our attention.

8

The Summit of Power

THE 1160s and the first half of the next decade were the years during which Henry the Lion consolidated his predominance in Saxony and Nordalbingia. During the same period he played an important part in the imperial and ecclesiastical policy of Frederick I, which he supported vigorously up to the end of the Emperor's second Italian expedition. Here the question arises whether, as is sometimes suggested, he then came to adopt a radically different view of Frederick's policy, which itself in those years took on a variety of forms with the purpose of healing the schism in the Western church and strengthening the power base of the Staufen dynasty.

The Emperor returned to Germany in the autumn of 1162 and remained for about a year: he had been away more than four years, and had important matters to settle. The diplomacy of Pope Alexander III, who was still in France, had not been idle meanwhile. In the summer of 1163 papal legates came to a diet at Nuremberg to negotiate with the Emperor through Archbishop Eberhard of Salzburg, but they accomplished nothing and had to withdraw. The Emperor's unforthcoming attitude led to a *rapprochement* between the Curia and Byzantium. During these years the Emperor Manuel I was extremely active in seeking to bring about a league of powers against Frederick I, including Pope Alexander, Louis VII of France, and the Norman king of Sicily. He was prepared to recognize Alexander as Pope if the latter would recognize him as sole Emperor. However, Louis VII opposed the plan and it came to nothing.

In the autumn of 1163 Frederick returned to Italy. Only a few of the German princes accompanied him, and Henry the Lion was not of their number. Frederick was planning a campaign against the Norman kingdom with the aid of his partisans in Upper Italy and the maritime powers of Genoa and Pisa. Before it could take place, however, Victor IV died at Lucca on 24 April 1164. His death offered an opportunity of ending the schism, but two days later Reinald of Dassel, without the Emperor's knowledge, brought about the election of a new anti-Pope, Cardinal Guido of Crema, who took the name of Pascal III. The Emperor approved Reinald's action after the event, but it was endorsed by only some of those who had supported Victor.

Meanwhile Alexander III enjoyed increasing support in Germany, where Conrad of Wittelsbach, elected archbishop of Mainz in 1163, openly took his side. Duke Welf VI had made contact with Alexander as early as 1160, soon after the Council of Pavia; he now definitely embraced his cause and approached Louis VII with a view to assisting the Pope.

In the late summer of 1164 an embassy came to Brunswick from the Byzantine Empèror. Henry the Lion returned at once from the region of Mecklenburg and Hither Pomerania, where he had been engaged in fighting the Obodrites. The purpose and outcome of the embassy are not known. Manuel probably hoped to gain Henry's support for his planned alliance, but was unsuccessful; in the next few months the closeness of the understanding between the duke and the Staufen Emperor became clearer than ever.

Frederick's difficulties in Italy were increased by the fact that Venice, fearing a threat to its independence from the imperial power, organized resistance against him in alliance with Verona, Vicenza, and Padua. Frederick managed to contain the alliance by making concessions to other cities, but was unable to subdue it by force of arms. In the autumn of 1164 he returned to Germany with little to show for his efforts. Accordingly he sought once again by diplomatic means to breach the unity of Alexander III's adherents in the West. Having failed in 1162 to come to terms with Louis VII of France for a resolution of the schism, he saw a fresh opportunity in the dispute between Henry II of England and the church. At the beginning of 1164 the king had attempted, by the Constitutions of Clarendon, to restore the supremacy of the crown over the clergy, especially in judicial matters. Thomas Becket, who as Chancellor had supported the king's ecclesiastical policy, had turned into an ardent champion of the church's independence since becoming archbishop of Canterbury in 1162. Refusing to accept the Constitutions of Clarendon, he took refuge in France and appealed to Alexander III. The Pope was in an awkward position, as he could not disavow the archbishop yet did not want an open breach with the king of England. He did his best to temporize, but the dispute inevitably led to an estrangement between him and Henry II.

Frederick I took a hand at this point. In the winter of 1164–5 he entered upon negotiations with King Henry, following consultations that probably took place at a diet at Bamberg in November 1164 and in which Henry the Lion no doubt played a prominent part. In April 1165 an embassy to the court at Rouen, headed by Reinald of Dassel, concluded an alliance which was to be cemented by a double marriage. Henry II's eldest daughter Matilda, aged 8 or 9, was betrothed to Henry the Lion, who was now about 35; and her younger sister Eleanor, aged about 4, was to marry the Emperor's only son Frederick, an infant of less than one year old. The idea of the double marriage no doubt came from Frederick I and Archbishop Reinald, but must have met with Henry the Lion's full approval. Gunzelin of Schwerin went on his behalf to the English court to confirm the engagement. The marriage to an English princess would appreciably increase Henry the Lion's prestige and power in Germany and elsewhere in the Western world. Henry II for his part promised to withdraw his support from Alexander III and recognize Pascal III as Pope. An English embassy, which Reinald accompanied on his return to Germany, was to swear an oath confirming this undertaking at an imperial diet to be held in Würzburg at Whitsun, at the end of May.

This diet, which we have briefly mentioned in connection with Bavarian church affairs, marked the culmination of Frederick I's struggle against Alexander III. Despite strong resistance from the clergy the Emperor forced through a decision calling on those present to swear that they would never recognize Alexander III or any Pope elected by his supporters. The Emperor himself first took the oath; then the secular princes, headed by Henry the Lion. Many of the prelates, however, avoided taking the oath or did so only with reservations. It was decreed that a similar oath should be taken throughout the Empire within six weeks; anyone who refused was to be deprived of his offices, fiefs, and property. The English envoys also made a declaration against Alexander on behalf of their king.

By imposing these decisions the Emperor had overstepped the mark, especially as he proceeded to enforce them ruthlessly. Conrad of Wittelsbach, for refusing to take the oath, was deposed from the archbishopric of Mainz and replaced by the Emperor's chancellor, Christian of Buch. In the period that followed Henry the Lion was wholly on the Emperor's side: as we have seen, he supported

Frederick's stern measures against the Alexandrine party in Bavaria and the deposition of Archbishop Conrad of Salzburg.

In foreign affairs, however, the diet of Würzburg did not bring the desired success. Henry II of England used its decisions to put pressure on the Curia in his quarrel with the church, but had no intention of breaking with Alexander III. The latter, who had returned from France to Rome in the summer of 1165, found his chief support in the Norman kingdom, ruled from 1166 by William II. From 1165 onwards the Emperor Manuel also resumed his efforts to form a grand coalition against Barbarossa. He proposed to Alexander III a union of the Eastern and Western churches, which would have healed the schism that had existed since the middle of the eleventh century. In return, however, he required that the Pope should recognize him as sole Emperor. To this Alexander could not agree, as it would have meant sacrificing a centuries-old Western tradition and depriving the Papacy of all influence over the Empire. Hence he finally refrained from endorsing the negotiations conducted by his legates in Byzantium.

In the face of this intense diplomatic activity by his opponents, Frederick I wished to secure a military decision as quickly as possible. In the autumn of 1166 he led a large army into Italy on a fresh campaign. Henry the Lion did not accompany him on this occasion, for several reasons. In the summer of that year he was occupied by affairs in Nordalbingia, the negotiations with Valdemar of Denmark and their joint action against the Obodrites; moreover, the coalition of princes against Henry was then forming in Saxony. In August, at the diet at the Boyneburg near Eschwege, the Emperor had been unable to dissuade the duke's opponents from resorting to arms; Henry was thus obliged to expect their attack, which took place a few weeks after the Emperor departed for Italy.

The Emperor's campaign was at first highly successful. After setting affairs in order in northern Italy, Frederick moved southwards in the spring of 1167 and by the end of May had conquered the greater part of the Papal state. He won a brilliant victory over a Roman army at Tusculum and, after a tough struggle, at the end of July captured the Leonine City of Rome on the right bank of the Tiber, including St Peter's church. There Pascal III was enthroned, and on 1 August conferred the imperial crown on Frederick's wife Beatrice. Alexander III had had to flee from Rome, and the Emperor seemed to have won a great triumph.

A few days later, however, disaster befell the German army encamped outside Rome. An epidemic of malaria, spreading rapidly in the August heat, is said to have killed more than 2,000 princes, knights, and squires. Reinald of Dassel and some German bishops were among the victims; so were Welf VII, the son of Welf VI, and the Emperor's young cousin, Duke Frederick IV of Swabia, who, shortly before the campaign, had married Gertrude, Henry the Lion's daughter by his first wife Clementia. Welf VII was his father's only son and heir to his many rights and possessions, so that his death was an exceptional blow.

The Emperor himself was taken seriously ill and could only with great difficulty lead the remnant of his army back to Upper Italy, where he was confronted by a flare-up of the resistance he had hitherto kept in check. In the spring of 1167 several north Italian cities had formed an alliance against him; it now expanded into a great Lombard League, embracing sixteen cities by the end of the year and still more thereafter, with the object of throwing off German rule in Upper Italy and restoring the independence of the communes. A year later the cities west of Tortona founded a stronghold for their joint defence, which they named Alessandria in the Pope's honour. The Emperor pronounced a ban on the League, but was not strong enough to enforce it. When he returned to Germany through Burgundy at the beginning of 1168, Italy was for the time being lost to him.

The year 1167 and the death of Reinald of Dassel mark a turning-point in Barbarossa's reign. His attempt, based on old legal titles and military strength, to restore the plenitude of imperial power in Italy had proved a failure; nor had he been able to reassert the authority of the Empire *vis-à-vis* the Papacy and the West European states. From this point onwards the Emperor had to adopt new policies both north and south of the Alps, to achieve his aim of a 'renewal of the Empire'.

The grave setback in Italy did not affect the Emperor's position in Germany: this was partly because the close understanding that had existed between him and Henry the Lion since the beginning of his reign remained unbroken in the next few years. The Emperor endeavoured to restore peace in Saxony by a compromise that would not materially weaken the duke's position. While still in Italy, in the autumn of 1167, he sent Archbishop Christian of Mainz and Duke Berthold of Zähringen to Saxony, and, as we have seen, his endeavours continued for some time after his return to Germany.

Although he regarded the Saxon princes as violators of the peace he did not want to take harsh measures against them, as he needed their assent to his plan to have his second son Henry, then aged three, elected 'king of Germany'. The election duly took place at the diet of Bamberg in June 1169, which Henry the Lion attended. At this diet the Emperor again attempted, without success, to bring about peace in Saxony; this was only achieved in the following year, at the diet of Erfurt.

Henry the Lion made use of the lull in hostilities during the winter of 1167–8 to celebrate his marriage to Matilda of England, to whom he had been betrothed in 1165. Towards the end of 1167 he sent an embassy under Provost Baldwin of Utrecht, a relative of the counts of Holland, to fetch the child-bride to Saxony. She was escorted by two earls and other English lords and brought a rich dowry with much gold and silver. The marriage was solemnized on 1 February 1168 by Bishop Werner in Minden cathedral. Henry granted a large estate to the church at Minden and later presented the cathedral with a precious relic. The festivities took place in Brunswick, but the marriage was not celebrated there because the small church in the castle precincts did not provide a sufficiently sumptuous setting.

Matilda was the ancestress of all later Welfs. Her marriage to Henry the Lion founded the alliance between the Welfs and the Angevins which was long a major factor in the politics of the Western world. Culturally, the English princess's new home bore no comparison with the Anglo-Norman realm. But, through the new duchess and her entourage, Saxony was increasingly open to intellectual and artistic influences from England and especially from southern France, where the court of Queen Eleanor at Poitiers was a centre of literary activity.

Pascal III died in Rome on 30 September 1168, having reigned only four years. The small group of cardinals who had supported him chose as his successor Abbot John of Strumi near Arezzo, who took the name of Calixtus III. After some hesitation Frederick I recognized him as Pope, but the anti-Pope's claim was by now of dwindling importance. At the same time Frederick continued his efforts, through the Cistercians, to come to terms with Alexander III, but without success as the Pope insisted on the Lombard League being party to any agreement. Accordingly the Emperor reaffirmed his challenge to the Pope at a diet at Fulda in June 1170. We do not know whether Henry the Lion was present on that occasion.

Earlier on, Frederick had again tried to soften up the political front against him. At the beginning of October 1168, before the election of the new anti-Pope could be known in Germany, he sent a secret embassy to Henry II of England and Louis VII of France, consisting of Archbishop Christian of Mainz—then the Emperor's chief adviser—the new Archbishop Philip of Cologne, and Henry the Lion. Little is known of its doings, but its composition shows it to have been of special importance. It was intended to mediate between the two kings, who were again at odds, and also to discuss with both of them ways of ending the schism. By way of Cambrai, where Count Philip of Flanders provided them with an escort, the envoys reached Henry II's court at Rouen. He gave them a friendly welcome, but Louis VII was less accommodating. A somewhat later English source even asserts that Louis refused to see them, as being themselves schismatics; but this is unlikely. In any case, the envoys had no success in healing the breach. Henry II and Louis VII made peace at the beginning of 1169, but it is not known what part the imperial mission played in this.

The Emperor also revived diplomatic contact with Byzantium, which had been dormant for some time. In 1170 Archbishop Christian of Mainz was sent to the court of Manuel I to endeavour to prise him away from Alexander's party. A plan was mooted for a marriage between a son of Frederick I and a Byzantine princess; next year the Greeks sent a return embassy to Germany, but as yet nothing was decided.

While the negotiations with Byzantium were still going on, Frederick executed a volte-face in his Western policy. As it was increasingly clear by the end of the 1160s that the Angevin alliance had not brought the desired result, Frederick again turned towards the French monarch. This change of front determined the shape of Western politics for a long time. Through the intermediary of the abbot of Clairvaux, Frederick and Louis met on the frontier between their kingdoms, at Vaucouleurs on the Meuse near Toul. At this meeting, the only one during their respective reigns, they did no more than agree to put down the depredations of mercenaries in the Franco-German frontier area. But this agreement later formed the basis for an alliance between the Hohenstaufen and the Capetians, which at the end of Barbarossa's reign took the form of a treaty of friendship between him and Philip II, Louis VII's son and successor. In the years following the Vaucouleurs meeting there were also negotiations for a marriage between the young Philip and a daughter of Frederick's, but these came to nothing.

Meanwhile relations eased considerably between the Hohenstaufen and the English monarchy. One reason was that Henry II, being held guilty of the murder of Thomas Becket in 1170, was forced largely to give way to Alexander III: he had to do penance and make concessions over the legal position of the English church. Before this, probably in 1169, the engagement between Barbarossa's eldest son Frederick and Eleanor of Anjou had been broken off: this Frederick was a sickly child, who died soon after, and his place as the Emperor's heir was taken during his lifetime by his younger brother, the future Henry VI. In 1170 Eleanor married Alfonso of Castile. However, this and other marriage plans for Henry II's children should not, as is sometimes suggested, be regarded as proof that the Angevin king was, from the early 1170s onwards, pursuing 'imperial' ambitions against Barbarossa, in which he sought to involve his son-in-law Henry the Lion.

Closely related as he was to the English royal family, Henry the Lion did not follow Frederick I in his switch of alliances; but their agreement in matters of imperial and ecclesiastical policy was not necessarily impaired at this stage. Little or nothing can be said of the relations between Henry the Lion and his father-in-law during these years, as the political correspondence—to use a modern term—between the two rulers has not survived. We hear occasionally of embassies from the ducal couple to the English court, but have no information as to their purpose.

When the fighting in Saxony came to an end in 1170, Henry the Lion was at the summit of his power. The extent of his dominions can be seen from his itinerary in 1171. Like the German king and other rulers of the time, Henry had to carry out long and often arduous journeys, accompanied by members of his retinue, so as to display his power by appearing personally in all the regions under his control. At the beginning of the year he left Saxony to spend several weeks in Bavaria. In March he was in Swabia, in the original Welf country north of Lake Constance; numerous local counts, lords, and Welf *ministeriales* attended a court held in the small locality of Oberteuringen south of Ravensburg. Whether he also met his uncle Welf VI in Swabia and discussed with him the question of the latter's inheritance is unknown.

On the way back to Saxony, at the beginning of May, he met the

Emperor at Donauwörth. At the end of June he was already in Nordalbingia; on St John's day (June 24) he met Valdemar I of Denmark on the Eider, and reached a settlement of the dispute over the distribution of booty after the latter's conquest of Rügen. It was also agreed on this occasion that Henry's daughter Gertrude—the widow of Duke Frederick of Swabia, who had died in Italy in 1167— would marry Knut, heir to the Danish throne. Early in August the duke was in Verden on the Aller, where he met Archbishop Baldwin of Bremen. At the beginning of September he was present, with a large suite, at the consecration of the first cathedral in Schwerin; at the same time he saw to the endowment of the bishopric with estates, and the division of tithes between the bishop and chapter. Then he returned to Saxony.

In 1172 Henry went on a pilgrimage to the Holy Land. He had probably planned this for some time; it was now rendered possible by the pacification of Saxony and, financially, by Matilda's dowry, the share of King Valdemar's booty from Rügen, and other revenues. The pilgrimage was a frequent custom of the time: many ecclesiastical and lay princes, including Welf VI, had visited the Holy Places. It also afforded Henry an opportunity of displaying his power and prestige in both the Western and the Eastern world.

He made elaborate preparations for the journey and for the government of Saxony during his absence. As his deputy there he appointed his former adversary, Archbishop Wichmann of Magdeburg. Two *ministeriales*, Ekbert of Wolfenbüttel and Henry of Lüneburg, were to look after Matilda, then probably aged 16, who was expecting her first child and therefore remained in Brunswick.

Henry left his capital in mid-January, accompanied by a large retinue including Archbishop Baldwin of Bremen, Bishop Conrad of Lübeck, Abbot Henry of St Giles's monastery in Brunswick, and other prelates. Among secular notables were the Obodrite Prince Pribislav and Count Gunzelin of Schwerin, with other counts and lesser nobility and many of the duke's *ministeriales* headed by the steward Jordan of Blankenburg, his brother Iusarius, and Henry, the marshal. In Regensburg the party celebrated the feast of Candlemas (2 February) and were joined by several Bavarian magnates, including the two younger brothers of the Count Palatine Otto of Wittelsbach.

The contemporary Cologne Royal Chronicle (*Chronica Regia Coloniensis*) states that the duke was accompanied by about five hundred knights. Arnold of Lübeck, then a monk in the suite of Abbot Henry of Brunswick, was to give a vivid account of the pilgrimage, with all its difficulties and dangers, in the first book of his *Chronicle*, compiled at the beginning of the thirteenth century as a continuation of Helmold of Bosau's work. He mentions that when the duke's camp was attacked in Serbian territory about 1,200 men took up arms in its defence. This may be an exaggeration, but in any case the expedition included a large contingent of knights with their equipment and followers.

Proceeding by ship from Regensburg, at the abbey of Heili-genkreuz Henry visited the grave of his mother Gertrude and was met by Henry Jasomirgott of Austria. In Vienna the pilgrims joined forces with Bishop Conrad II of Worms, who was on his way to Byzantium to continue the Emperor's negotiations with Manuel, begun by Archbishop Christian of Mainz. Henry Jasomirgott accompanied them into Hungary and furnished ships for the further route down the Danube, while the baggage-train and horses followed by land.

Arriving at the Hungarian court at Gran (Esztergom), the pilgrims found that the young King Stephen III, who was married to Henry Jasomirgott's daughter Agnes, had died suddenly on the previous night; there were rumours of poison. Agnes returned to Vienna with her father; Henry the Lion and Bishop Conrad pursued their journey, with an assurance of safe conduct from the Hungarians. Shortly before they reached the Byzantine frontier at Branichevo, downstream from the confluence of the Morava and the Danube, the ships were caught by dangerous rapids. Henry's was wrecked on some rocky cliffs; help came from a nearby castle, but Count Gunzelin and Jordan of Blankenburg were only saved by swimming to the river-bank.

At the frontier an envoy of the Emperor Manuel greeted the pilgrims and provided a further escort. Here the party abandoned their ships and proceeded through the 'Bulgarian forest', a pathless area south-east of Belgrade. As the horses were unable to drag the heavy wagons through the marshy ground, some of the provisions and gifts were reloaded on to horses and mules and the rest jettisoned. One night the combined party's camp was attacked by Serbs, who, however, were beaten off without great loss. The expedition con-tinued by way of Nish, Philippopolis (Plovdiv), and Adrianople (Edirne), reaching Byzantium on Good Friday, 14 April 1172.

On Easter Sunday Manuel welcomed Henry in a style that the Byzantine court generally reserved for kings. The duke, who had beforehand presented the Emperor with horses, arms, and other costly gifts, came with his suite to the hippodrome, where Manuel had erected stately pavilions for himself and his entourage. The Emperor and his guest then proceeded along a route carpeted with purple and overspread by golden canopies to St Sophia, where they heard Mass. During the ceremony the duke sat in an armchair beside the Emperor's throne. After Mass the Emperor referred to him as his 'brother' or 'son', which must have been especially flattering to the duke's self-esteem.

After the banquet which followed, Bishops Conrad of Lübeck and Conrad of Worms began, in the presence of the Emperor and duke, to dispute with Greek theologians concerning the issue between the Greek and Latin churches as to the procession of the Holy Spirit. Against the Greek doctrine that the Holy Spirit proceeds only from the Father, Abbot Henry of Brunswick adduced numerous passages of Scripture in support of the Western dogma that the Holy Spirit proceeds from the Father and the Son. His arguments found favour with the Emperor, who was anxious for a settlement of the old dispute between the churches. Later the Empress presented the duke with so many furs and costly garments that, according to Arnold, he could have clothed all his knights in them.

Conrad of Worms remained in Byzantium to pursue his embassy, which as far as we know did not lead to any specific result. Henry the Lion left his baggage-train and many of his retinue in Byzantium and continued his journey to Palestine on a ship of the Emperor's. After weathering a violent storm he landed at Acre and made for Jerusalem. He was received outside the city by Knights Templar and members of the Order of St John, and was solemnly greeted by the clergy in Jerusalem itself.

Amalric I, the Latin King of Jerusalem, entertained the ducal party for three days, during which Henry showed great munificence. He presented the church of the Holy Sepulchre with a large sum of money and three perpetually burning lamps to be erected in different parts of the building; these were to be maintained by means of the revenue from two houses that Henry bought for the purpose. He caused the Holy Cross chapel within the church to be adorned with precious mosaics, and its gates covered with silver plate. He made valuable presents, especially of arms, to the Templars and Hospitallers, and provided the large sum of 1,000 silver marks to buy land, the income from which was to provide soldiers' pay in time of war. He himself purchased many valuable relics.

From Jerusalem Henry visited the Valley of Jehoshaphat, the Mount of Olives, Bethlehem, and Nazareth. Accompanied by Templars he went to the Jordan and ascended the *Mons Quarantana* in the wilderness near Jericho, where traditionally Christ fasted for forty days. According to a chronicler in Normandy, he planned to travel further but was dissuaded by Amalric and the Templars; nothing more is known of this, however.

After his return to Jerusalem he was again Amalric's guest for a few days, and at the beginning of July set out for home. The party divided at Acre, whence Henry with most of his suite proceeded by land to Antioch, escorted by Templars. Bishop Conrad of Lübeck fell ill at Acre; he and some of the duke's retinue embarked there but soon had to land at Tyre, where Conrad died and was buried.

From Antioch, where he was warmly received by Prince Bohemund III, Henry made contact with Prince Mleh, the ruler of Cilician Armenia. The latter offered him safe conduct through his territory, but Henry had been warned of possible treachery and decided to go by sea to Tarsus. There he was received by an impressive escort representing the Seljuk Sultan Kilij Arslan of Iconium. After a march of several days through wild and arid country they reached a castle near Iconium (Konya): here the Sultan greeted Henry as a blood relation, declaring himself to be descended from a high-born German lady. He presented costly gifts to the duke and his suite. Henry received silken garments, horses with ornamental saddles, tents made of felt, and camels for transport; also two hunting leopards trained to ride horses, and slaves to look after them. This is the foundation of the later legend that Henry brought a lion back to Brunswick from the Holy Land. He made an attempt to convert the Sultan to Christianity; the latter was non-committal, but released some Christian prisoners.

The journey continued by way of Nicaea and Bithynia to Byzantium, where Henry collected the baggage he had left behind and visited the Emperor at his summer residence. The subject of their conversation is not known. The Emperor again offered precious gifts, but the duke protested that Manuel had been generous enough; however, he asked for and received numerous relics in ornamental settings. He then set out for Germany by the same route as he had come by. In December 1172 he was back in Bavaria and visited Frederick I in Augsburg. At the beginning of the new year he returned to Brunswick, where his daughter Richenza had been born in his absence. He presented the relics he had brought with him to St Blaise's in Brunswick and other Saxon churches.

The motive for Henry's pilgrimage was primarily religious, as is emphasized by Arnold of Lübeck and other sources; but it may be asked if he did not also have political aims. Some sources, dating from after his downfall, suggest that he may have come to an agreement with Manuel against Frederick I and the German Empire. Many recent historians have taken the view that his journey to the East was primarily political, and that his agreement with the Eastern Emperor was one ground for the later accusation of high treason.

However, the idea of a plot against the Staufen Emperor bears no relation to the political situation in Germany at that time, when the Emperor and the duke were in perfect accord. No doubt German–Byzantine relations were discussed at Henry's two meetings with Manuel. On this account it has recently been suggested that Henry may have played the part of an unofficial envoy of Frederick's, alongside the official mission of Bishop Conrad of Worms: while loyal to the Staufen Emperor, he could offer Manuel greater concessions than Conrad was able to do. Thus, according to one theory, he may have offered Manuel bases in Italy in return for a *rapprochement* with the Western Empire, but found when he got home that Frederick I was not prepared to make such a concession. But nothing is known of any such offer by the duke, and he would hardly have made it without Frederick's knowledge. Neither the duke's interviews with Manuel nor Bishop Conrad's mission brought about any progress in the German–Byzantine negotiations, which came to an inconclusive end in 1174.

There is thus no ground for the suspicion that the duke engaged in treasonable conversations during his pilgrimage; nor, on the other hand, is there any probability in a story that is first found in a fifteenth-century source but may rest on earlier reports. This is that when Frederick I was in Saxony during Henry's absence in 1172 he induced the duke's castellans by threats and promises to swear that they would surrender their castles to him if Henry were to meet his death in the Orient. This was supposedly the cause of the quarrel between the Emperor and Henry on the latter's return. The story is to all appearances a rumour put about by the Welf party after Henry's fall, to justify his behaviour during these years.

After the duke's return, relations between him and the Emperor remained good for the time being. In 1173 and 1174 Henry spent much time at the imperial court until Frederick set out on his fifth expedition to Italy in the autumn of 1174. In Saxony peace was on the whole maintained between Henry and his opponents. Only in eastern Saxony, outside the area of the duke's direct control, after the death of Albert the Bear hostilities broke out between the Ascanians and the Landgrave Louis III of Thuringia over the latter's claim to the county of Weimar, which had become Ascanian property some time earlier. At the beginning of 1175 Henry the Lion intervened on the landgrave's side by invading the territory of Count Bernard of Anhalt, a son of Albert the Bear. He crossed the Bode with a large force, sacked the locality of Gröningen near Halberstadt, and captured and burnt the stronghold of Aschersleben. The Ascanians, however, were able to retain possession of Weimar.

Barbarossa for his part devoted the years after his return from the fourth Italian expedition to enlarging the Hohenstaufen power base in Germany, so as later to be able to resume imperial policy in Italy with good hope of success.

The chief opportunities that presented themselves in Germany were in Swabia and on the upper Rhine, which had in the past been bastions of Staufen domestic policy. The duchy of Swabia was vacant, since the Emperor's young cousin Frederick IV had died in Italy in 1167, leaving no children of his short-lived marriage to Henry the Lion's daughter Gertrude. Barbarossa granted the duchy to his own son Frederick, then aged three, and kept it for the time being in his own hands. Two years later young Frederick died; Conrad, the Emperor's third son, was now given the name of Frederick along with the duchy, which remained in his father's control. The extensive holdings of Duke Frederick IV, especially in Franconia, also passed to the Emperor on his death.

The disaster in Rome in 1167 claimed as its victims the heirs to several noble families of Swabia. Frederick took advantage of these deaths to further his own territorial policy, either by purchasing lands to which there was no heir or by concluding agreements by which they would fall to him in the future. In this way he enlarged his domain from central Swabia southwards to the area of Lake Constance, where the Welfs had till then predominated. Thus in the period from 1167 to 1180, by means of agreements with Count

Rudolf of Pfullendorf, whose only son had also died of the plague in Italy, he acquired by degrees the extensive possessions of that family between Lake Constance and the upper Danube.

The great question affecting the balance of power in Swabia was who should inherit the possessions and rights of Welf VI, whose only son Welf VII had died in the epidemic in Italy. Welf senior, who was then about 60, had taken to leading a riotous life on his estates, and sought to earn the reputation of a generous prince by gifts to his proprietary monasteries and other churches. To defray the cost of his extravagant life-style he restored to the Emperor, probably in 1173 or 1174, his imperial fiefs in Italy, the principality of Sardinia, the duchy of Spoleto, the margraviate of Tuscany, and the Matildine lands. Frederick I paid his uncle a large sum in exchange, though he had already to a large extent incorporated these territories in the administration of upper and central Italy.

To forestall too great a preponderance of the Hohenstaufens in south-west Germany, Henry the Lion came to an agreement with Welf VI—presumably after much negotiation—whereby Welf promised him the succession to his allodial lands and other rights. This was natural enough in itself, since Henry the Lion's property in Swabia and the Swabian–Bavarian border area was in many places in close proximity to his uncle's. In return Henry promised to pay a large sum of money. The date of this agreement is not known; it was probably not before 1175. Henry, however, did not execute the financial clause, thinking that as Welf VI's next male heir he would get the property anyway. Accordingly Welf VI revoked the agreement with Henry and concluded one with his other nephew, Frederick I; this was probably not until 1178. The Emperor undertook to pay the money, and Welf made over his estates at once; Frederick kept part of them, but regranted the major part to Welf as a fief.

After his return from the Holy Land, Henry the Lion embarked on vigorous building activity in the castle precincts at Brunswick. We have unfortunately no dates as regards the rebuilding of the old Brunonian fortress, which probably began some time earlier. The fact that the lion monument was erected in front of the new castle in 1166 suggests that the latter was virtually completed by then. In any case, the new Dankwarderode castle was clearly modelled on the royal *palatia*, especially that erected by the Salian Emperors at Goslar. However, the new castle at Brunswick was larger than the imperial residences built by Frederick I at this time. The biggest of them, at Gelnhausen, was in fact smaller than the hall of Dankwarderode; the latter came to be called a *Pfalz* in the time of Duke Henry's sons, and there can be no doubt that it was meant to challenge comparison with the royal residences.

The date at which work was begun on the new church is attested by sources. In 1173 the duke had the church dating from the first half of the eleventh century pulled down and began to erect a considerably bigger one. Planned as a basilica with three naves, a transept, a crypt, and a raised choir, it resembled a cathedral—as it later came to be called—rather than a mere collegiate church. (At Goslar the eleventh-century church of SS Simon and Jude, founded in the *palatium* precincts by the Emperor Henry III, was in later times often called a cathedral for the same reason.) The rebuilt church was also rededicated. Whereas the original building had been placed under the patronage of SS Peter and Paul, Blaise, and John the Baptist, for the new edifice the two former saints were replaced, early in the thirteenth century, by St Thomas of Canterbury. The rebuilding was carried out quite quickly for the time, and was practically complete when the duke died in 1195.

In the years during which the rebuilding of the monastery church was begun, the ducal court did much to encourage artistic activity in Saxony. We shall in due course evaluate Henry the Lion's role as a patron of the fine arts, literature, and science of his time. Here we shall only mention one work that gives a good idea of the political ideology of the duke and his entourage in the 1170s.

This is the Gmunden Evangeliarium or gospel book, so called after the castle in Upper Austria where it was long preserved. It was written, by the duke's command, between about 1173 and 1180 in the monastery of Helmarshausen, then one of the leading schools of writing and illumination in Germany, and presented by the ducal couple to St Blaise's in Brunswick. The writer, Herman of Helmarshausen, was the most famous artist in the school in the second half of the twelfth century, and the work is undoubtedly the finest illuminated manuscript produced there at that period.

The dedicatory poem that names the duke as patron of the work emphasizes his noble birth and that of his consort. Henry is extolled as a descendant of Charlemagne: according to the ideas of the time, any ruler with Carolingian blood was endowed with a special legitimacy. For this reason, the poem continues, England judged him alone to be a worthy spouse for Princess Matilda, and their posterity would bring to the land salvation and the peace of Christ.

The idea of the special dignity of the ducal couple is still more clearly expressed in the so-called coronation picture, the best-known miniature in the volume. The upper part, representing the heavenly sphere, shows Christ in glory with his apostles, angels, and saints, particularly those that were revered by Henry himself or especially honoured in England. On one side are John the Evangelist, John the Baptist, and St Blaise; on the other St Peter, Pope Gregory the Great, and the recently canonized St Thomas Becket. The lower half of the picture represents the temporal world. The duke and duchess, kneeling in the centre, receive two crowns from the Saviour's crossed hands. On either side, as if bearing witness to the honour paid to them, are ancestors with their names inscribed. On Henry's side we see his parents Henry the Proud and Gertrude; next to them, however, instead of Henry the Proud's parents, Henry the Black and Wulfhild, the picture shows Gertrude's parents, the Emperor Lothair III and his consort Richenza. On the other side of the picture are, beside Henry's duchess, her father Henry II of England and his mother Matilda (daughter of Henry I), who was the consort of the Emperor Henry V and subsequently queen of England for a brief period. On the extreme right is another female figure who is not named and cannot be identified with any certainty; she does not wear the head-dress of a married woman.

Thus the ancestors of the ducal couple depicted in the miniature are above all those entitled to an imperial or a royal crown. The four crowns they wear are exactly similar to those that are being bestowed on Henry the Lion and Matilda. At the same time, this emphasizes how far the duke has risen above his parents, who are uncrowned, as is the female figure on the extreme right. The banderoles at the four corners of the miniature refer expressly to the crown of eternal life; but the earthly crowns bestowed on Henry and Matilda express the idea that they are deserving of royal rank.

This picture is one of the main arguments for the view sometimes put forward in recent research that Henry the Lion intended in the 1170s to make himself a king in his north German territory. The quasi-royal power that he wielded in large parts of Saxony, and the way in which he exercised the imperial prerogative in Nordalbingia and the Baltic area, would have been constitutionally legitimized by the existence of a Welf kingdom.

Such advancement to royal rank would not have been unique in twelfth-century Germany. In 1158, at a diet in Regensburg, Frederick I had conferred a royal crown on Duke Vladislav II of Bohemia; he and his descendants were permitted to wear a royal circlet on certain feast days and to be crowned by the bishop of Prague or, as his deputy, the bishop of Olmütz (Olomouc). In this way Barbarossa revived the royal dignity which Henry IV had in 1085 bestowed, on a personal basis only, on Duke Vratislav, the grandfather of Vladislav II. Frederick I's action was a recognition of the special position of Bohemia within the Empire, of which it had only gradually become an integral part.

It is noteworthy, however, that the idea of royal rank for Henry the Lion is only attested in this symbolic form. No other contemporary or later source offers any suggestion that the duke entertained such an idea or broached the matter at any time with Frederick I. It may have been an idea that was vaguely mooted at the duke's court around that time but did not assume any concrete form. In the same way, about the middle of the twelfth century there were ideas in Frederick I's entourage of the Emperor claiming to be ruler of the world, without Barbarossa himself seriously endorsing them. So it must remain an open question whether Henry the Lion really intended to make himself king on the strength of his power in north Germany. What is clear, however, is that the idea of kingship was bound to foster his self-conceit, born of the long Welf tradition as to the family's quasi-royal dgnity. Thus in the early 1170s we have the beginning of a development that was eventually to lead to conflict and to the breakdown of the long-standing amity between the Emperor and the duke.

9

Condemnation and Deposition

AFTER his return from Italy in the spring of 1168, Frederick I remained in Germany for six and a half years, longer than at any other time during his reign of almost forty years. He devoted this period to the systematic extension of royal power in the Empire, not only in Swabia and Alsace but also on the middle Rhine and in East Franconia. He also endeavoured to build up a large imperial territory in east central Germany, in the region of the Mulde, Pleisse, and Eger rivers. To the north of the Harz, the crown territory around Goslar was once more firmly in his hands from the late 1160s onwards; but he avoided pursuing an expansionist policy in this area at Henry the Lion's expense.

As all his active diplomacy failed to achieve any real success against Alexander III, Frederick was obliged once again to seek a solution in Italy by military means. During his absence the Lombard League had developed into an important political factor, and in central Italy too the imperial power had been seriously eroded.

In the autumn of 1174 the Emperor set out on his fifth Italian expedition with a comparatively small feudal levy, reinforced by mercenaries. Henry the Lion and other lay princes of the Empire did not take part; Frederick's main support came from the ecclesiastical princes. Archbishop Christian of Mainz had been in northern Italy since 1171 as an imperial legate, making diplomatic preparations for the campaign. Despite the limited size of his army, the Emperor did not take long to re-establish his rule in western Lombardy. The main object of his attack was the League's fortified city of Alessandria. Contrary to expectation, he was not able to overcome it rapidly: the siege lasted through the winter of 1174–5. As a relief army drew near, Frederick advanced to confront it, but could not risk a pitched battle.

As the cities were prepared to compromise, a truce was arranged in April 1175 at Montebello near Piacenza. The Lombards submitted once more, and a definitive peace was to be negotiated by a commission of three representatives from either side; if they failed to agree, the consuls (councillors) of Cremona were to act as arbitrators. Frederick was prepared to make far-reaching concessions. However, the negotiations broke down because the cities insisted that the Emperor should make his peace with the Pope as well and that Alessandria should be recognized as a member of the League, while the Emperor demanded that it be destroyed.

Thus fighting again broke out in the autumn of 1175. The Emperor's position was awkward, because he had disbanded part of his army after the truce of Montebello. Troops recruited in Germany by Archbishop Philip of Cologne were still awaited. Frederick therefore decided to appeal personally to Henry the Lion for military aid, but the latter refused.

The sources give contradictory accounts of the meeting between the Emperor and the duke. The very brief contemporary records say nothing of such a meeting, which is only mentioned by chroniclers of the late twelfth and early thirteenth century, after both the protagonists were dead, and it has often been treated as legendary on that account. Certainly an event of such importance to the fortunes of the Empire impressed the minds of subsequent generations, who embellished it with more and more anecdotal features. But there is no reason to doubt that the king and duke met face to face, especially as the accounts we have are probably based on older, lost sources.

Otto, of St Blaise in the Black Forest, in his *Chronicle* dating from the beginning of the thirteenth century, states that meeting took place at the imperial fortress of Chiavenna north of Lake Como, which then belonged to the duchy of Swabia. This is indeed the most likely place: a meeting in that area between the end of January and the beginning of February 1176 would fit in well enough with what we know of the protagonists' movements. The story found in a somewhat later Saxon source that the Emperor summoned the Saxon princes to Partenkirchen, where Henry alone refused military aid, seems hardly probable. Quite untenable is Arnold of Lübeck's statement that Barbarossa crossed the Alps and held a diet at which he put his request to the duke: nothing is known of any such diet in Germany that year.

The meeting at Chiavenna, at which the Empress Beatrice was present as well as the two princes' attendants, was a dramatic affair. The Emperor certainly made an urgent appeal to his cousin for help, and apparently in his agitation fell on his knees to overcome the duke's resistance. Some sources expressly say that he did so; others merely remark that his attitude was humbler than became his royal majesty. The gesture would have been less of a personal humiliation for men of that day than it would appear to later observers.

According to Arnold of Lübeck the duke was so disturbed that he at once raised up the Emperor; other sources say that he did not trouble to do so. Two chroniclers of the early thirteenth century, Provost Burchard of Ursberg in Swabia and the compiler of the *Sächsische Weltchronik*, allege that Henry's steward, Jordan of Blankenburg, dissuaded his master from helping the Emperor, saying proudly: 'Let the imperial crown lie at your feet, my lord; one day it will be on your head.' The story in this form is certainly touched up, but not a pure invention: it serves to illustrate the overweening self-conceit of the Welf and his followers. The Stade Annals, by contrast, have the Empress raising Frederick to his feet and saying: 'Rise, my lord, and remember this fall, which may God remember also.' We see from this how strong a memory of the occurrence at Chiavenna persisted in the mid-thirteenth century.

As to the reasons for Henry's refusal, the explanation by Arnold of Lübeck, close to the duke though he was, is unconvincing. According to this, Henry said he was prepared to aid Frederick to raise an army with gold, silver, and other means, but not to bear arms himself, as he was old and exhausted by his many campaigns in Italy and elsewhere. (Henry's age was then about 45.)

Here again, Otto of St Blaise probably gives the right account. He states—as do the Marbach Annals, compiled shortly afterwards in Alsace—that Henry said he would help the Emperor if the latter would confer on him Goslar as a fief, 'the richest city in Saxony'. Frederick, according to Otto, refused this as a shameless piece of blackmail, whereupon Henry left Chiavenna in deep disappointment.

Henry's demand for the imperial advocacy of Goslar—for it was not only the city that was in question—is in line with his ambitions in Saxony. If he could succeed in gaining possession of the advocacy with its rich revenues from the Rammelsberg mines, which had already been within the Welf sphere of influence for more than a decade from the beginning of the 1150s, this would have set the seal on his policy in the Harz area. On the other hand it is quite understandable that the Emperor should have rejected the demand as blackmail, greatly though he stood in need of Henry's help. At a time when Frederick was increasingly concerned to accumulate territory in different parts of the Empire, the crown property in the Harz district was more important to him than at the beginning of his reign, when there seemed to be other ways of building up a strong imperial power. By granting the advocacy he would have been giving up the principal economic support of the crown in north Germany and forgoing the possibility of a successful territorial policy in the northern foreland of the Harz mountains.

But the conflict that broke out at Chiavenna is not to be regarded only from the point of view of the territorial rivalry between Hohenstaufen and Welf that was extending to more and more parts of the Empire. Moreover, it is uncertain whether at this time Welf VI had already broken off the agreement making Henry the Lion his heir, and had begun to approach Frederick I for the same purpose.

In refusing to meet Henry's wishes the Emperor was no doubt moved by basic political considerations. The tenor of the interview and Henry's unyielding attitude made it clear that he regarded himself not as a vassal in the presence of his liege lord but as a partner with equal rights, offering voluntary aid at a price. Barbarossa realized that the excessive power Henry had acquired in the course of time and the almost kingly prestige he enjoyed in both East and West threatened to disrupt the feudal fabric of the German state.

The fact that Henry the Lion was prepared to accede to the Emperor's wish on his own terms is the best refutation of the view, often repeated by historians of the nineteenth and early twentieth century, that he refused aid because of his basic opposition to the Emperor's Italian policy, which (on this view) he had supported with reluctance from the beginning. Henry was not in fact an opponent of that policy, which he supported as long as it seemed to favour his own designs in Germany. Nor can it be thought that he had meanwhile come closer to Alexander III's party or that—as was alleged from time to time in the context of his trial—he maintained treasonable relations with the Lombard cities.

The duke was under no feudal obligation to take part in the campaign, as Frederick had proclaimed no general levy. He did, however, have a moral duty to stand by the Emperor in the latter's difficulties. If his own position in Saxony was perfectly secure at this time, it was above all because Frederick had again and again protected him against his Saxon opponents. It was the tragedy and the condemnation of Henry the Lion that he ignored the debt of gratitude. Thus Chiavenna put an end to the political understanding that had existed between Emperor and duke for about twenty-five years and had largely governed the course of political events in the Empire. It also destroyed the close human bonds that had united the two cousins for decades, and was thus a turning-point in the history of Frederick I and Henry the Lion.

Although the reinforcements furnished by Philip of Cologne and other German princes were few in number, the Emperor on his return to Upper Italy decided to take the offensive. However, on 29 May 1176 his small cavalry army was defeated at Legnano, north-west of Milan, by a superior force of Lombard knights and Milan infantry. For some days Frederick himself was thought to have been killed. The military importance of the defeat was not very great, as only part of the imperial troops were engaged; it was more a prestige victory for Frederick's opponents. None the less, he decided to negotiate once more. There seemed to be a basis of understanding, as the Cremona consuls came forward with new peace proposals; Frederick was prepared to accept these, but this time the communes refused.

The Emperor thereupon resolved on a decisive change in his church policy, and entered on negotiations with the Curia which showed him to be a master of diplomacy. By November 1176 he had concluded a preliminary treaty at Anagni that was to provide a basis for enduring peace. Frederick undertook to recognize Alexander as the rightful Pope and to restore his regalia and possessions. He waived his own claim to the Matildine lands and engaged himself to include the Lombard communes and the kingdom of Sicily in the peace settlement. The Pope in return promised to release Frederick from excommunication, to recognize him as Emperor and his son Henry as king of the Romans, and to validate the ecclesiastical measures taken by Frederick in Germany during the schism.

This preliminary peace was to a large extent a victory for the papal claims, but in the tough negotiations of the ensuing months the Emperor's representatives were able to modify it considerably in his favour. Frederick also managed to drive a wedge between the Curia and the Lombards, enabling him to step up his demands on the latter. The Pope, anxious to come to terms as far as the church was concerned, proposed that the Emperor should for the present conclude an armistice with the Lombards for six years and with Sicily for fifteen. The vexed question of the Matildine lands was to be omitted from the treaty, so that for the time being they remained in the Emperor's possession. On the basis of this compromise, peace was finally concluded between the Emperor and the Pope at Venice at the end of July 1177, putting an end to the schism that had lasted 18 years. At a ceremony in St Mark's Alexander received the Emperor, whom he had already absolved, into the bosom of the church. Frederick did obeisance to the Pope, kissing his toe after the custom of the time. The Pope raised him up, gave him the kiss of peace, and bestowed his blessing.

Although formally a triumph for the church, the treaty of Venice was in fact anything but a victory for the Papacy. Above all, the Emperor was able largely to preserve his influence on church affairs in Germany. The archbishops and bishops appointed by him were confirmed in their offices after acknowledging Alexander as Pope: this applied in particular to Christian of Mainz and Philip of Cologne. Conrad of Wittelsbach, who had been deposed from the see of Mainz in 1165, was compensated with Salzburg, where he replaced Archbishop Henry, who had occupied the see since 1174.

Two decisions concerning Saxony were clearly adverse to Henry the Lion's church policy. In Bremen, the circumstances of the appointment to the archbishopric in 1168 were to be re-examined. If it was found that the election of the Ascanian Siegfried—who had maintained his claim to Bremen even after being installed as bishop of Brandenburg—had taken place canonically, he was now to be given the see in place of Archbishop Baldwin. In Halberstadt Bishop Gero, who had possessed himself of the see, was deposed and Ulrich, whom Henry had deprived of his office, was reinstated.

By another provision still more unfavourable to Henry the Lion, all grants made by Baldwin and Gero were declared invalid: church property alienated by them in the two dioceses was to be restored. As willing tools of the duke they had enfeoffed him with church estates on a large scale, so that he now forfeited much property in addition to his previous influence in the two dioceses. These arrangements concerning Bremen and Halberstadt, which were already embodied in the preliminary treaty of Anagni, show how decisively the Emperor's attitude towards Henry had changed within a short time of Chiavenna.

After the peace of Venice Frederick remained in Upper Italy for about a year and then proceeded to Arles, where he was crowned king by the archbishop as a symbol of his rule over the whole of Burgundy. In October 1178 he returned to Germany, where further arduous tasks awaited him.

Henry the Lion had gone from Chiavenna to Bavaria, where he met Henry Jasomirgott on the Enns, and then to Saxony. A court held at Westminster by Henry II of England in November 1176 was attended by the Lion's envoys as well as those of Frederick I, Manuel I, and other crowned heads; however, no agreement was entered into at this time against Barbarossa by Henry and his father-in-law.

Henry the Lion had not regarded his position as threatened by the preliminary treaty of Anagni: this is best shown by the fact that in the summer of 1177 he undertook a campaign in the border area between Mecklenburg and Pomerania. The initiative for this last expedition of the duke's against the Slavs came from Valdemar of Denmark, who had meanwhile reasserted Danish supremacy in the Rügian territory of Hither Pomerania. When the Pomeranian princes, having built new fortresses on the Swine river, carried out pirate raids on Danish merchant ships, Valdemar proposed an alliance against them. Accordingly, in the early summer Henry advanced against the strong border fortress of Demmin on the Peene with an army that included the Margrave Otto I of Brandenburg, the eldest son of Albert the Bear, while Valdemar's fleet sailed up the mouth of the Oder. For ten weeks, from the end of June to the beginning of September, the Saxon army besieged Demmin. Despite the use of heavy siege engines the stronghold continued to resist; an attempt to capture it by diverting the Peene was also unsuccessful.

When Henry learnt that his old adversary Ulrich had reoccupied the see of Halberstadt following the treaty of Venice he realized that this would be the signal for fresh battles in Saxony, in which he could no longer expect the Emperor's support. He therefore decided to raise the siege of Demmin and return to Saxony. The constructor of his siege engines offered to destroy the town by fire, but Henry refused, as it would only cause fresh fighting in the border area. After the Pomeranian princes had undertaken to give hostages, pay tribute, and refrain from invading the duke's territory, he broke off the siege and returned to Brunswick, without having achieved his object of improving the security of his realm by subduing the Hither Pomeranian border area.

In February 1178 Bishop Evermod of Ratzeburg died, and there seems to have been a dispute in the chapter as to his successor. The duke, however, finally secured the election of the Premonstratensian Provost Isfried from Jerichow, who was devoted to his cause. This was Henry's last success in Nordalbingia. In the same year, on 30 December, Prince Pribislav of Werle was killed in a tournament at the duke's court at Lüneburg. His inheritance was contested by his son Henry Borwin, who was the duke's son-in-law, and Niklot, son of the Vratislav who was executed in 1164; but Henry was unable to intervene on this occasion.

In the autumn of 1177 Ulrich of Halberstadt had begun to repossess the church lands that Gero had alienated. When he demanded that Henry return the fiefs granted to him, he met with a firm refusal. Ulrich thereupon excommunicated Henry, who retaliated by destroying the bishop's castle of Nornburg on the important road from Halberstadt to Brunswick. To improve the defence of his cathedral city Ulrich began in the winter of 1177–8 to erect a castle on the Hopelberg south of Halberstadt.

At about the same time fighting broke out in Westphalia between the archbishopric of Cologne and the duke's supporters led by Bernard of Lippe, who successfully combated the archbishop's forces. Philip, the archbishop, returned to Germany in the spring of 1178 and intervened actively in the hostilities in Saxony, using as a pretext his claim to the inheritance of Count Otto of Assel, which had been repossessed by the duke, and to the estates of another relative, Count Christian of Oldenburg, which had fallen to Henry after the count's death in 1167. The archbishop and Ulrich of Halberstadt concluded an offensive and defensive alliance against Henry, probably at the beginning of the summer, each undertaking to assist the other even if his own claims were satisfied. The archbishop led an army into the Westphalian part of the duke's dominions, destroying castles and localities including the town of Höxter, and advanced as far as Hamelin. Archbishop Wichmann of Magdeburg, who had pursued a policy of neutrality since the peace of 1170, joined with Bishop Eberhard of Merseburg to bring about an armistice between Archbishop Philip and the duke, whereupon Philip withdrew his forces.

Henry, however, did not observe the armistice for long, as he wanted at any cost to prevent Ulrich of Halberstadt continuing to strengthen his castle on the Hopelberg. Wichmann once more intervened and restored peace in eastern Saxony. Soon afterwards the castle was destroyed by fire, which was universally laid to the duke's charge. Wichmann then persuaded the neighbouring princes to help the bishop rebuild the fortress, while Henry sent a large force against

Halberstadt under the Count Palatine Adalbert of Sommerschen-burg. This army was severely defeated by Count Bernard of Anhalt in a battle in the marshland north of the city; over 400 knights are said to have been taken prisoner. With the beginning of winter the fighting in eastern Saxony ceased for the time being. It is uncertain whether Bishop Ulrich released the duke from excommunication at this time or later.

Barbarossa attached much importance to pacifying Saxony. At an imperial diet in Speyer on 11 November 1178, a few weeks after Frederick's return to Germany, Henry the Lion made grave charges against his enemies; but they too were present, headed by Arch-bishop Philip of Cologne, and accused the duke in their turn. It is a sign of Frederick's changed attitude towards Henry that he now opened formal legal proceedings, summoning both parties to a diet to be held at Worms in mid-January. Henry was offered the opportun-ity there of rebutting the charges against him—a clear indication that Frederick now regarded him as a defendant rather than a plaintiff.

Thus began the legal proceedings against Henry the Lion, which lasted more than a year till the final judgment pronounced at a diet at Würzburg in mid-January 1180. It is strange that contemporary sources give only an incomplete account of the trial, which was of crucial importance not only to the history of the Empire in the next few decades but also for its further constitutional development. We have only one documentary source, a diploma issued at a diet at Gelnhausen on 13 April 1180, about three months after the conclu-sion of proceedings against the duke, whereby the Emperor, having consulted with the princes, enfeoffed Archbishop Philip of Cologne with part of Saxony as a new duchy of Westphalia. The original of this important document was unfortunately destroyed in 1945 at the place to which it had been removed for safety. It had been so badly damaged by damp in the Middle Ages that at an early date several fourteenth-century copies had to be called in aid to establish the text. This applies especially to the first lines, which give an account of Henry the Lion's trial. The text of this long sentence, and its interpretation, have been the subject of lively dispute among scholars up to the present day. Moreover the narrative sources give highly contradictory information as to the proceedings and especially the dates set for the successive hearings. Thus many important questions cannot be answered with certainty.

The duke's trial was unquestionably political, but it was conducted in full accordance with contemporary legal standards. Two phases can be clearly discerned: one of customary law (*Landrecht*) and the other of feudal law, the second beginning only after the first was concluded. In the first phase the princes were the accusers. They charged the duke with violating the public peace by attacking their possessions and by high-handed acts against churches. Henry ignored the summons to Worms, where the diet opened on 13 January 1179; many princes attended, including Welf VI and numerous Swabian counts and lords in their capacity as peers of Henry the Lion and members of the same tribe or 'stem'. It was probably here that a judgment was issued to the effect that Henry would be outlawed in the event of further contumacy.

The diet at Worms also took further decisions that affected Henry's attitude. With the consent of the assembled princes Frederick endowed his sons partly with Hohenstaufen property and partly with fiefs of other lords, as well as castles and *ministeriales*. These were chiefly in Swabia, and Frederick's agreement with Welf VI over the latter's inheritance was concluded on this occasion if not earlier; at all events, in the course of the same year Frederick disposed of estates that Welf had ceded to him.

Henry the Lion for his part now concerted with other Swabian families who likewise felt threatened by the Emperor's territorial policy. Among them were the counts of Zollern and those of Veringen near Sigmaringen; but other families too were involved in the conspiracy against the Emperor, as it was later expressly called. We have no details of what took place, but the Emperor seems to have had little difficulty in quelling the opposition movement in Swabia.

It is impossible to be certain whether a second summons was issued from Worms to a court day not otherwise known. The next attested stage in the procedure under customary law was a diet, again attended by great numbers, at Magdeburg on 24 June 1179. As Henry again failed to appear he was placed under a ban (*Acht*), perhaps on 29 June and probably in accordance with the Worms judgment. This, however, constituted only a preliminary step towards complete outlawry.

At Magdeburg an old enemy of the duke, the margrave of Lusatia, Dietrich of Landsberg of the house of Wettin, accused him of high treason and challenged him to settle the issue by a duel. On what Dietrich based this grave charge is not known. It is unlikely that he adduced Henry's relations with foreign powers, in particular his dealings several years earlier with Manuel of Byzantine. According to Arnold of Lübeck the charge was based on a Slav attack on the march of Lusatia, for which the duke was blamed; but this probably only took place in the autumn of 1179.

Henry, who was at Haldersleben at the time of the diet, declined to fight a judicial duel but asked the Emperor for an interview, which took place soon after in or near Haldersleben. He endeavoured to make his peace with the Emperor, who however said he would only mediate between Henry and his opponents if the duke would pay him an indemnity of 5,000 silver marks. However, Henry refused to pay this high price for the lifting of the ban. The last attempt at compromise having thus failed, legal proceedings had to pursue their course.

The proceedings under *Landrecht* having reached an interim conclusion by the pronouncing of the ban, the Emperor now himself instituted a suit under feudal law. His charge was that by failing more than once to appear at the king's court of justice Henry had violated one of a vassal's chief obligations. For this he was to be tried by the princes of the Empire as his fellow-vassals.

The chronology of this second form of procedure is not certain either. To begin with, we do not know the opening date. The Emperor may have brought his charge at Magdeburg after the ban was pronounced; but it is more likely that he did so after the failure of his negotiations with the duke, at a further diet held in mid-August at Kayna near Gera. Feudal procedure required threefold notice at intervals of six weeks. It is not clear from the sources, however, whether there were in fact three summonses for successive dates or whether they were combined into a single 'peremptory summons'. The next diet, as far as we know, which conducted proceedings against Henry the Lion was at Würzburg on 13 January 1180, about eighteen weeks after Kayna. The duke again failed to comply with the summons under feudal law or to send a spokesman who could answer for him, and he was accordingly condemned at Würzburg for persistent contumacy. By unanimous decision of the princes he was deprived of his two duchies and all imperial fiefs, which reverted to the crown. When the Gelnhausen document speaks in this connection of overt *lèse-majesté* on the duke's part this refers to his failure to appear in court, not to any treasonable behaviour as has sometimes been suggested. It is noteworthy that neither in the customary nor in the feudal proceedings was any mention made of the duke's refusal of aid at Chiavenna.

After the Magdeburg diet, the fighting in Westphalia and eastern Saxony had broken out again in all its violence. While Archbishop Philip of Cologne was still with the Emperor in east Saxony, Henry sent an army consisting mainly of contingents headed by the three Nordalbingian counts of Schwerin, Holstein, and Ratzeburg, but also of troops furnished by other counts, against Philip's followers led by Count Simon of Tecklenburg, who had occupied Welf territory near Osnabrück. On 1 August the duke's forces were victorious at the Halerfeld north-west of Osnabrück. Many of the enemy were killed or captured; Simon of Tecklenburg was only set free after swearing fealty to the duke. At about the same time Bernard of Lippe and Count Conrad of Rheda near Gütersloh attacked the archbishop of Cologne's stronghold in central Westphalia. The town of Soest held out, but Medebach (south-west of Korbach) was captured and sacked. However, Henry partially deprived himself of the benefit of these successes, as he demanded that the prisoners be handed over to him. Some of his followers complied; others, such as Count Adolf III of Holstein, declared that they had fought the war at their own expense and had a right to the ransoms. This was the beginning of a rift between Henry and the Schauenburger.

The fighting in eastern Saxony was primarily around Halberstadt and Haldensleben. As Bishop Ulrich was raiding the duke's territory from the rebuilt fortress of Hornburg, and at this time probably again pronounced excommunication upon him, Henry resolved on retaliation. From Brunswick, where he then was, he sent a force which invaded the bishopric, destroyed the Hornburg, and captured Halberstadt itself in a surprise attack on a Sunday (23 September). The town offered no serious resistance; many inhabitants took refuge in the churches, but a fire broke out and spread rapidly, the buildings being mostly of wood. The cathedral and several other churches were burnt. Many of the clergy and citizens—one source even speaks of 1,000—died in the fire or were put to the sword. The charred relics of St Stephen, the patron of the cathedral, were saved with difficulty. Bishop Ulrich at first held out in the castle by the cathedral but was finally captured with his immediate suite and taken to Brunswick.

The duke, while regretting the destruction of churches, the deaths of the clergy, and the damaged relics, intended to exploit his victory. The aged bishop was kept in captivity at the Ertheneburg, and was only released at Christmas (which the duke celebrated at Lüneburg) when he promised to absolve Henry and reinvest him with his Halberstadt fiefs. One of Henry's oldest and bitterest enemies, he died some months later.

The fighting for Haldensleben began a few days after the sack of Halberstadt. Archbishop Wichmann was again on the side of the duke's opponents, having attended the diets at Worms, Magdeburg, and Kayna. There was also a dispute between him and Henry the Lion over the lands of the Count Palatine Adalbert of Sommerschenburg, who had died without male heirs in the first half of 1179. His sister Adelheid, abbess of Quedlinburg, could not keep a hold on the estates and sold them to the archdiocese of Magdeburg. However, Henry the Lion, probably without any legal justification, laid claim to the inheritance and seized a portion of it.

In his fight against the duke Archbishop Wichmann received military support from the other princes of eastern Saxony, especially the Margrave Otto of Meissen and his brothers and the Landgrave Ludwig III of Thuringia. Still more important to him was the army of the archbishop of Cologne, about 4,000 strong, consisting mainly of the notoriously savage Brabantine mercenaries.

The centre of the struggle was the town of Neuhaldensleben on the Ohre. The besiegers, though superior in numbers, were unable to overcome its strong fortifications. The inhabitants set fire to the marshy soil of their city; the blaze quickly spread to the siege engines and destroyed them. There was also a violent dispute among the besiegers over the claim of the archbishop of Cologne to exercise command on account of the size of his contingent. Otto of Meissen and his brothers withdrew in dudgeon, and, when Philip of Cologne and the Thuringian princes did the same, Wichmann had to give up the siege.

The duke now carried out a plundering raid through the archbishop's territory, destroyed Calbe on the Sale, and advanced close to Magdeburg. At about the same time, Pomeranians and Ljutici, at his instigation, invaded Lusatia and the eastern part of the see of Magdeburg, devastating Jüterbog and setting fire to the neighbouring monastery of Zinna.

Thus by the end of 1179 Henry could regard himself as the victor of the hostilities in Saxony. The next year began with a lull in operations. After their return from the diet of Würzburg at which Henry was deprived of his fiefs, the Saxon princes concluded an armistice with the duke which was to last till 27 April, the Sunday after Easter. The reasons for this surprising step are not known. It may have been due to the difficulty of winter campaigning; perhaps the princes also wanted to induce the Emperor to proceed rapidly to a settlement of the succession in Saxony which would take account of their wishes.

It is noteworthy in any case that Frederick departed from the custom which then prevailed of not regranting escheated fiefs until a year and a day had elapsed: on this occasion, fourteen days before the expiry of the armistice he made a regrant of Saxony at the great diet of Gelnhausen. Thus the charter of 13 April issued to Archbishop Philip of Cologne no longer speaks, as previously, of the duke and duchy of Saxony, but refers to Henry the Lion as the former duke of Westphalia, and his territory as the *ducatus* of Westphalia and Engern.

After close consultation with the princes and with their consent, the Emperor divided the duchy of Saxony into two *ducatus*. The first, extending into the Cologne diocese and including the whole see of Paderborn, was granted, with all the rights and privileges specified in detail, to the church of Cologne in recognition of Philip's services to the Empire. The new duchy, which has no name of its own in the Gelnhausen document, was granted to the archbishop as a banner-fief (*Fahnenlehen*). As the archbishops of Cologne had enjoyed ducal rights west of the Rhine since Conrad III's time, they now possessed a twofold duchy.

The rest of former Saxony was enfeoffed to the Ascanian Bernard of Anhalt. He is only referred to as duke of Westphalia and Engern, but there is no doubt that his rule also extended to Eastphalia in so far as that was subject to ducal authority. The Ascanians had thus reached their goal. The ducal rank in Saxony for which Albert the Bear had fought but which he had held for only a few years had now reverted to his family and remained in their possession for centuries. If Bernard of Anhalt and not his eldest brother Margrave Otto of Brandenburg was raised to the dukedom, this was to prevent a strong ducal power once again arising in Saxony; moreover Bernard had played an important part in the fighting against Henry the Lion.

Two other important decisions were taken at Gelnhausen. The county palatine of Saxony, vacated by the death of Adalbert of Sommerschenburg, was bestowed on the Landgrave Ludwig III of Thuringia, who thus extended his family domain northwards; and the dispute over the archbishopric of Bremen was settled. On the death of Baldwin, Henry the Lion's loyal supporter, in 1178, the chapter had hastily elected Canon Berthold of Cologne, ignoring the rights of the Ascanian Siegfried under the treaty of Venice. Henry the Lion, who at first accepted this election, protested to the Curia when Berthold sought and received investiture from Frederick I. In view of the evident irregularity Berthold's election was pronounced invalid at the third Lateran Council in March 1179. The Bremen chapter now at last declared for Siegfried, on whom Barbarossa conferred the investiture at Gelnhausen. This was a further important success for the Ascanians.

The condemnation of Henry the Lion caused a great stir in the Western world. Henry II of England was particularly concerned by his son-in-law's fate, but could not offer military aid as he was involved in a dispute with his eldest sons, Henry and Richard. It is not clear whether he tried to persuade Philip II, the new king of France, and Count Philip of Flanders to take action against the Emperor. In any case both of them assured Frederick, through envoys, that they had never had any idea of taking up arms against him on Henry the Lion's account.

Henry himself attempted to get help from Valdemar of Denmark. The two met on the Eider in 1180, probably in spring before the expiry of the truce in Saxony. According to the Danish historian Saxo, Henry advanced right across the bridge into Denmark, instead of at most half-way as he had done on previous occasions—an important point, given the protocol which governed royal meetings in those days. Saxo also states that Valdemar offered help on condition that Henry first give back the church lands he had seized. It is questionable, however, whether he was really prepared to give aid to Henry, which would have been a breach of his fealty to the Emperor; moreover Valdemar had every reason to welcome a weakening of the Saxon duchy.

At Gelnhausen a general campaign against the duke had been arranged to open on 25 July 1180. This was more than a year and a day after the original ban, so that Henry was by this time finally outlawed.

At the end of April, however, violent hostilities again broke out in Saxony on the expiry of the armistice. They began with an attack by Henry on Goslar, the defence of which had been entrusted by the Emperor to the Landgrave Ludwig. Failing to capture the city, Henry destroyed the metallurgical works and smelting furnaces and then invaded the landgrave's territory. Ludwig hastened to its protection but was severely defeated at Weissensee north of Erfurt. He himself, his brother, and many knights were taken prisoner by the duke, who returned with his captives to Brunswick.

At a diet at Regensburg at the end of June the Emperor proclaimed the *Oberacht* (sentence of complete outlawry) against Henry, as he had failed to purge his original contempt within a year and a day. At the same time Frederick began discussions with the Bavarian magnates about the regranting of the duchy, but as yet without result.

Frederick then went to Saxony to lead the campaign against the deposed duke. At a diet at Werla on the Oker north of Goslar, attended by many ecclesiastical and secular lords, he set three time-limits extending to 11 November, by which date Henry's adherents were called upon to cease supporting him on pain of losing their fiefs. For the defence of Goslar Frederick ordered the nearby Harzburg, in ruins since Henry IV's time, to be rebuilt.

Before the Emperor arrived in Saxony, a final breach had taken place between Henry and Count Adolf III of Holstein over the question of the Halerfeld prisoners. Adolf joined the Emperor's army, and there began a massive abandonment of Henry by vassals and *ministeriales*, many of whom had chafed under his harsh regime. Among the greater feudatories, the counts of Wöltingerode, Scharzfels, Ilfeld, and Dannenberg, together with some lesser nobles, went over to the Emperor, who thus secured important fortresses without battle, especially in the Harz area. The movement spread to many of Henry's *ministeriales* in the ensuing weeks and months, including some, such as the lords of Heimburg, Herzberg, Peine, and Weida, whose fathers had been among the duke's chief assistants. Jordan of Blankenburg, however, remained firmly loyal, as did the burghers of Henry's cities: Brunswick, Lüneburg, and Haldensleben were his most reliable strongholds.

The Emperor's rapid success enabled him to disband a large part of his army at the beginning of September and to advance into Thuringia. At a diet at Altenburg in mid-September, after consultation with the princes, Bavaria was partitioned, like Saxony, and regranted. Henceforth the duchy comprised only the Bavarian heartland, with which Frederick invested Otto of Wittelsbach, then aged about sixty, on 16 September; the title of count palatine was transferred from him to his youngest brother, also named Otto. The grant of Bavaria to the Wittelsbachs reflected the family's power and influence in Bavaria and was also a reward for the unstinting service

Otto had rendered to the Hohenstaufens for decades in both Germany and Italy. Henceforth the Wittelsbachs were to rule Bavaria for over 700 years.

Styria, which had enjoyed considerable autonomy within the duchy of Bavaria, was now transformed from a march into an independent duchy under Ottokar of Steyr, who was raised from a margrave to a duke. Frederick also dissolved the vassal relationship in which the counts of Andechs had stood to the duke of Bavaria as margraves of Istria and Carniola. Henceforth they were to bear the title of dukes of Merania (the coastal part of Istria), Croatia, and Dalmatia.

While the Emperor was still in Altenburg, Henry the Lion had gone to Holstein to recover the countship of Adolf III, who had deserted him. Having lost a large part of east Saxony, he attempted to carry on the fight from Nordalbingia. He was aided by the fact that the lesser nobility of Holstein took his part under their leader Marcrad. Adolf's castles, Plön and the strong fortress of Segeberg, fell into his hands; the latter withstood a long siege but was compelled to surrender for lack of water. A breach also took place soon afterwards between Henry and Count Bernard of Ratzeburg. While the count was at the ducal court at Lüneburg at Christmas in 1180 Henry accused him of treason, imprisoned him for a time and seized the Ratzeburg. When Bernard was set free he joined the Emperor's party. Thus of the three counts in the colonial area east of the lower Elbe, only Gunzelin of Schwerin remained as a firm supporter of the deposed duke.

Henry used the first months of 1181 to strengthen the fortifications of Lübeck and the castles of Nordalbingia. While the Emperor was still in south Germany, the war in Saxony broke out again with an attack on Neuhaldensleben, led by Archbishop Wichmann of Magdedeburg. The Ohre and Beber rivers provided a good natural defence, and the citizens resisted vigorously under Henry's commander Bernard of Lippe. Wichmann resorted to an unusual stratagem by damming the Ohre to the east of the city. The river was swollen with rain at that season, so that the town was flooded and the inhabitants finally had to climb to their roofs for safety. The duke was unable to help them, and at the beginning of May they surrendered with his approval and evacuated the town. It was then sacked by Wichmann and the inhabitants of Magdeburg, who resented it as a rival to their trade.

At the end of June 1181 the Emperor returned to Saxony to

continue the fight against the deposed Henry, and advanced north-ward with the main body of his army. To guard the Emperor's rear Philip of Cologne set up a permanent camp near Brunswick, while the new Duke Bernard took up his position at Bardowick. Realizing that he could no longer prevent the Emperor invading Nordalbingia, Henry the Lion fled, with a few of his supporters, along the course of the Elbe to Stade, having first destroyed the Ertheneburg.

Here, at the beginning of July, Frederick crossed the Elbe and turned against Lübeck, where Henry had left a strong garrison under count Simon of Tecklenburg. The Emperor was much helped by the fact that Valdemar of Denmark, obedient to his feudal duty, block-aded Lübeck with a strong fleet; while the land forces besieging the city were reinforced by those of the Obodrite Prince Niklot of Werle and Duke Bogislav of Pomerania.

The citizens, seeing that resistance was hopeless against such odds, addressed a message through Bishop Henry to the Emperor, who allowed them to send envoys to Henry the Lion as lord of the city. The envoys returned with Henry's permission to surrender, whereupon the citizens opened their gates, having first asked Frederick to confirm the liberties and rights granted them by the duke. The Emperor agreed to these in full, and promised that the canons of Lübeck and Ratzeburg would continue to receive a share of the Lübeck tolls. Count Adolf, in return for his services against the duke, was invested with half the revenue from the Lübeck tolls, mills, and exchange banks. The Emperor entered the city in August 1181, and Henry the Lion's authority over it thus came to an end: the ducal city became a royal one under the protection of the Empire.

While the Emperor was awaiting the surrender of Lübeck, some other decisions were taken with important results for the Baltic area. Frederick I and Valdemar concluded an alliance, sealed by the betrothal of a daughter of Valdemar's to Duke Frederick of Swabia. The Emperor, however, did not recognize Valdemar's claims to Slav territory. Instead, in the camp at Lübeck he invested Duke Bogislav of Stettin (Szczecin) with his Pomeranian duchy, presenting him with an eagle banner and thus making him a prince of the Empire. Probably at this time too, Niklot of Werle did homage to the king of Germany as his feudal lord.

After the capture of Lübeck the rest of Nordalbingia soon submit-ted to the Emperor, who could now return south of the Elbe. Henry the Lion had few bases left except Stade; realizing that his situation was hopeless, he gave up resistance. He asked the Emperor for safe conduct to Lüneburg, which Frederick had allowed the Duchess Matilda to retain, as it was part of her marriage portion. On the way Henry is said to have remarked: 'I used not to require anyone's escort hither, but to grant it to others.' All his attempts to achieve a personal meeting with the Emperor or to lighten the severity of his punishment were in vain: Frederick demanded that he submit unconditionally to the princes' sentence, to be delivered at an imperial diet. This did not take place at Quedlinburg, where the Emperor held court in September or October, but at a great diet on 11 November in Erfurt, attended by Henry and most of his opponents. Here the Lion, escorted by Wichmann of Magdeburg, prostrated himself and begged the Emperor's forgiveness, while the princes confirmed the forfeiture of the two duchies and all Henry's countships. The Emperor at the same time granted to Archbishop Siegfried of Bremen the fortress and town of Stade with all its privileges; the Bremen church received back all the fiefs that it had granted to Henry under compulsion. However, the sentences of outlawry (*Acht* and *Oberacht*) under customary law were remitted at the Emperor's instance. Thus Henry regained possession of his wide allodial estates in Saxony, as far as they were lawfully acquired. In this way it became possible for the Welfs, not at once but in the future, to build up a territorial base once more. In the last years of his life Henry made dispositions concerning Welf property in Swabia, showing that at least part of his allodial estates in that duchy must have been restored to him also.

On the other hand he was now obliged to leave Germany for three years, to betake himself to Henry II's court and not to return without the Emperor's express approval. Some English sources state that he was banished for seven years and that the period was reduced at Henry II's intercession. This is unlikely: the sources no doubt only wished to make the most of Henry's support for his son-in-law.

The fall of Henry the Lion is in many ways a turning-point in twelfth-century German history. The proceedings against him brought into view constitutional developments that were previously adumbrated but now took on a more or less definitive character.

It became necessary for the crown to destroy the Welf power that threatened to burst the bounds of the German state, once the duke began to question the subordination of his own authority to the monarchy. It is not true, however, as is sometimes suggested, that the Emperor took such offence at the Chiavenna incident that he resolved from then on to destroy his Welf cousin. Henry was himself responsible for the catastrophe that befell him, by his inordinate self-conceit and misjudgement of political realities: this led him to refuse to recognize the rule of law as binding on himself, and instead to put matters to the test of arms.

Frederick, for his part, conformed closely to the procedural standards evolved by customary law. Henry the Lion and the Welf party, then and afterwards, claimed that he was unjustly dealt with because his trial ought to have taken place in Swabia, but this is not so: the law was satisfied by the participation of Swabian judges in the diet at Worms in January 1179 which pronounced the first sentence in accordance with *Landrecht*.

Necessary as it was from the standpoint of imperial power to prevent the Welf exceeding his ducal rank, the unfavourable effects of his deposition on the history of northern Germany must also be recognized. It meant the collapse of the grandiose attempt to transform the Saxon stem duchy into a single consolidated political unit extending from the Baltic far into Westphalia, from the Frisian border and the North Sea to the Werra and the Saale. From now on Saxony was increasingly fragmented into separate territories, a process that had already begun in other German lands. After the Lion's fall many lay and ecclesiastical lords successfully tried to throw off their dependence on the duke of Saxony and create a local domain for themselves. Thus the duchy of the archbishops of Cologne was confined to the extreme west of the Saxon tribal area. The Ascanian dukes lacked, in many parts of Saxony, the strength that would have enabled them to build up a genuine ducal power. Their often-used title of duke of Saxony, Engern, and Westphalia represented a claim that could at no time be translated into reality.

The break-up of the wide dominions of Henry the Lion had adverse effects especially in Nordalbingia and neighbouring Mecklenburg, the areas which the duke had largely made into a self-contained political unit and which remained to the end an important buttress of his power. Thereafter the bishops of the three sees he had created soon asserted their direct dependence on the Empire and were able to resist all attempts of the Saxon dukes to bring them back to vassal status. The counts of Holstein, Ratzeburg, and Schwerin set about creating the basis for a territorial sovereignty of their own; Bernard of Anhalt's efforts to assert ducal power in Nordalbingia were fruitless.

The lack of a strong ducal regime in the north-east soon led to a complete change in the political balance of power in the western Baltic. The dynastic ambition of the Danish royal house, developed in the successful reign of Valdemar I, was seen in the fact that his son Knut II, who ascended the throne in 1182, refused several summonses to do homage to Frederick I. From the outset he pursued his father's policy in Hither Pomerania and Mecklenburg, and in 1185 compelled Bogislav I to become his vassal. He made his influence felt in Mecklenburg and Holstein and paved the way for their absorption into the Danish sphere, which he achieved at the end of his reign. However, Danish predominance in the Baltic did not, as is often said, materially reduce the scale of German settlement in the area. The counts and the church with their various institutions, who were the chief promoters of this activity, were able to continue it even in times of political unrest.

Still more far-reaching were the effects of Henry's deposition on the internal framework of the German state. The transformation of the Empire from the old stem duchies with their loose structure to smaller but much more compact principalities had begun gradually in the first half of the twelfth century. The conversion of the march of Austria into a duchy in 1156 was an important step on this road. The further dismemberment of Bavaria and the destruction of Saxony—the two last tribal duchies—brought the transformation to a climax: the stem duchy was now finally replaced by the territorial duchy.

Closely connected with this was the formation of the so-called 'younger estate' of princes of the Empire (*Reichsfürsten*). Up to now, the composition of this estate had not been clearly defined. It included all who held office from the king, as well as the many imperial counts (*reichsunmittelbar*—depending directly on the Empire). From this large group there now emerged a smaller but more coherent estate of the realm, comprising only those princes who held office directly from the crown. These included the many ecclesiastical princes who were invested with the sceptre by the king since the concordat of Worms—holders of the 'sceptre-fief' (*Zepterlehen*), as it was later called. A much smaller group, at first, were the lay princes, invested by the king with a banner, symbol of the military summons (*Heerbann*), whose principalities came to be known as 'banner-fiefs' (*Fahnenlehen*).

The great majority of counts were mediatized and became vassals of the princes. The decisive part played by the new type of imperial princes in the partition of Saxony and the granting-out of the two newly created duchies is emphasized in the Gelnhausen charter. As it was feudal law, invoked against the duke, that first made his over-throw possible, so the same law now became fundamental to the structure of the Empire. The gradation in the form of a feudal pyramid with the king at the top was reflected in the *Heerschild*, the military hierarchy that was embodied in law-books of the thirteenth century but no doubt goes back as far as the twelfth.

How was it that Barbarossa, who pursued a very conscious policy of dynastic and territorial power, did not retain for the crown any of the escheated imperial fiefs? This surprising fact is generally accoun-ted for by the *Leihezwang*, referred to—only as a custom, it is true—in thirteenth-century law-books, whereby the king was supposed to regrant escheated fiefs within a year and a day. The origin of this principle has often been associated with the trial of Henry the Lion, where, it is said, the princes demanded that it be given the status of a law and made part of the imperial feudal code. However, nothing is known of an imperial law to this effect in 1180, and it is doubtful whether there ever was such a general principle in Germany even at a later date. There was no lack of attempts by the monarch to keep escheated property for the crown, even though they were unsuccessful.

When Frederick I began to regrant the escheated fiefs within a few months of Henry's condemnation under feudal law, he was not forced to do so by legal rules but rather by political circumstances. In proceeding against the duke he had needed the princes' help, and he needed it almost more in executing the judgment: without their military aid it would have been impossible to do so. The two new dukes, Philip of Cologne and Bernard of Anhalt, were those who had been most successful in the fighting of 1179. By the Gelnhausen decree Frederick secured their active help in the further contest with the Lion. The other Saxon princes who had been summoned to the campaign also certainly expected considerable profit from a share-out of the rights and possessions of the deposed duke. Even in the absence of express evidence, it is natural to suppose that the prompt dismemberment and regranting of Saxony took place at the demand of the princes, anxious to make sure of their hold on the booty.

Thus the princes and other magnates of Saxony and Bavaria might rightly consider themselves victors over the duke. His fall meant the disappearance of their fiercest adversary, who had always ruthlessly disregarded their rights and against whom they had time and again taken up arms. Although Henry's fall brought no appreciable territorial gain to the Hohenstaufen monarchy, the Emperor too could nevertheless regard it as a success. The political constellation had altered decisively in his favour. He was now the most powerful man in the Empire, incomparably stronger than any of its other princes. Moreover, the restructuring of the German state with the princes feudally dependent on the monarch seemed to provide a firm foundation for imperial power. The vital question was whether this order would prevail or whether the centrifugal forces that were also inherent in feudal law would gain the upper hand. Thus the events accompanying the fall of Henry the Lion bring into prominence the tension between a strong central power and the forces of federalism that has been a recurrent problem in German history.

Exile and Closing Years

TOWARDS the end of July 1182 Henry left Brunswick to join his father-in-law Henry II of England, in whose dominions he was to spend his term of exile. He was accompanied by his consort Matilda, their only daughter Richenza, and their first and third sons Henry and Otto. The name of Richenza being quite unfamiliar in the Anglo-Norman realm, she was henceforth known by her mother's name Matilda. The couple's second son Lothair, a boy of 7 or 8, remained in Saxony for reasons unknown to us. A number of loyal counts, nobles, and *ministeriales* accompanied Henry at the outset, but most of them soon returned to Germany and made their peace with the Emperor. Only a very few remained, such as Jordan of Blankenburg, who had been Henry's steward for many years and seems to have shared the whole period of his exile.

The duke first betook himself with his suite to Normandy; the king was then in the mainland part of his realm, engaged in putting down the troubles stirred up by his sons, especially Henry 'the Young King'. Henry II and the ducal family met at Chinon in Touraine in August or September.

Although Henry the Lion was allowed part of the income from his Saxon possessions, the English court seems to have borne the brunt of the cost of maintaining the duke and his entourage. Exchequer records contained in the pipe-rolls, together with mostly brief references in English chronicles, are our chief source of information on this subject; the amounts indicate that Henry II enabled his son-in-law to live in a princely style.

After going on a pilgrimage in the autumn to the shrine of St James at Compostela, Henry spent the Christmas of 1182 with his family and Henry II at Caen. During his absence in Spain Matilda stayed at the king's court at Argentan in Normandy. There, through her brother Richard Lionheart, she met the troubadour Bertrand de Born, one of the most celebrated Provençal poets of the time. He dedicated two of his finest love-songs to her, extolling the charms of the young princess (she was then about 26), whom he called Helen for her surpassing beauty and praised for beguiling the tedium of a court.

According to an English chronicler, Matilda bore a son at Argentan. If so, the child must have died at birth or soon after, as no more is heard of it. Henry the Lion and his family probably remained in Normandy during 1183 and the first months of 1184. By the spring of that year Henry II had settled matters in France to the extent that he was able to return to England in June. He was accompanied by Matilda, who—probably in July or August—gave birth at Winchester to her youngest son William, the ancestor of all subsequent Welfs.

Henry the Lion in all probability meanwhile attended the court held by Frederick I at Mainz at the end of May (Whitsuntide) 1184, a brilliant pageant of chivalry at which the Emperor bestowed the accolade on his two eldest sons, King Henry of Germany and Duke Frederick of Swabia. The principal sources, it is true, do not mention Henry the Lion's presence at this court, but it is indicated elsewhere: for instance the Exchequer records in that year an item for the duke's journey to 'Saxony', which probably means Germany in general. Henry presumably attended the court in the suite of Archbishop Conrad of Mainz, in the hope of obtaining the Emperor's pardon. He may even have hoped to recover the duchy of Bavaria, Otto of Wittelsbach having died in 1183, but this is questionable. In any case he had no success. At the end of July he landed in Dover and rejoined his family at the court of Winchester.

In these years Henry II seems to have made several attempts to reconcile the Emperor with his son-in-law. A fresh opportunity offered when Archbishop Philip of Cologne and Count Philip of Flanders came to England in the late summer of 1184, ostensibly to visit St Thomas's shrine at Canterbury but actually on a diplomatic mission. The archbishop was to prepare the ground for a marriage between Richard Lionheart, heir to the Plantagenet throne since the death of his brother Henry, and the Emperor's daughter Agnes; the plan came to nothing, however, as Agnes died in the same year, shortly before her mother Beatrice.

Henry II received the envoys with much honour at Dover and entertained them on a grand scale in London. He also seems to have succeeded in bringing about at least a personal *rapprochement* between Henry the Lion and the archbishop, hitherto one of his fiercest opponents. It may have been at Philip's suggestion that, soon after his departure from England, Henry II sent an embassy to Lucius III, Alexander III's successor, to ask him to mediate between the Emperor and Henry the Lion. The embassy arrived at the papal court at Verona in the second half of October: a fortunate time, as the Emperor was then also in Verona to settle with the Pope important political and ecclesiastical matters in Germany and Italy. Lucius's mediation was successful: the Emperor agreed to Henry's return to Germany, and the Pope released the duke from the oath he had sworn at Erfurt in 1181.

Although Henry was now free to go back to Saxony at once, he and his family remained in England through the winter. In the spring of 1185 he and Matilda, with their suite, crossed to Normandy, whence they returned to Brunswick in the autumn. Which of their children accompanied them is not quite certain, but in any case their eldest son Henry went with them to Germany, where we find him repeatedly in his father's entourage. Otto may also have returned to Saxony for a short time. Curiously, William, then less than a year old, remained in England and was brought up at his grandfather's expense.

Matilda, the daughter of the ducal couple, also remained at the English court, where many attempts were made to find a husband befitting her rank. In 1184 King William of Scotland asked for her hand from Henry II as his overlord. As the two were within the prohibited degrees, the envoys sent to Verona at that time tried to obtain a dispensation; the Pope refused, so the marriage did not take place.

Two years later King Béla III of Hungary sent an embassy to ask for the princess's hand. Henry II, however, temporized from day to day, which according to an English chronicler was his habit. Accordingly Béla applied instead to King Philip II of France for the hand of his sister Margaret, widow of Henry II's eldest son; Philip at once agreed to the match. A few years later Matilda married Godfrey, heir to the important county of Perche in southern Normandy.

During Henry the Lion's three-year absence, conditions in north Germany had changed drastically. This was especially the case in Nordalbingia: instead of the law and order that Henry had brought about, the province was a scene of rivalry between the new duke and the local counts and other lords.

Arnold of Lübeck describes the altered conditions by citing the words: 'In those days there was no king in Israel, but each man did what seemed good in his own eyes.' Duke Bernard regarded himself as the duke's rightful successor here as in Saxony proper, but could not make good his claim. Count Adolf III of Holstein was now the most powerful man in the region of the lower Elbe. He expelled supporters of Henry the Lion from his county, and for a time extended his rule to Ditmarsh and the county of Stade. When Duke Bernard came to the Ertheneburg in 1182 to receive the homage of his new vassals, only the counts of Ratzeburg, Schwerin, Dannenberg, and Lüchow appeared to swear fealty. Adolf III disregarded the summons, and Bishop Isfried of Ratzeburg refused to do homage to the duke on the ground that he had already sworn an oath to Henry the Lion.

The Ascanian Duke Bernard had the walls of the Ertheneburg pulled down and used the material to build the Lauenburg on the opposite (north) bank of the Elbe, a few miles upstream. He also transferred the Elbe crossing to the new site, so as better to control the trade route leading from the Empire to Lübeck; however, the Lübeck citizens complained to the Emperor, who rescinded the measure.

When Bernard thus began to levy tolls and claim possessions that had belonged to Henry the Lion, the counts of Holstein, Ratzeburg, and Schwerin joined forces and destroyed the Lauenburg in 1182. The Emperor obliged them to make amends and re-erect the fortress, but in the next few years Duke Bernard had no influence on events in Nordalbingia.

As we have seen, this change in the power situation in the northeast of the Empire gave Knut VI an opportunity to reassert the Danish claim to hegemony in the Baltic. From 1184 onwards he intervened in the Slav princes' disputes. He received the submission of the warring Mecklenburg princes Henry Borwin, Henry the Lion's son-in-law, and his cousin Niklot; in 1185 Bogislav of Pomerania became a vassal of the Danish king, who soon afterwards adopted the style 'king of the Danes and Slavs'.

Knut's refusal to do homage to Frederick I had led to acute tension between him and the Emperor, and this was increased by his action in withholding part of the promised dowry of his sister, betrothed to Duke Frederick of Swabia in 1181. When he refused to pay the full amount Barbarossa revoked the marriage contract and sent the princess back to Denmark.

In Bremen, after the death of the Ascanian Siegfried in 1184 the chapter elected Canon Hartwig of Uthlede, who had for many years been Henry the Lion's notary, to be their new metropolitan with the title of Hartwig II. He received the regalia from Frederick I and was consecrated by Pope Lucius III. Although he owed his canonry to Henry the Lion and had till then been regarded as a supporter of the Welf party, he refused to meet the deposed duke after the latter's return to Saxony.

In the mid-1180s events in north-western Germany and on the lower Rhine were dominated by the tension that arose, owing to differences of policy in church matters, between Frederick I and Archbishop Philip of Cologne, who had till then been a loyal supporter of the Emperor. Frederick later accused Henry the Lion of inciting both Knut and the archbishop against him, but the truth of this is uncertain. We know very little of Henry's activity in the years after his return from banishment. He probably stayed mainly in Brunswick and administered his patrimony from there; but his attempts to enlarge it were in vain, especially as the Emperor refused the help which Henry no doubt sought from him.

In the relatively few charters issued by Henry after his deposition he is styled 'duke' without any addition. In a charter by Archbishop Conrad of Mainz, dating probably from 1186, he appears as a witness simply as 'duke'. The ducal seal was also adapted to his change of status. Until his fall the various seals used by his notaries were of the kind then usual with territorial princes, representing a fully-armed rider on horseback with shield and banner. After the recovery of Bavaria the inscription read: 'Henry by the grace of God duke of Bavaria and Saxony'. As the equestrian seal was regarded first and foremost as a token of princely rank, and as Henry was not entitled to display a feudal banner after the loss of his imperial fiefs, from then onwards he adopted a much smaller seal with a lion statant and the inscription 'seal of Duke Henry'.

Towards the end of 1187 all dissensions in the West were thrust into the background by the news that the Seljuk Turks led by Sultan Saladin had, in July, annihilated an army of Christian knights in the bloody battle at Hattin near Lake Gennesaret, and had in the next two or three months conquered the rest of the Holy Places in Palestine. The crusading movement flared up again throughout Europe, with the Emperor taking the lead. Although Frederick had experienced the hardships and difficulties of the Second Crusade and was now some sixty-five years old, he held a great diet at Mainz in March 1188, known as the 'Diet of Christ', at which he took the cross, followed by his son Duke Frederick of Swabia and many other magnates. The Crusade was set to begin in the spring of 1189. Frederick took this step out of religious zeal and because he regarded it as the Emperor's duty, as head of Christendom, to draw the sword against the infidel and rescue the Holy Sepulchre. Richard Lionheart of England and Philip II of France also took the cross in 1188.

However, Germany had to be pacified before the Crusade could begin. At the diet of Mainz, Philip of Cologne had submitted and been restored to the Emperor's favour. In Saxony, Frederick held a diet at Goslar at the end of July and beginning of August 1188, to which Henry the Lion was bidden. According to Arnold of Lübeck, Henry was offered a choice between three courses. He could be restored to some of his former rights at once if he would give up the remainder, or he could take part in the Crusade at the Emperor's expense and then be reinstated in his former position. If he refused both alternatives he must promise to leave Germany for another three years together with his son Henry, then aged about fourteen. Whether the offers, especially the second, were actually made in this form is very doubtful. Certainly Frederick had no idea of completely reinstating the Lion. In any case, the upshot was that Henry agreed only to go into exile with his young son and spend another three years with his father-in-law Henry II. In return the Emperor promised that Henry's possessions would not be touched during his absence.

In other respects also, both political and military, Frederick had made good preparations for the Crusade. His son King Henry was to be regent while he was abroad. Negotiations were conducted with the rulers of the countries through which the crusading army had to pass, and assurances received of peaceful passage and supplies. At the beginning of May 1189 the army set out from Regensburg. It was very large for its day, though the figure in contemporary sources of 20,000 knights with their attendants and baggage is much exaggerated. The most notable of the lay princes from Lower Saxony who took part was Count Adolf III of Holstein.

At the beginning of April, at Eastertide, Henry the Lion left Saxony for England with his son Henry, leaving Matilda to look after his affairs in Brunswick. His other sons Otto and William were already in England. On landing in Dover he found that Henry II was still on the Continent, where he was involved in combat with Philip II of France and his own rebellious son, Richard Lionheart. Henry the Lion thereupon went to Normandy, where he met the king. A few weeks later, on 6 July, Henry II died. Richard Lionheart succeeded to the throne without opposition; he crossed from the Continent to England at the beginning of August, accompanied by Henry the Lion and the latter's son.

On 28 June, a few days before her father, the Duchess Matilda had died in Brunswick at the age of only thirty-two or thirty-three; she was buried in the recently completed eastern part of the new cathedral. On hearing of her death Henry, despite his sworn promise to the Emperor, returned to Saxony to safeguard his rights. He sent his son Henry in advance and followed some time later, in a royal vessel that his brother-in-law Richard had placed at his disposal.

The absence of many of his Saxon opponents and of the Emperor himself on crusade seemed to Henry a good opportunity of recovering his former power. The results of his first attempts in this direction were promising. Archbishop Hartwig of Bremen, who had refused to meet Henry on his first return from exile, had meanwhile run into severe financial difficulties in his diocese. This time he at once took the side of his former lord and invested him with the county of Stade, at which town they met at the end of September. In this way Hartwig hoped to recover the Ditmarsh district, which belonged to the county but of which he had lost control.

Henry also found increasing support in the Welf heartland in the east of Saxony and Nordalbingia. In the latter district he was joined by Counts Bernard of Ratzeburg and Helmold of Schwerin and above all by the minor nobility of Holstein, whom Adolf III had temporarily expelled; they now soon occupied the counts' fortresses at Hamburg, Plön, and Itzehoe. Count Adolf of Dassel, Adolf III's uncle, who was administering the area in his absence, was able to hold only Lübeck and the fortress of Segeberg.

Meanwhile Henry himself led a large army against Bardowick. According to a later story of doubtful authenticity, when the duke was on his way into exile in 1182 the citizens of the town had closed their gates and mocked him from the battlements. This time their resistance was punished by a fearful revenge. After a brief siege at the end of October Henry captured the city and destroyed it, including the churches and cemeteries, so thoroughly that instead of a flourishing trade centre it became an insignificant spot. The male inhabitants were taken prisoner and deported, only women and children being spared. The ruined cathedral was afterwards rebuilt; a later legend relates that Henry inscribed on it the words *Vestigia Leonis* (the lion's footprints).

At the beginning of November Henry crossed the Elbe northwards to crush the last resistance in Holstein. When he approached Lübeck the citizens, warned by the fate of Bardowick, opened their gates without a fight, after Henry had promised safe passage to Count Adolf of Dassel and his men and to Adolf III's wife and mother, who were in the town. Segeberg, however, held out despite a prolonged siege in which the local peasantry were called on to take part, and was finally relieved by the Schauenburger's supporters. Meanwhile Henry had attacked Lauenburg, which was held by Duke Bernard, captured it, and thus gained an important base on the Elbe.

At the same time he scored another major success. In 1187 or 1188 Count Adolf III had founded a settlement of merchants in Hamburg—later known as the Hamburger Neustadt—on the right bank of the Alster, opposite the existing Wikort. The new settlement, on the site of the destroyed fortress, was to be provided with a harbour. The merchants' leader was one Wirad of Boizenburg, probably a former *ministerialis* of Henry's who had been a toll collector at Boizenburg on the Elbe. The count granted him and his fellow-settlers, among other privileges, the right to own the land they lived on and to be governed by the Lübeck code.

On 7 May 1189, shortly before the Crusade began, Frederick I issued a charter of privileges to the Hamburgers at the request of the count, who was then with him at Neuburg on the Danube. Among other rights this exempted them from customs duties in the lower Elbe area as far as the sea. Although falsified by spurious additions in the thirteenth century, this imperial diploma is still regarded as the birth certificate of the port of Hamburg.

Henry the Lion at this time succeeded in persuading the citizens of the new town of Hamburg to desert Count Adolf; Wirad, Henry's former servant, was probably instrumental in this. In return, in a charter that is unfortunately lost, Henry granted the merchants immunity from customs duties at several stations on the Elbe upstream from Hamburg.

Meanwhile the future King Henry VI, to whom Duke Bernard had appealed for help after Henry the Lion's return, held a diet at Merseburg in October 1189 at which he summoned the German princes to do battle against him. Within a few weeks a large army assembled at Hornburg under the king's command, including the troops of Duke Bernard and those of Mainz and Cologne. Despite the unfavourable season the king advanced against the heavily fortified Brunswick, whose defence Henry the Lion had entrusted to his son Henry. The town was well off for supplies, and the siege was unsuccessful. Before long a severe winter set in, and fighting was suspended at Brunswick and in Nordalbingia. On his retreat from Saxony Henry VI sacked the Welf city of Hanover.

During the lull Henry the Lion sent his son Henry to his brother-in-law Richard Lionheart, who was then in the south of France preparing for the Crusade. At the beginning of February 1190 the young prince was at his uncle's court at La Réole on the Garonne. The reason for his journey is not known. The Welfs could have expected no help from the king of England at that time; it is more likely that Richard urged Henry the Lion to make his peace with King Henry.

During the events in Germany an unexpected situation had arisen in the West. King William I of Sicily had died on 18 November 1189. As he had no children by his marriage to Joanna of England his lawful heir was his aunt Constance, the consort of Henry VI. The magnates of mainland Italy acknowledged her claim, but in Sicily a Norman national party proclaimed as king Count Tancred of Lecce, a relative of William I whose legitimacy was disputed.

A separate kingdom of Sicily could only be welcome to the Roman Curia, as it averted the danger of a union of the Empire with the kingdom of southern Italy and Sicily, which would have encircled the Papal State. Clement III, who had become Pope in 1187, at first adopted a waiting attitude. He did not yet invest Tancred with the kingdom, over which he was suzerain, but he allowed the archbishop of Palermo to crown Tancred in January 1190.

Henry VI, however, was not prepared to renounce his wife's claim to the inheritance, and, as a conflict was thus inevitable, he desired first to come to an understanding with Henry the Lion. The latter for his part was ready, as the fighting that resumed in Holstein in the spring of 1190 was not going well for him. An army led by Count Bernard of Ratzeburg, Helmold of Schwerin, and the steward Jordan of Blankenburg was defeated by Adolf III's lieutenant, Adolf of Dassel. Helmold and Jordan were captured and released only on payment of a large ransom.

Through the mediation of the archbishops of Mainz and Cologne, with whom Henry the Lion had met in March, negotiations took

place between him and King Henry; the two met in July at the diet of
Fulda, when peace was concluded. The duke had to agree to dis-
mantle part of the fortifications of Brunswick and to raze the fortress
of Lauenburg. The king allowed him half the revenue from the city of
Lübeck; Adolf III was to have the other half, and his county was
to remain undiminished. Archbishop Hartwig II of Bremen was
deposed at the Fulda diet and departed for England. Henry the Lion's
second son Lothair was made a hostage for the fulfilment of the terms
imposed on him, while the eldest son Henry was to contribute 50
knights to the king's forthcoming campaign in Italy.

The opening of the campaign was delayed by the news that
Frederick I had died on 10 June 1190 while bathing in the river Saleph
in Asia Minor. Henry VI set out at the turn of the year 1191,
accompanied, as agreed, by the Lion's eldest son, who now begins to
be referred to in documents as Henry of Brunswick. Lothair, his
younger brother, had died at Augsburg in October 1190; the Welf
faction suspected poison, probably without cause.

King Henry's first object was to be crowned in Rome, as Clement
III had promised him; but the Pope died at the end of March 1191,
before the German army reached the city. To succeed him the
cardinals chose the eldest of their number, Cardinal Hyacinth, aged
about eighty-five, who took the name of Celestine III. Despite his
age he pursued a firm policy and, like his predecessor, was an
opponent of Henry VI's plans in Sicily. After negotiation with the
new Pope and the city of Rome—the Pope was himself crowned on
Easter day, 14 April—the coronation and anointing of Henry and
Constance took place on the 15th.

The statement of a later source that the Pope's conditions for the
coronation included a demand that Henry the Lion be restored to his
former rights is quite improbable. So is the statement in the Steterburg Annals that young Henry was a kinsman of Pope Celestine's,
and that in the hope of future reward he used all his influence with the
Pope in favour of Henry VI's cause. There is no evidence of the
alleged kinship between the Welf and the Pope, who belonged to a
noble Roman family.

After the coronation Henry VI at once proceeded southwards
against the Norman kingdom, Celestine having tried in vain to
dissuade him. Meanwhile Tancred had strengthened his position by
an offensive and defensive alliance with Richard Lionheart, who, like
Philip II of France, had spent the winter of 1190–1 in Sicily with his

crusaders. Henry VI encountered no great resistance in the northern frontier areas of the Norman kingdom, but was checked at the end of May before Naples, which was strongly fortified and held out against the besiegers. As the summer heat increased the imperial army was visited by plague, and the Emperor himself fell gravely ill.

During this campaign Henry of Brunswick took a spectacular step: he deserted the Emperor and secretly absconded from his army. The details are uncertain, as the sources give conflicting accounts. According to Arnold of Lübeck the Welf's flight took place at the beginning of the campaign in southern Italy, while the other sources connect it, more convincingly, with the siege of Naples. According to the Steterburg Annals the reason for Henry's action was that after the death of his brother Lothair he wanted to escape the plague that was ravaging the German army. Probably he and his attendants made their way in June or at the beginning of July, first to Naples and then by sea to Rome.

In Rome on 5 August Pope Celestine granted an imperial privilege to the Welfs whereby Henry the Lion and his sons could not be excommunicated by anyone except the Pope, his successors, or a legate commissioned for the purpose, unless they committed an offence which of itself entailed this penalty. Although the papal document speaks in general terms of a request by the deposed duke, it seems certain that his son obtained the privilege in Rome by his own efforts and brought it with him to Saxony, where he arrived at the end of August or the beginning of September. Having incurred the guilt of felony vis-à-vis the Emperor it was important to him to secure some form of moral support from the Pope. The grant of the privilege deprived the Welfs' ecclesiastical opponents of an important weapon—one which had been successfully used by Bishop Ulrich of Halberstadt in 1177–9. However, despite this mark of favour to the Welfs, the Pope avoided an immediate breach with the Emperor. Only in August 1191, when Henry VI had to raise the siege of Naples and abandon the further campaign against the Norman realm, did Celestine come into the open; he then invested Tancred with Sicily and in the following year made a concordat with him on terms favourable to the Curia.

During the Emperor's Italian campaign Henry the Lion had not complied with the peace terms agreed at Fulda: he neither dismantled the Lauenburg nor ceded half the Lübeck revenue to Adolf of Dassel, the Schauenburger's representative. He endeavoured to increase his power in the land by means of his strongholds in Nordalbingia, and Adolf III, who returned from the Holy Land in the spring of 1191, was obliged to take up arms. In the next few years Henry the Lion was probably for the most part in Brunswick, and did not take a direct part in the fighting in Nordalbingia. Adolf was able to recover his duchy with the help of the Ascanians, Duke Bernard and the Margrave Otto of Brandenburg. After he had captured Hamburg and Stade, Lübeck had to open its gates to him in the summer of 1192.

Tension also arose in the east of Saxony towards the end of 1191, when Henry VI, still in Upper Italy, called on the Saxon princes to take up arms against Henry the Lion, their old enemy. At an assembly summoned to Goslar by Archbishop Wichmann of Magdeburg, the pro-imperial princes agreed to take the field against the Welf in the summer of 1192.

Henry VI was back in Germany in December 1191. Welf VI had died on 15 December aged about seventy-six, bequeathing his last possessions to the Emperor, who was thus able to enlarge the Staufen patrimony in Swabia.

In the Welf camp the young Henry of Brunswick was more and more the effective leader; Henry the Lion, with advancing years, was more inclined to accept a compromise. The Steterburg Annals even allege that he sent an embassy assuring the Emperor that he had no part in his son's defection and offering, by way of compensation, military help in a new Italian campaign, but that the duke's Saxon opponents persuaded the Emperor to decline the proposal. Whether it was really made in such terms we cannot say. In May 1192, at a Whitsun diet at Worms, the Emperor pronounced the full sentence of outlawry upon the young Welf for his desertion.

Soon afterwards the Saxon princes assembled with their troops, as agreed, at Leiferde near Brunswick. As the Emperor sent no reinforcements they did not venture to attack the town but contented themselves with plundering the neighbourhood. They lost their leader with the death of Archbishop Wichmann in his cathedral city in August. Previously Provost Gerhard of Steterburg had succeeded in bringing about a truce between the Welfs and their adversaries, which was prolonged beyond its original time-limit.

The truce suited Henry the Lion also. He had fallen out with Liudolf of Dahlum, one of his chief *ministeriales*, whom he had made bailiff (*Stadtvogt*) of Brunswick, on account of some prisoners taken in skirmishes outside the city. Liudolf and his followers fled from

Brunswick and carried on hostilities against Henry with the help of another of the latter's *ministeriales*, Ekbert of Wolfenbüttel. Young Henry now had a free hand thanks to the truce with the Saxon princes, and could suppress the rebels. However, he failed to subdue the town of Stade and so restore the authority of his dynasty in the northern part of the old Welf dominions.

At this time events in Saxony were of secondary importance to Henry VI. His increasing arrogance in connection with the appointment of bishops met with growing resistance in western Germany. After a disputed election at Liège at the beginning of 1192 he rejected both candidates and installed a bishop of his own choice. When Archdeacon Albert of Liège—a brother of the duke of Brabant, who had been elected by a majority of the chapter and confirmed in office by the Pope—was murdered by German knights at Reims, the crime was generally imputed to the Emperor, though doubtless unjustly. This had fateful consequences, as nearly all the princes on the lower and middle Rhine banded together against him; the alliance extended to other parts of Germany also, and its members entered into contact with the Welf opposition. By the end of 1192 Henry VI had on his side only the duchy of Swabia, Leopold V of Austria, and the imperial *ministeriales*, while his opponents enjoyed support in England, Sicily, Denmark, and also the Curia.

In this almost desperate situation the Emperor was saved by an unexpected stroke of luck. At the siege of Acre King Richard Lionheart had quarrelled with his feudal suzerain Philip II of France and also with Leopold of Austria: after the city's surrender he had torn down the banner that the Austrian had hoisted in the crusaders' camp in token of his claim to a share of the victors' spoils. The French ports being closed to him, Richard with much hesitation decided to return to England via Germany. However, he was wrecked at Aquileia and in December 1192 was captured near Vienna by his enemy Duke Leopold, who imprisoned him in his castle of Dürnstein in the Wachau and negotiated his ransom with the Emperor, the sum being fixed at 100,000 silver marks. After receiving half this amount Leopold handed over his captive, who was now confined to the Emperor's castle of Trifels.

With Richard's capture the opposition in western Germany lost its chief mainstay abroad and began to disintegrate. The Emperor showed great skill in exploiting the situation. By threatening to hand Richard over to Philip II he induced the English king to agree to the huge ransom and to promise military help for the imperial campaign against Sicily. After tough negotiations, concluded at Worms at the end of June 1193, Richard was released from the military obligation but had to promise to pay 50,000 marks in addition to the original 100,000, unless he were able to keep a certain promise to the Emperor concerning Henry the Lion. What this promise was does not appear from the very general terms of the agreement, but in any case Richard was unable to perform it and had to pay the full ransom. It has been supposed that Richard was to persuade his brother-in-law to revoke the engagement that had existed for some years between his son Henry of Brunswick and Agnes, the only child and heiress of the Count Palatine Conrad of Staufen. Henry VI at this time wanted to strengthen the alliance between the Staufens and Capetians by marrying his cousin Agnes to Philip of France. It is uncertain, however, whether this was really the subject of the bargain which Richard failed to keep.

As Philip of France and Richard's own younger brother John strove to prevent his release, Richard offered to do homage to the Emperor for his kingdom and pay 5,000 pounds a year for it as a fief, thus assuring himself of the protection of his new suzerain. In February 1194 he was at last released and returned to his kingdom. As a guarantee of his intentions he gave as hostages to the Emperor Henry the Lion's two younger sons, Otto and William, who were then in England.

Henry the Lion, who had lost his chief ally by Richard's capture, now placed his last hopes in his son-in-law Knut VI of Denmark. In the summer or autumn of 1193 he sent his son Henry to ask for Knut's help in recovering Nordalbingia. However, this was incompatible with Danish ambitions in the area, and the young Welf returned empty-handed.

A change in Staufen–Welf relations was heralded by the fact that the marriage between young Henry of Brunswick and Agnes of Staufen took place, despite all opposition, towards the end of 1193. The Countess Palatine Irmingard, who did not want her daughter to marry Philip of France, took advantage of her husband's absence to summon Henry secretly to her castle of Stahleck on the Rhine, where the couple were married on the spot. The Count Palatine Conrad acquiesced in the marriage despite initial vexation, but Henry VI was incensed at the thwarting of his planned alliance. The young Welf also became heir to the dignity of count palatine and to his father-in-law's extensive allodial property. After vainly urging Conrad to dissolve the marriage, the Emperor restored Henry of Brunswick to favour at a diet at Würzburg in January 1194.

Conrad also undertook to bring about a reconciliation with Henry the Lion, whom the marriage had taken by surprise and who did not at first approve of it. The Count arranged for a meeting to take place between the Emperor and Henry the Lion at the end of February at Saalfeld, to restore relations between the two families. On the way from Brunswick to the meeting, in the Harz near Bodfeld, Henry fell from his horse on a steep path and suffered a contusion or fracture of the shin-bone. He was taken to the nearby monastery of Walkenried and sent messengers to excuse his absence. The Emperor was at first sceptical, but was convinced by Provost Gerhard of Steterburg that the injury was a genuine one. He then decided to go to Henry himelf, and they met in March 1194 in the palace of Tilleda on the Kyffhäuser mountain.

Here the Emperor and Henry the Lion were finally reconciled. Henry VI once again confirmed the Welf in his allodial possessions. Henry of Brunswick took part in Henry VI's campaign in south Italy until the autumn of 1194, when he returned to Germany with the Emperor's consent. After a short stay in Brunswick he betook himself to the Rhenish Palatinate. As to his brother Otto, then aged about seventeen, Richard I had tried to persuade the Emperor to allow him to join the Italian campaign and to be released from his hostageship. Henry VI refused this, as he mistrusted the Welfs, but granted Otto some alleviation of his condition. Towards the end of 1194 Otto was released and went at once to the English king, who shortly afterwards made him count of Poitou.

Henry the Lion's youngest son William, who was also a hostage with the Emperor, was about ten years old at the beginning of the Italian campaign. Henry VI confided him to Leopold V of Austria, who soon afterwards had a fatal fall from his horse. Feeling his end approaching, he entrusted the boy to King Béla III of Hungary, who was to restore him to his father in Brunswick. The Emperor, however, prevented this for the time being; we do not know how long William continued to be a hostage for Richard I.

On Easter eve of 1195 (1–2 April), Henry the Lion's health took a sudden turn for the worse. According to Gerhard of Steterburg, who in his Annals describes the last months of Henry's life in almost hagiographic terms, he bore the illness and acute pain with extreme fortitude. As the warm weather set in his condition turned to dysentery, but he refused all forms of medicine. At the end of July there was a violent storm over Brunswick and the cathedral was struck by lightning which set fire to the roof timbers. Henry, unlike his attendants, kept his calm and presence of mind, and the blaze was extinguished by heavy rain. Feeling the approach of death, he summoned his son Henry from the Palatinate and also Bishop Isfried of Ratzeburg, who had been his confessor for some years and who now gave him absolution and the last sacraments. He died a few days later, on 6 August, and was buried in the cathedral to the right of his consort Matilda.

In recent decades there has been a keen controversy concerning Henry's tomb and the question whether his remains were those discovered during excavations in 1935, when the authorities of the time proposed to deconsecrate the cathedral and transform it into a 'national shrine', having as its centre a new monument to Henry the Lion and Matilda. Excavations in the great vault under the tombs of the ducal couple, which were in some ways very inexpertly carried out, brought to light a stone sarcophagus next to an almost decomposed wooden coffin with a large leather casing inside it and, near by, a small stone coffin for a child. In the sarcophagus lay a skeleton, well preserved except for the skull, which must have been originally 162 cm. long (nearly 5'4"). On the other hand the body which had been sewn into a leather casing and then buried in the wooden coffin had crumbled away; there was long fair hair in the place where the skull had been. In the child's coffin were some bones of a babe in arms.

On the basis of this evidence and of his investigations, the anthropologist Eugen Fischer believed that the remains in the stone coffin were those of Henry the Lion, that Matilda was buried in the wooden coffin and one of her infant children in the other. The preserved skeleton showed a marked shortening of the left leg, due to a malformation of the hip. The sprain (luxation) at the hip was, it was supposed, connected with the injury due to Henry's fall from his horse a year before his death; but the Steterburg Annals expressly state that only the shin-bone was affected on that occasion. In any case a later orthopaedic opinion, based on published photographs, was to the effect that the malformation of the hip could not be due to an accident shortly before death, but must have been a congenital disability. If it was really the duke's skeleton he must have limped from childhood; but there is nothing to suggest he did, and it is very improbable in view of the hardships he had to undergo on his campaigns and constant travels.

Further doubt is thrown on the idea that the sarcophagus contains the mortal remains of Henry the Lion by the fact that anthropo-logical measuring data which have only recently become available suggest that the skeleton is not male but female. It has therefore been suggested that not Henry but Matilda was buried in the stone sarcophagus; that the duke's body was first encased in leather and then placed in the wooden coffin, and that for unknown reasons it was never transferred to a stone sarcophagus. But this too is purely hypothetical; nothing is known of a physical disability of the duchess, and the skeleton is probably too short to have been hers.

It is no longer possible to decide the controversy, as the matter was not thoroughly investigated at the time of the excavation. Moreover later members of the Welf dynasty were buried in the vault under the cathedral nave. In the course of centuries the flood-water of the Oker has on several occasions done severe damage to the tombs, so that clearing work was necessary when the crypt was subsequently opened. In 1935 the vault was likewise found to be in a very disordered state. It is quite possible therefore that the original arrangement of the coffins was subsequently altered. For all these reasons it is quite unlikely that the remains in the stone sarcophagus are those of Henry the Lion.

Patronage of the Arts
and Sciences

NONE of the German princely courts in the second half of the twelfth century were of such importance to the cultural life of the time as that of Henry the Lion. The wealth that Henry accumulated in the course of time enabled him to act as a patron on a grand scale, providing valuable stimulus to the fine arts, literature, and science in a variety of fields. In this respect the Hohenstaufens were altogether less influential than the Welfs, for the court of Welf VI was also an important centre of the arts and sciences at this time; a change did not begin to manifest itself until the turn of the century.

The first impressions of Henry's youth in Bavaria and Swabia were enriched by new ideas from his campaigns and journeys in Italy, France, England, and the Levant. Above all the family connection with the Angevins gave a decisive impulse to intellectual and artistic life in the ducal entourage. The knightly culture that was coming into flower in the south of France was fostered at the court in Poitiers of Henry II's queen, Eleanor of Aquitaine. Through her daughter, the Duchess Matilda, and her entourage the new style of courtly poetry was introduced to Henry the Lion's circle. This led to the composition, after French models, of two major poems that are among the first specimens of the early courtly epic to have originated on German soil.

Henry's role as a patron appears most impressively in the fine arts, especially architecture. It was thanks to him that Brunswick became a city of art; its buildings were also intended to display his power. This was shown by the development of the citadel into a princely residence, for which, as we have seen, the palace and its surroundings in nearby Goslar supplied a model.

Unfortunately we have exact dates only for the rebuilding of St Blaise's church. In 1173 the duke had the older, smaller church pulled down and work began on a new one designed not only to proclaim the duke's greatness far and wide but also to provide a worthy setting for some of the costly relics he had acquired in the Orient. The building went ahead relatively fast. In September 1188 the altar of Our Lady in the choir, donated by the ducal couple, was already consecrated by Bishop Adelog of Hildesheim; a year later Matilda was buried in the church. The nave must have been virtually completed at the time of the duke's death in 1195. The chief patrons were now St Blaise and St John the Baptist, to whom St Thomas of Canterbury was added at the beginning of the thirteenth century; the church was consecrated to all three saints in 1226.

The new church was built as a cruciform basilica with the crossing square as module, with a crypt and a raised choir. Like the palace church at Goslar, dating from the eleventh century, it was more like a cathedral (as it was commonly called in later years) than a mere collegiate church. With its relatively sparse ornamentation it belongs to the tradition of Saxon church building, which from the end of the eleventh century onwards was much influenced by the Hirsau school of architecture. This is seen, for instance, in the massive western end with a gallery originally intended as a place from which the duke could assist at services. In other respects the building shows independent features. Whereas in the church at Königslutter, begun by Lothair III and finished under Henry the Lion, only the eastern part was vaulted, at Brunswick, for the first time in Lower Saxony, vaulting was used for all three aisles of the nave. The church thus marks the beginning of a new era in church building in this part of Germany, and served as a model for several contemporary or somewhat later churches.

When Arnold of Lübeck, formerly a cleric at Brunswick, recorded Henry the Lion's death in his *Chronicle* and extolled his work in biblical language, he compared the duke, whom he also celebrated in verse, to King Solomon. This suggests that Henry may have seen himself as a latter-day Solomon and in his own mind compared the church, erected after his return from the Holy Land, with Solomon's temple—an analogy that was quite usual with medieval church-builders. It cannot be proved that he thought in this way, but the idea is supported by some of the earliest parts of the church's furnishing.

The first of these is Our Lady's altar, the marble top of which rests on five bronze columns with capitals. This has frequently been compared with the altar in Solomon's temple. The inscription on a leaden plate in the capital of the centre column, which was also a repository for relics, states that the altar was consecrated to Mary, the mother of God, in 1188 by Bishop Adelog of Hildesheim at the behest of the ducal couple. It refers to Henry the Lion as 'son of the daughter of the Emperor Lothair' and to Matilda as 'daughter of King Henry II of England, a son of Matilda, Empress of the Romans', showing that the deposed duke wished to emphasize that he and his consort were of imperial descent.

The reference to Solomon's temple is still clearer in the great seven-branched bronze candelabrum that now stands in the choir. According to old tradition, the duke had it specially cast and erected in the church. The earliest documentary reference to the candelabrum dates from a year after his death. There was already such a candlestick in the Jewish tabernacle, according to the Old Testament, and there was certainly one in the second temple in Jerusalem. After some hesitation the Christian church adopted the seven-branched candlestick for its own sacred buildings, its significance being variously interpreted. In the twelfth century it was generally thought of as representing the seven gifts of the Holy Spirit. It has been supposed that Henry may have had it placed by his wife's tomb as a symbol of death and resurrection, but this is uncertain. Stylistically the candelabrum is strongly influenced by Rhenish–Lotharingian cast bronze of the time, while the four lions supporting the base show some resemblance to the castle lion; the work may have been executed in Brunswick by an artist from the Rhineland. St Michael's monastery at Lüneburg also possessed a seven-branched candlestick said to have been commissioned by the duke. This was melted down at the end of the eighteenth century; reproductions of it show a strong resemblance to the one at Brunswick.

The third feature of the cathedral that most probably dates from Henry the Lion's time is a large wooden crucifix, the so-called Imervard cross. Christ is represented with outstretched arms, bearded and with long hair; he wears a long garment with a knotted girdle at the hips. On the ends of the girdle are the words 'Imervard me fecit', indicating the artist's name. The crucifix was also a reliquary: the back of the head is hollowed out and once contained a number of relics. It is of the so-called 'Volto Santo' type, found chiefly in medieval Italy, Spain, France, and England and modelled on the much venerated crucifix of the 'Holy Face' in Lucca cathedral. The latter is recorded in Lucca in the eleventh century at latest, but the one now in Lucca cathedral is not the original: it is an imitation of a cross dating from the late twelfth or early thirteenth century. Since the Imervard cross is severer in design than the present Lucca cross, it was presumably modelled on the one that is now lost. Its probable date is around 1170.

An especially valuable processional cross, which according to the Steterburg Annals was presented by the duke in 1194 and which was kept for centuries in the entry arch to the choir, is no longer extant: it was burnt at the beginning of the nineteenth century—an extraordinary piece of vandalism, to modern ideas—by order of the cathedral preacher. According to earlier descriptions it showed the Saviour surrounded by a group of followers. Its destruction is particularly unfortunate as it was probably a prototype of the well-known triumphal cross in Halberstadt cathedral.

Apart from these works of art, the earliest mural paintings on the eastern side of the building have been dated *circa* 1200 and attributed to a cleric in Henry the Lion's entourage. This supposition is based on an old inscription on a pillar of the nave—partly damaged and subsequently reconstructed, perhaps incorrectly—naming a certain Johannes Gallicus as the artist. According to the theory, this Johannes and his brother Eilbertus belonged to a rich family of cloth dealers in Hildesheim named Wale; and Johannes may be identical with a Canon Johannes who was chancellor to the Emperor Otto IV and may have been employed as a notary during the last years of Otto's father, Henry the Lion. This theory, however, is untenable if only on stylistic grounds: the painting of the eastern side of the cathedral did not begin until 1240–50.

While Brunswick cathedral, despite later enlargements and alterations, still basically appears as it did in the late twelfth century, the neighbouring Dankwarderode castle, which Henry did much to develop, has had varied fortunes in the course of time. After being much neglected in the late Middle Ages, in the seventeenth and eighteenth century it was incorporated in a larger complex of buildings. The Romanesque remains of the castle were only discovered after a fire in the 1870s, and were used as a foundation for the reconstruction of the ducal palace.

Like its model, the imperial residence at Goslar, this was a two-storied edifice. The lower part, which had a heating system, was used as an assembly hall in winter. It was divided lengthwise by a row of pillars supporting the ceiling. The ceremonial hall which comprised the whole upper storey had large arcaded windows, the capitals of which show the influence of the church at Königslutter. On the south side are the residential rooms, which have not been reconstructed, and further south-east the two-storied chapel with three aisles; only one of its towers was rebuilt as part of the restoration work. Unfortunately we do not know when this imposing structure was created. Probably the duke began it soon after the outset of his reign, so that it was near completion when the lion monument was set up in front of the castle.

The castle lion is certainly the best-known work of art connected with the duke, and it has a special place as the first large free-standing piece of sculpture in medieval art. The sources expressly state that it was erected in 1166, at the height of the duke's contest with his opponents. Recent metallographic analysis makes it certain that it was cast in the Brunswick area, using ore from the Harz mountains.

Its prototype was formerly sought in the 'aquamanile', a small bronze ewer in the shape of a lion, and the portal lions in north Italian churches. However, the immediate model for the lion's pose is undoubtedly the antique she-wolf from the Capitol in Rome, which stood near the Lateran palace from the eighth century at latest. The lion's tense attitude, with wide-open jaws, symbolizes the duke's resolve to dominate over his enemies. In the Middle Ages domination was expressed above all in the right to judge, and lions were traditional symbols of jurisdiction. Thus the lion of Brunswick is not only an expression of the duke's power but also recalls the fact that justice was administered here in the palace court, by the duke himself or in his name.

Besides the impressive castle area in Brunswick there are two other buildings whose beginnings, as we have seen, are closely associated with Henry the Lion: the cathedrals of Ratzeburg and Lübeck. The foundation stone of Lübeck cathedral was laid in the duke's presence in 1173, the year in which work was begun on the new church in Brunswick. It is not known at what date a beginning was made on the cathedral building at Ratzeburg, at the northern tip of the island; it may have been some years earlier. In both cases the duke, as we saw, did much to encourage the building by contributing the large sum of 100 silver marks a year. After his fall this was no longer paid, and the work slowed down; only in the first three decades of the thirteenth century were both cathedrals completed.

It has often been said that the Brunswick cathedral was the model for the other two, but this is only partly correct. Both of them, like the Brunswick church, are cruciform basilicas with the nave walls resting on pillars, proportioned on the crossing square as a module. At Ratzeburg, where less ground space was available, the nave consists of three bays and not four. In all three buildings the aisles are vaulted throughout. However, there are marked differences between them as regards decoration and numerous architectural details. Lübeck cathedral shows signs of the influence of churches built about the same time in Westphalia, for instance St Patroclus's at Soest; this is natural, as the localities were then closely connected. The cathedral at Ratzeburg has strong stylistic links with Premonstratensian churches in central Germany, such as that at Jerichow in the Altmark, which again is natural since the first bishops and canons of Ratzeburg were Premonstratensians from that area: Isfried, for instance, was a provost at Jerichow before becoming bishop of Ratzeburg.

The differences between the two cathedrals and the Brunswick church are also due to the fact that the former are not of dressed stone but of brick. Together with the church at Segeberg, which is of about the same date, they are the earliest large brick buildings in the colonized territory east of the lower Elbe.

There are no sources to indicate whether Henry the Lion initiated, or provided the means for, the building of other churches in Saxony. If he had, it seems likely that there would at least be an oral tradition to that effect. Recently it has been suggested that the church at Mandelsloh, north of Neustadt am Rübenberge, which is very large for such a small village, may have been founded by the duke; but there is no evidence to support this, and Mandelsloh was in any case a private estate belonging to the bishop of Minden.

Henry's generous patronage also did much to encourage the art of illuminating manuscripts. In twelfth-century Germany the writing and painting school at Helmarshausen on the Weser was in the forefront of the illuminator's art. Henry, who was advocate of the abbey from 1152 onwards, probably commissioned three works which are among the most important pieces of German book illumination of the period. These are: a small psalter now in the Baltimore Museum; a psalter in the British Museum, of which only a few fragments survive; and the Gmunden Evangeliarium, which we have already mentioned for the light it throws on the political conceptions prevailing at the ducal court.

The Baltimore psalter bears no indication of who commissioned it, but the style shows it clearly to be a product of the Helmarshausen school, where it was probably executed between 1145 and 1160.

Whether it belonged, as has been suggested, to the Duchess Clementia and was made at the time of her marriage to the duke is uncertain. The London psalter, on one of its few intact pages, bears a representation of the crucified Christ with Henry and Matilda in a double arcade at the foot of the cross, in an attitude of prayer and with inscribed banderoles—a prelude to the devotional pictures of the later Middle Ages. It may have been executed at the time of their marriage in 1168 or soon after.

The highest achievement in the way of book illumination at this time is without doubt the magnificent Gmunden Evangeliarium, which dates from the mid-1170s. It was commissioned by Henry the Lion at Helmarshausen and intended for St Blaise's in Brunswick, as is indicated by the dedicatory poem and miniature at the beginning of the code. The upper part of the picture shows the Mother of God (Theotokos) enthroned in a mandorla, with St John the Baptist and St Bartholomew (also venerated at St Blaise's) on either side. In the lower half the duke hands a book to St Blaise, no doubt the Evangeliarium itself, while St Giles—patron of the Ägidienkloster in Brunswick—holds the Duchess Matilda by the hand.

The author of this work is known. The dedicatory poem states that the monk Herman executed the precious work to the glory of God and by the duke's command, conveyed to him through the abbot. This Herman was the outstanding artist at Helmarshausen in the last three decades of the twelfth century. He not only executed the exquisite miniatures of the Evangeliarium but, as we know today, also copied the entire volume. He is also the scribe of the London psalter, so far as it survives, while its miniatures are by another hand.

The writing and painting school of Helmarshausen belongs to an old Saxon tradition, but the style of the figures and decoration also shows the influence of book illumination in northern France and England. Links have been pointed out between the Gmunden Evangeliarium and manuscripts from St Albans in southern England. Here again we may suppose that the ducal court played a role as intermediary. A typical feature of Herman's work is the close connection of New Testament scenes with allegoric symbols interpreted by texts in banderoles. The artist's power of symbolism is especially clear in the coronation picture in the last part of the Evangeliarium, at the beginning of St John's gospel. No doubt Helmarshausen gave a strong impulse to book illumination elsewhere in Saxony at this time, but we know of no other manuscripts connected with Henry the Lion and his artistic circle.

The third branch of the fine arts which the duke fostered on a large scale was that of goldsmithing. Costly receptacles were made for the numerous relics which he brought back from his pilgrimage to Jerusalem and Byzantium, and bestowed on St Blaise's and other churches. Several of these reliquaries today form part of the 'Welf treasury', formerly and more appropriately known as the 'treasury of relics of the house of Brunswick–Lüneburg'. The larger and more valuable part of this collection is in the Kunstgewerbemuseum in West Berlin; some pieces are in the possession of American museums which acquired them in the early 1930s. It cannot be said with certainty that all the items in this treasury that date from the second half of the twelfth century were commissioned by Henry the Lion; nor do we know whether they were executed in Brunswick, in workshops on the Rhine, or in Hildesheim, where the goldsmith's art was then flourishing. The collection has suffered losses in the course of time. One reliquary that has disappeared must have been of great value; according to an inventory dating from the end of the fifteenth century, it represented a church with five towers and bore an inscription stating that it was commissioned by 'Duke Henry of Saxony and Bavaria'.

One of the finest specimens in the Welf treasury is the so-called 'dome reliquary'. According to an old tradition it once contained the head of St Gregory of Nazianzus, which the duke is said to have brought back from the Levant. The reliquary is of Rhenish origin and was probably commissioned by the duke around 1175. It may have been executed in Brunswick by an immigrant from the Rhineland. It shows a close similarity of style with a very valuable item in the collection, a portable altar inscribed with the maker's name, one Eilbert of Cologne. It remains an open question whether Eilbert made the altar in Cologne or whether he was an artist from Cologne who worked for the duke in Brunswick or Hildesheim. It is not certain whether he was the same person as Canon Eilbert of Hildesheim, who figures in a charter of the duke's in the second half of the 1170s.

A particular group within the Welf treasury consists of arm reliquaries dating from the second half of the twelfth century. Arnold of Lübeck relates that Henry brought back many arms of apostles as relics and had them set in gold, silver and precious stones. Two arm reliquaries, those of St Innocent and St Theodore, bear inscriptions naming Duke Henry as donor. These, and another by the same craftsman which contained the arm of St Caesarius, were probably made in Brunswick. Two other especially costly arm reliquaries, that of St Lawrence and the 'Apostle's arm' now in the Cleveland Museum, were probably also commissioned by the duke, but their technique suggests that they originated in Hildesheim. The St Lawrence reliquary may be by the same craftsman as the St Oswald reliquary now in the Hildesheim cathedral treasury, which may thus also be connected with the ducal court. Another arm reliquary commissioned by the duke is now in the cathedral treasury at Minden. There is an old tradition that Henry presented Minden cathedral with an arm of St Gorgonius. The duke also had a reliquary made in the shape of a cross to contain a fragment of the True Cross which he presented to the Holy Cross monastery at Hildesheim in 1173. The so-called reliquary of the Emperor Henry II, now in the Louvre, is probably also one of those commissioned by Henry the Lion. Stylistically it is very similar to goldsmith's work of this period from the Brunswick–Hildesheim area. It features an effigy of the Emperor and of certain kings closely related to the English royal house, and may have been made shortly after Henry the Lion's marriage to Matilda.

Surveying these numerous works from the realm of fine art which owe their existence to the duke, one may think of him as the moving spirit of an artistic community. There would appear to have been, in or near Brunswick, what in modern terms might be called a ducal workshop, which, thanks to Henry's great wealth, enjoyed opportunities for artistic creation in many fields, far surpassing those of any rival craftsmen. Its products had, moreover, a symbolic value, being a clear reflection of the duke's power and quasi-royal dignity. But Henry also had another motive. As the Steterburg Annals tell us, in his last years he strove by good works to please the King of Heaven. Deprived of companionship and feeling the approach of death, the duke no doubt felt a deep religious need to gain salvation by works of piety. Rich as was the artistic activity in Henry the Lion's environment, one cannot speak in terms of a typically Welf style, clearly distinct from some other style characteristic of the Staufens. The works in the creation of which Henry was decisively involved present a variegated picture, mingling traditional forms with fresh inspiration.

Of the literary monuments that probably originated in Henry the

Lion's entourage, the most important is an epic poem, the *Rolands-lied* (Song of Roland), whose author names himself at the end of the work as *der Pfaffe* [priest] *Konrad*. Nothing else is known of him, but the markedly Bavarian dialect and frequent references to Bavaria and Regensburg make it very probable that he was a Bavarian and held some clerical office at the ducal court at Regensburg. The date of the work is disputed. In the epilogue Conrad states that a Duke Henry, at the request of his noble spouse, the daughter of a mighty king, procured the original French book [the *Chanson de Roland*] in order to have it translated into German. He goes on to say that he turned it first into Latin and then into German, without any addition or omission. The language is in part highly archaic, and the work has often been assigned to the second quarter of the twelfth century. In that case the 'Duke Henry' could only be Henry the Proud or Henry Jasomirgott, who were successively married to Gertrude, daughter of the Emperor Lothair III. As against this, the opinion has increasingly prevailed that the author's patron was Henry the Lion, husband of Matilda of England. The claim that the duke spread Christianity and converted the heathen can only apply to him. The fact that the poem refers at one point to the relics of St Blaise, whereas the French *Chanson* speaks of St Basil, suggests that the poet belonged to the entourage of Henry the Lion and may have spent some time at his court in Brunswick. As there is no mention of Henry's journey to the Holy Land, present-day scholars generally assign the work to the first years after his marriage to Matilda, i.e. 1168–72. There is little to support the most recent view that the ducal couple brought the French original to Saxony on their return from exile and that Conrad composed his work in Brunswick after Matilda's death and during Henry's last years, i.e. in about 1193–5. If Matilda had been dead, the epilogue would certainly have mentioned the fact.

The medieval poems centring on the figure of Roland relate to Charlemagne's Spanish campaign of 778. When the Emperor had to withdraw from Spain owing to a renewed Saxon rebellion, the rearguard of his army was attacked by the Basques in the pass of Roncesvalles in the Pyrenees. Many Frankish nobles were killed, including Roland (Hruodland), warden of the Breton marches. These events, embellished by legend in subsequent centuries, were first given literary form in the *Chanson de Roland* around 1100. This original version, which has not survived, was later reworked and translated more than once. The *Rolandslied*, the earliest treatment of the theme in German, was probably based on a lost French version dating from about the middle of the twelfth century: it is uncertain whether this version was identical, or largely so, with that in the Bodleian Library in Oxford.

While basically conforming to the French original, Conrad's poem differs in one important respect. In the French epic, Roland's chief motive is love of country: he is a bold and fearless champion, fighting for the greater glory of the Frankish realm. The *Rolandslied*, on the other hand, is imbued with the idea of a holy war against the infidel, the crusading ethos transposed into the time of Charlemagne. Religious themes take the place of political ones. Roland is the ideal Christian knight: he does not fight for his own sake or for earthly glory, but piously accepts martyrdom and death. Thus the *Rolandslied* is not only the first treatment of its subject-matter in German, but also an important link in the development of the Roland theme in Western literature as a whole. Henry the Lion for his part would naturally take a special interest in a poem representing his ancestor Charlemagne as a champion of Christendom.

Like the story of Roland, another recurrent theme of Western literature, that of Tristan and Isolde, was in all probability first treated in German in the entourage of Henry the Lion. The work in question is *Tristant und Isalde* by Eilhart of Oberg, which again raises a number of critical questions that cannot be answered with certainty.

Members of the Oberg family, named from a village near Peine, belonged to the Welf ministerial class at the end of the twelfth and beginning of the thirteenth century, but were also vassals of the bishops of Hildesheim, such double dependency being frequent at this period. In the immediate entourage of Henry the Lion we only know of a cleric, John of Oberg, in 1190. However, a year earlier one Eilhart of Oberg, with his father John (Johannes) and others of his family, figures as witness to a charter whereby Bishop Adelog of Hildesheim conferred parish privileges on the chapel founded by Duke Henry on his own estate in Oberg, during the period of Henry's absence in England. Between 1196 and 1207 this Eilhart witnessed a number of documents for the Count Palatine Henry (son of the Lion) and later for the Emperor Otto IV, and he is finally mentioned in an inventory of the property of Count Siegfried II of Blankenburg, drawn up after 1209. Despite the doubts that have been expressed from time to time, we may consider him to be identical with the Eilhart of Oberg who is named, at the conclusion of *Tristant*, as the author of that work.

Its date is still a matter of controversy. In the first place, only about 1,000 lines, roughly a tenth of the original, have survived, in three portions of manuscript dating from soon after 1200. The only complete version we have is a thirteenth-century revision preserved in three manuscripts of the fifteenth century. Some passages are also to be found in the *Eneide* of Henry of Veldeke, the chief example of early courtly epic in German, showing that the author of one work must have been acquainted with the other. Henry of Veldeke had already composed most of his epic when it was removed from his possession in 1174; about a decade later it was restored and he was able to complete it. If he made use of Eilhart's poem, this must date from the early 1170s; if, on the other hand, the *Eneide* is the older work, *Tristant* must be assigned to the late 1180s. The language of *Tristant* is very archaic compared to the *Eneide*, and its versification and rhyming are awkward in many places, which would suggest that it is the earlier work of the two. *Tristant* would thus be a youthful work of Eilhart's, whom we do not otherwise encounter as a poet. In that case, however, it is curious that there is no reference to Eilhart in documents earlier than the end of the 1180s. Thus the dating of *Tristant* must remain uncertain.

The story, derived from Celtic myth and legend, of the fatal love potion that united Tristan to Isolde, the bride of King Mark, was elaborated in the course of time and took on a new artistic form in France, in an epic dating from the middle of the twelfth century. This work, by an unknown author, has not survived; it provided a model for many subsequent versions, including that by Eilhart. Presumably the Welf *ministerialis* learnt of it from Matilda or her entourage. Although no patron is mentioned as in the case of the *Rolandslied*, we may assume that the ducal couple commissioned this work also. This would strengthen the view that it originated in the 1170s, when the Welf court was particularly active in encouraging the arts.

Even if Eilhart did not compose his work until about 1190, however, he is in any case the first poet known to us by name from the Welf region of Lower Saxony. There is little probability in the view sometimes expressed that he wrote his work in the middle or lower Rhine country, where Veldeke lived, or in Thuringia. The language of *Tristant* is too free from dialect features to be assigned to a particular area.

We can say nothing of the poem's relationship to the French original, as the latter is lost. By comparison with later Tristan poems such as that by Godfrey of Strasburg, Eilhart shows a lack of sensitivity to the theme of courtly love (*Minne*). To him the potion is a dire stroke of fate, taking away the hero's power of independent action. His main theme is not Tristan's love but his knightly deeds. Thus the work still has much of the popular epic (*Spielmannsdichtung*) about it, which accounts for its becoming the basis of the prose version of Tristan and Isolde in a late medieval *Volksbuch*.

While in the case of *Tristant* the sources leave important questions unanswered, we are well informed as to the origin of a work that testifies to the duke's strong interest in the learning of his time. This is the *Lucidarius*, a compendium of general and especially theological knowledge that was intended primarily for layfolk. It exists in two versions, of which the shorter is certainly the earlier. According to the rhymed preface, the duke instructed his chaplains in the city of Brunswick to compile, on the basis of Latin models, a German work which he stipulated should be in prose. The 'master', as he is styled in the preface—what we should call the chief editor—would have preferred verse, we are told, but the duke considered prose a better medium for expressing the truth. He also wished the work to be called *Aurea gemma*, symbolizing the value of its contents, but the clerical compilers opted for *Lucidarius*, a title that was commonly used for works of this kind, denoting a source of light or enlightenment. The date of the work is not known; in its earliest form it may be assigned to Henry the Lion's last years, when we know him to have been particularly interested in the intellectual life of his time. His decision to have it in prose, and his reason for doing so, are a pointer to the future, and entitle him to no small credit for the development of German literary prose in the Middle Ages.

The work is a survey of universal knowledge, beginning with cosmography. It treats of heaven and earth, paradise and hell. It briefly describes the three known continents, explains the nature of elements, constellations, the weather and other natural phenomena, and the origin of human life. The second book contains an introduction to Christian doctrine, including the truths of faith and also the customs and rules of everyday religious life. The third book, perhaps a later compilation, is an eschatological treatise on the Last Things, the Judgement, and the eternal life of those redeemed by God.

The main source was the *Elucidarium* of Honorius

Augustodunensis, a theologian of the first half of the twelfth century who remains a mystery in many ways but who probably lived for some time in Regensburg. His work, an encyclopedic compendium of the knowledge of his time, was highly popular within decades of its composition. The compilers of the *Lucidarius* imitated its question-and-answer form, with a pupil or 'youth' eliciting replies from the 'master'. They also made use of Honorius's other writings, such as *Imago mundi* and *Gemma animae*. Their close knowledge of his work is accounted for by the fact that during Henry the Lion's rule very close relations existed between the clergy at Brunswick and that at Regensburg. In addition the Brunswick chaplains used the works of other theologians, e.g., for their second book, a treatise on liturgy by Rupert of Deutz. Altogether the *Lucidarius* reflects the high theological standard of the duke's chaplains and the Brunswick clergy in general.

By the duke's desire, the compilers of the *Lucidarius* kept its didactic purpose steadily in mind. Knowledge that had been confined to the clergy was now to be made available to the laity. The authors therefore eschewed difficult questions of dogma and confined themselves to subjects of importance to layfolk. As the first book of universal knowledge in the German language, the work became extremely popular; more than fifty manuscripts of it are known. In the fifteenth century it was taken over by the printers of *Volksbücher*, and with some modifications it was more than once reprinted in early modern times. It thus had a lasting effect on German education, such as Henry the Lion could not have foreseen when he commissioned the work.

No other literary monuments are known to have originated in the duke's circle. The lyric poetry that was being developed by the troubadours of Provence was not yet practised at his court. Thus we have only two poems—though very important ones—that are associated with Henry's name. Nor can we speak, as has sometimes been done, of a specifically Welf school of poetry distinct from, and supposedly more archaic than, the Staufen type of literature that was soon to come into greater prominence.

Henry's Personal Appearance and Character. The Judgement of Historians

HENRY THE LION is certainly one of the most popular, but also one of the most controversial of medieval German rulers. On the one hand he has been extolled as a champion of nationalism and one of the chief pioneers of German colonization in the East; on the other he has been upbraided for deserting Frederick Barbarossa at a crucial moment and occasioning a serious setback to the latter's imperial and Italian policy. Historians of the nineteenth and twentieth century have often fallen into the danger of transferring modern ideas to the twelfth century, failing to take due account of the fact that the Middle Ages, like any other period, has its own values and can only be understood in the light of them.

At an early date, legend laid claim to the duke's personality and gave a fanciful colouring to particular events in his life. In the course of centuries, the legend that took shape in the Brunswick area around 1200 spread far and wide beyond Lower Saxony and even outside Germany, with constant variations on its original form. The Lion's life and exploits were a theme much loved by poets, and poetic licence combined with legend to transform reality. At the same time, legend and poetry together ensured that the Welf hero's personality remained constantly alive in the imagination of later times, with truth and fiction interwoven as is usual in popular ideas of history.

Let us therefore try in the first place to form a notion of the duke's personality as far as contemporary evidence allows. Henry's physical appearance is comparatively easy to recognize. However, the skeleton that was found in the crypt beneath the monument to the ducal couple in Brunswick cathedral during the excavations of 1935 is of no use as evidence, since, as we have seen, it is in all probability not that of the duke.

The monument itself, which probably dates from 1230–40, is one of the finest and most impressive pieces of Lower Saxon sculpture of the thirteenth century. The artist who created it had never seen the duke or the duchess, who died before her husband. His object was to depict ideal figures of a princely pair according to the notions of his time. Henry appears as a fairly young man, clean-shaven and with curly hair. In his right hand he holds a model of the cathedral to show that he is its founder; the sword in his left hand proclaims him to be an upholder of justice. No other symbols of princely rank are visible. Matilda reposes on his left. Round her head is a broad circlet with decorative plaques, but this is not a royal coronal. The duchess, who was noted for her piety, is portrayed with her hands raised in prayer. It is noteworthy that the duke is about a head taller than she.

Quite a different impression is given by the pictures of the couple that were made during their lifetime, namely three miniatures in the two liturgical manuscripts commissioned by the duke at Helmarshausen. We have referred to the artistic and symbolic importance of these in another connection. The question here is whether they can tell us anything as to the couple's stature and appearance. The two miniatures in the Gmunden Evangeliarium, which show the couple full-length, are more informative than that in the London psalter, where they are seen kneeling at the feet of the Crucified. The monks at Helmarshausen who executed the miniatures were undoubtedly acquainted with the duke and duchess, but, as was common in the early and later Middle Ages, their object was not to paint a lifelike portrait but rather to represent a typical prince of the period; however, some individual features are unmistakably discernible.

In all three miniatures Henry, like the other princes in the coronation picture, wears a beard and a small moustache according to the custom of the time; his hair is dark, parted in the middle, and reaches nearly to his shoulders. His eyes are also dark. Matilda, in the coronation picture, is noticeably taller than Henry. It has been suggested that this is because she is standing while he is kneeling, and it is true that only in the depiction of Henry can the bend of the lower leg be clearly seen. But a close comparison of this coronation picture with the dedicatory portrait of the Evangeliarium, which is by the same artist, suggests that Matilda is also kneeling in the former picture, though her robe conceals the fact. It is unlikely, moreover, that the couple would receive their crowns from the divine hand in two different postures, the duke kneeling and the duchess standing. It would thus appear that Matilda was in fact taller than Henry.

Although these miniatures are not portraits in the modern sense, they are probably fairly good likenesses of the ducal couple.

This supposition is confirmed by a description of Henry's appearance by one of the Emperor's justices, Acerbus Morena of Lodi, who continued a work of history begun by his father Otto describing Frederick I's deeds in Lombardy. Under the year 1163 he inserted short descriptions of the Emperor and some personalities in his entourage, whom he no doubt met during Frederick's second Italian expedition. Henry the Lion, who was then somewhat over thirty and in the prime of life, was, according to Acerbus, of strong physique, average height, and well proportioned limbs; he had a broad face, large black eyes, and almost black hair. Acerbus adds that he was magnanimous, rich, and powerful, of most noble descent, and a grandson of the Emperor Lothair. When Acerbus, an Italian, says that Henry was of average height, we may suppose that he was short for a German; the description also indicates that the Italian blood of the Este family was more visible in this descendant of theirs than in his cousin Frederick, who shared the same ancestry through his mother Judith.

As to the duke's character, we have to rely solely on contemporary judgements of him and his acts. We have no record of personal utterances that might give an idea of his temperament. Rahewin, who continued Otto of Freising's *Gesta Friderici* after the latter's death, gives a description of Henry and Welf VI in the context of their military aid to Frederick in northern Italy in 1159. He does so in terms borrowed from the Roman historian Sallust, applying the latter's antithesis of the Elder Cato and Caesar almost literally to Henry the Lion and his Welf uncle respectively; this was a common practice of medieval chroniclers, who sought to heighten the effect of their narrative by citing ancient prototypes. However, some of the qualities that Rahewin claims for Henry are independently attested: his physical prowess, personal courage, keenness of mind, and delight in the art of war. Henry's intrepidity was repeatedly shown in campaigns in Germany, Italy, and the Slav country: a typical example was his personal bravery in subduing the Roman rebellion on the day of Barbarossa's coronation. The Wendish campaigns, over difficult territory with bad roads and with problems of organizing supply, called for especial strategic skill, which can also be clearly seen in Henry's co-operation with Valdemar of Denmark.

All these wars were fought with great ferocity on both sides. The cruelty of which Henry was capable is shown in the razing of the town of Bardowick, which he ordered in a fit of rage. But such methods were no rarity at the time. Frederick I's battles with the north Italian cities, culminating in the total destruction of Milan, were in many ways unsurpassed for harshness and inhumanity.

A marked characteristic of Henry was his love of power, which amounted to an obsession. He went about the enlargement of his domains with the greatest ruthlessness, insisting on his own real or supposed rights, unscrupulously ignoring the just claims of his rivals, and using force to create *faits accomplis* which they had eventually to recognize. A typical instance from his early years was his seizure of the Stade inheritance; but subsequently he behaved in similar fashion over the refoundation of Lübeck and the founding of Munich.

Money also played an important part in his policies. Next to the Normans of Sicily and the English kings, Henry was one of the richest princes in the West. He was probably wealthier than Frederick Barbarossa. He made use of his wealth to achieve political ends, and did his best to increase it by exacting a financial price for political or military aid. We have already noticed Helmold of Bosau's remark that his campaigns against the Slavs were not a matter of Christianity but of money—a criticism confirmed by the complaint of the Obodrite Prince Pribislav, also reported by Helmold, concerning the exploitation of his fellow-countrymen in Wagria. When the Danish historian Saxo accuses Henry of greed and ambition and observes that his friendship was purchasable rather than useful, there is a kernel of truth in these charges, even allowing for the fact that Saxo's work is strongly anti-German and that he generally adopts a hostile attitude towards the duke.

The financial aspects of the duke's policy can best be followed, thanks to the quality of the sources, in Nordalbingia and in his negotiations with Valdemar of Denmark; but no doubt the picture was the same in the rest of Saxony and in Bavaria. The tough struggle for Goslar and the rich silver mines of Rammelsberg tells the same story of thirst for gain. With all his wealth, moreover, the duke lacked the generosity of style with which his uncle Welf VI was able to make friends.

Henry's pursuit of power, which despite setbacks was successful for many years, and his growing wealth increased his self-confidence, which was already great, to the point of arrogance and over-estimation of his own power. He ruled his subjects with a heavy hand. Not only the conquered Slavs, but his own vassals and *ministeriales* felt increasingly oppressed. The steadily rising opposition exploded with full force at the moment of his fall.

Henry lacked the diplomatic skill which again and again enabled his cousin Frederick to weather a difficult situation. The Lion adhered stubbornly to his own purposes without realizing that political conditions had begun to change since the beginning of the 1170s. He has sometimes been described as a coolly calculating realist, but in the crucial years of his reign he did not display that quality.

His appetite for power was often indulged at the expense of the church and led to violent disputes with ecclesiastical princes. But inferences should not be drawn from this, as is sometimes done, concerning his personal attitude to religion. He was deeply and uncritically devout, interested in the intellectual life of the time but unaffected by new trends in religious matters. The idea that God had set him over many of his fellow-men and that he must prove himself worthy of this grace by good works recurs constantly in the formalized language of his charters. Religion played an important part in his pilgrimages to Jerusalem and Compostela, even though the journey to the Levant was also much concerned with prestige. In his last years, especially after Matilda's death, his religious feelings became deeper still and found concrete expression in the many endowments of those years.

Such a man, and the vicissitudes of his fate, were naturally of strong interest to contemporaries. The amity between the Hohenstaufen and the Welfs, that continued for over two decades from the accession of Frederick I, is reflected in the historical writings of that period. The chroniclers close to the Welfs, and the court historians of the Hohenstaufen, agree in their opinion of Henry the Lion. Helmold of Bosau, for all his criticism of Henry, depicts him as a mighty and successful fighter against the heathen Slavs, and also emphasizes his important role in Frederick's imperial and Italian policy; while Rahewin, to take one example from the Staufen camp, also points out how greatly Henry assisted Barbarossa in the Empire and Italy.

The chronicles of the late twelfth and early thirteenth century bring out clearly the opposing views of Staufen and Welf partisans in their accounts of the rift between the Emperor and the duke at Chiavenna, the duke's trial, and his deposition. The conflict between

Frederick and Henry was, for a long time to come, the main theme of all works describing the history of those decades. Arnold of Lübeck, a convinced adherent of the Welfs, is at pains to explain and justify Henry's acts, illegal though he admits them to be. On the other hand Godfrey of Viterbo, chaplain to Frederick I and Henry VI, who formerly described Henry the Lion as the 'jewel of the fatherland', later denounces him as a traitor to the Empire, deserting Frederick for the sake of 'Greek gifts'. No less severe is the judgement of Giselbert of Mons in his Chronicle of Hainault (*Chronicon Hanoniense*), who portrays Henry's refusal of aid to Frederick as particularly flagrant and calls him 'well-nigh the proudest and most ruthless of all men'.

Outside Germany, the historical sources of the time that give an account of Henry the Lion are almost all Anglo-Norman or Danish. It is notable that the English chroniclers of the late twelfth and early thirteenth century, despite the close political and family connections between Henry and the English royal house, are inclined to favour the Emperor's side of the conflict; while Saxo Grammaticus's *Gesta Danorum* is imbued with national pride and castigates Henry not only for avarice but for the 'underhandedness' of his policy.

During the thirteenth century the popular image of the duke took on more and more anecdotic and legendary features, associated in part with the lion monument and Henry's pilgrimage to the Holy Land. In Brunswick, probably as early as about 1200, it was related that the duke had brought back from the Orient a lion which he had helped to vanquish a dragon. The beast had remained faithful to Henry even beyond the grave; it finally died at the duke's tomb in Brunswick cathedral, the doors of which still bore the marks of its claws. This local legend subsequently absorbed elements of the 'wanderer's return' theme, familiar in the West, wherein a hero is kept in distant lands by adverse fate; the time for his return expires and his wife is about to wed again; then at the last moment the hero, believed dead, returns to his wife and possessions. The legend of Henry the Lion, thus embroidered, finally developed into a tale of love and adventure, popular in other countries as well as Lower Saxony and the rest of Germany. At an early date it reached Scandinavia. The original pre-literary state of the legend may be seen in the carvings, dating from about 1230, on the church door at Valthjofstad in Iceland, one representing a fight with a dragon and the other a lion couched on a grave.

The legend first found literary form in the epic *Reinfried von Braunschweig*, composed by an Alemannic poet in about 1300. Reinfried, representing Henry the Lion, is a prince who journeys to the Holy Land and has strange adventures there; he is shipwrecked on a mountain, is rescued by a fabulous creature, and eventually reaches home just as his wife is about to remarry. He brings back from the East a lion which follows him everywhere and dies on its master's grave. Later the subject was treated in other literary works: several mastersingers, including Hans Sachs, were to use it as a model for their poems. It made its appearance in historiography in the *Cronecken der Sassen* of 1492 by Konrad Bothe of Brunswick. In the fourteenth century it appears in Czech literature, where it provided the material for a *Volksbuch*; in the seventeenth century this was translated and became known in Russia. There is a pictorial representation of the legend, dating from the fifteenth century or the beginning of the sixteenth, in a room of the former monastery of St Castor at Karden on the Moselle.

The endeavour of Renaissance historians to penetrate to original sources is seen in their treatment of Henry the Lion as in other matters. In *Saxonia*, dating from the beginning of the sixteenth century, the Hamburg city councillor Albert Krantz portrays the duke in a very favourable light on the basis of contemporary accounts.

During the Reformation and Counter-Reformation the picture of Henry was much influenced by religious differences. An example from the Protestant side is afforded by a pamphlet entitled *Papsttreu Hadriani und Alexanders III. gegen Kaiser Friedrichen geübt* ('The papal loyalty of Hadrian and Alexander III towards the Emperor Frederick'), which was published at Wittenberg in 1545 and to which Luther wrote a foreword. In this work—a free translation of the relevant part of a history of the Papacy, in Latin, by an English theologian—Henry is depicted as a traitor, bribed and incited against the Emperor by Pope Alexander. On the other hand many Catholic historians of the early seventeenth century saw him as a loyal son of the church who helped significantly to end the schism by refusing to go to the Emperor's aid in Italy.

It was a considerable advance when, at the end of the seventeenth century, dynastic history took the place of confessional history. During the period from about 1680, when the Welf dynasty in Hanover was in the ascendant, history became a powerful instrument of policy. The story of the medieval dynasty was of consequence both in the struggle to obtain the Electoral dignity (the duke of Hanover became the ninth Elector of the Empire in 1692) and in the Welf claim to the duchy of Saxony-Lauenburg after the extinction of the Ascanian line. Henry the Lion, the mighty ancestor, was to give a fresh impetus to Welf policies. For the opening of a new opera house in Hanover in 1689 the court commissioned a work entitled *Enrico il Leone*, embodying motifs from the legend and glorifying Henry after the baroque fashion of the period.

The intensive study of Welf history is closely associated with the name of Leibniz, who was invited to Hanover in 1676 to direct the recently founded ducal library and was later, as court historiographer, commissioned to investigate and compile the history of the Welfs. The famous philosopher collected a great deal of material for this purpose, not only in the archives and libraries of the Welf lands but on a journey, lasting many years, to South Germany, Vienna, and Italy; however, his other plans eventually took precedence and the historical work was still incomplete at the time of his death in 1716. The accumulation of sources was added to by his successors in the posts of librarian and court historian, but the great work was not completed until Christian Ludwig Scheidt took over both posts in 1748. In 1750–3 he published the four imposing volumes of *Origines Guelficae*, the third of which is devoted to a full account of Henry the Lion and his sons.

The *Origines Guelficae*, with their wealth of documentary and other material, were for a long time the main source for the history of the Welf dynasty up to the middle of the thirteenth centry. They are still of some value for the life of Henry the Lion, though many of their evaluations are out of date. The first biographies of the duke, dating from the eighteenth century, are more like essays, and their moralistic comments are strongly influenced by the pragmatic conceptions of the age. The first life of the duke that deserves to be called a scientific biography is *Heinrich der Löwe, Herzog der Sachsen und Bayern*, published by the Swedish historian Carl Vilhelm Böttiger in 1819 when he was a *Privatdozent* in Leipzig.

After the Romantic movement rediscovered the Middle Ages, historical interest centred on the German Emperors and other great rulers of those centuries. In 1823–5 Friedrich von Raumer published his *Geschichte der Hohenstaufen und ihrer Zeit*, the first major account of a period of the High Middle Ages; here, though Raumer is at pains to do justice to the duke, Henry the Lion definitely takes second place to the Emperor Frederick.

A revaluation of Henry the Lion was announced in the 1830s by *Geschichte des teutschen Volkes*, whose author, Heinrich Luden, was a pioneer of the *kleindeutsch* school of German history in the nineteenth century. He saw the duke as the champion of a national policy who achieved lasting results to the north and east of Germany while the Emperor neglected the rights and interests of the crown, obsessed as he was by 'the spell of a passion for Italy'. The new idea of Henry as a convinced opponent of Barbarossa's Italian policy became topical in and after 1848, as the controversy between *grossdeutsch* and *kleindeutsch* parties was intensified by the argument over the proper bounds of a German national state. This may be seen in an article, 'Die modernen Ghibellinen', which appeared at the beginning of 1849 in the *kleindeutsch* organ *Die Grenzboten*. This expressed the severest condemnation, up to that time, of the imperial policy of medieval Germany, against which Henry the Lion's actions were upheld as a model: his refusal of help at Chiavenna was depicted as a conscious rejection of a misguided Italian policy.

A decade later, when the question of Germany's future was still a subject of passionate discussion, the opposition between the *grossdeutsch* and *kleindeutsch* camps and their rival assessments of Henry the Lion found expression in the controversy between Heinrich von Sybel and Julius Ficker concerning German imperial policy in the Middle Ages. Both, it is true, mention Henry the Lion only incidentally in their various writings, but their arguments have been repeated in scholarly discussions ever since. Sybel, representing the *Kleindeutsche*, regards the duke as the first German prince who openly broke away from the imperial policy that the nation, according to him, had followed only with reluctance since Otto I's time. Like King Henry I before him, the Welf saw the possibility of a national policy in the East and made it a reality. Ficker, on the other hand, as a *Grossdeutscher* and 'universalist', contends that the Welf's refusal to aid Barbarossa's Italian policy in the 1170s was dictated by self-interest and not by patriotism, while the general approval of his deposition showed that the German nation was on the Emperor's side.

In the 1860s this controversy concerning medieval imperial policy was more reflected in propaganda than in historical research. Scarcely any trace of the discussion, impassioned though it was, can be found in the two biographies of Henry the Lion that appeared in that decade, by Hans Prutz and Martin Philippson respectively.

After the foundation of the second German Empire in 1871 it might perhaps be thought that *kleindeutsch* ideas of medieval history would have prevailed in the German popular mind, but this was not so. By and large, the policy of the medieval Emperors was commended; not, however, on Ficker's universalist grounds, but on a different basis which had, not long previously, been given the name of 'Ghibellinism'. This view of history drew a bold parallel between the Hohenstaufen Empire and that of the Hohenzollern, in which the majesty of the Middle Ages seemed to have been revived. In subsequent years this idea was constantly repeated in poetry and art, for instance in the great memorial to Frederick I on the Kyffhäuser mountain.

Because the nineteenth-century Welfs were in opposition to the Hohenzollern Empire, Henry the Lion was often represented as having been no more than a rebel against the Empire and his liege lord. According to Bismarck's harsh judgement in his memoirs: 'As regards the policy of the Guelfic efforts, their earliest historical landmark—the revolt of Henry the Lion before the battle of Legnano, the desertion of Emperor and Empire, for reasons of personal and dynastic advantage, at the crisis of a most severe and perilous struggle—is decisive for all time.'

For a long time the dominant view of Henry the Lion in German historiography was that of Ranke and his school. Ranke's references to the Lion reflect his purpose of illustrating the tension between universal and national tendencies in the German Middle Ages as in other periods. While in the introduction to his *History of the Prussian Monarchy* he still depicts Henry as a champion of national interests and one of the first important examples of a territorial prince, in his subsequent *Universal History* he emphasizes the opportunities that could have sprung from co-operation between the Emperor and the duke. 'On their agreement rested the future of the German Empire and of the world. Together they could have asserted German dominion over Italy and the Papacy, but they came to no understanding.'

Ranke's pupil Wilhelm von Giesebrecht, whose great *Geschichte der deutschen Kaiserzeit* was read widely and not only by specialists, came in the course of his work to place increasing emphasis on power politics, not least in relation to Frederick I's reign. The Emperor had to take up his cousin's challenge if he was to maintain the power of the crown. According to Giesebrecht Henry 'no doubt possessed a statesman's genius', but 'his great qualities were besmirched by greed, disloyalty, and pride' and he thus brought about his own ruin.

Up to the end of the nineteenth century Henry the Lion was judged mainly from the political point of view, but thereafter research began to concentrate on legal and constitutional aspects. The many analyses of the duke's trial and the lively controversy it aroused among scholars have given us deeper insight into the judicial processes of medieval Germany.

Among other German historians since the beginning of the present century, Karl Hampe more than once summed up the results of these and other investigations. Besides his accounts in *Deutsche Kaisergeschichte zur Zeit der Salier und Staufer* and his work on the High Middle Ages, especial mention should be made of his balanced estimate of the duke in *Herrschergestalten des deutschen Mittelalters*. The English biography of Henry the Lion by Austin Lane Poole (1912), later known for other important works on medieval history, is more of an extended essay than a full-scale work.

In the first years of the National Socialist regime influential Party circles set about creating a new image of medieval German history, in which nineteenth-century *kleindeutsch* arguments were revived and combined, often in a highly inconsistent way, with Nazi doctrines of race and popular ideology. Like Sybel and other *kleindeutsch* historians, they extolled Henry I (the Fowler) and Henry the Lion as the champions of a policy devoted to promoting and safeguarding German colonization in the East. The two rulers were to be given their due place in the historical consciousness of the German people, which specialist writers had allegedly denied them. Brunswick cathedral with the duke's tomb, and the Quedlinburg abbey where Henry I is buried, were to be secularized and transformed into 'national shrines'. In the cathedral not only was the crypt rebuilt but scenes were painted on the upper side walls of the nave glorifying Henry the Lion as a promoter of German settlement in the East. After 1945 the cathedral once more became a place of worship, and the paintings were very properly effaced.

As Nazi foreign policy became increasingly imperialistic from 1938 onwards, the Party version of history changed abruptly. The idea of the medieval Empire as a 'force for European order' was coined to provide a basis for the current ideology. An artificial 'idea of the Germanic Reich' was set against the Christian–universal concept of the Empire; Charlemagne and the medieval German kings and Emperors were proclaimed as its exponents. The estimate of Henry the Lion altered, as he was now thrust into the background in relation to Barbarossa. In *Das Reich als europäische Ordnungsmacht* by the Nazi historian Karl Richard Ganzer, a work much used for propaganda purposes during the Second World War, it was actually stated that the duke's 'particularist designs' involved the Empire in a grave crisis. On the other hand, Hans Martin Elster in his biography of Henry the Lion (1940) adhered to the line of glorifying the duke one-sidedly from a *kleindeutsch* and Welf point of view.

Serious German scholars, it must be emphasized, took no part in this refurbishing of history. They took increasing interest in Henry the Lion from the beginning of the 1930s onwards, but chiefly with the object of studying Henry's regime in his two duchies in the light of the constitutional and regional investigations that had been successfully applied to other German lands, and thus gaining a deeper insight into the development of the medieval Empire.

Today we see ever more clearly that the twelfth century in Germany was a period of transition from older, less rigid, and more personal forms of rule to those of an institutional, territorial state. In German constitutional history, the century was that in which the modern state began to take shape.

In Saxony, this change of political structure is linked with the personality of Henry the Lion. It was his purpose to combine together his various seigniorial rights on the basis of a large new territorial duchy and to create a unified dominion on the grand scale. Although his attempt to create a self-contained political entity comprising the whole Saxon tribal area was unsuccessful, his policy made it possible for the Welfs in later times once again to achieve a leading position in North Germany and in the history of the German Empire. The recovery of the Welf dynasty began in the middle of the thirteenth century, the extinction of the Hohenstaufen having put an end to the latter's dominant role in Germany after barely a century.

To us, Henry the Lion is not the champion of a 'national' policy, nor is he a 'rebel against the Emperor and the Empire': he is the first important representative of the new estate of German territorial princes, and one of the great creative forces of German history by reason of his work in laying the foundations of a modern state and his contribution to the variety of German culture.

But modern research has also made us recognize another important fact. The alternative 'Frederick Barbarossa or Henry the Lion', which dominated our history books for so long, has increasingly shown itself to be false. Inevitable as was the conflict between these two mighty leaders, we should not forget that it was preceded by nearly twenty-five years of co-operation between them, which alone made it possible to consolidate the power of the state at home and to secure for the Empire a strong position in foreign affairs. In this way the age of Frederick I and Henry the Lion illustrates in full clarity the opportunities, but also the conflicts and tensions, that have time and again characterized German history.

Sources and Bibliography

Note. In accordance with the character of this work, I have refrained from providing an exhaustive critical apparatus with running footnotes. The following indications are intended to provide the necessary references and enable the reader to follow up particular questions that could only be treated in summary fashion. Given the abundance of specialized literature on the history of Henry the Lion, if only for reasons of space I have as a rule confined myself to citing the latest works, but it is not difficult, through them, to make use of earlier research. I do not enter into controversies that have already been resolved; my views on questions that are still in dispute will be found implicitly in the text. For specialized literature on questions of imperial history in this period I would refer to the relevant sections of my 'Investiturstreit und frühe Stauferzeit', in Gebhardt-Grundmann, *Handbuch der deutschen Geschichte*, vol. i (9th edn., 1970, pp. 323 ff.; this has been published separately as a paperback (1973) with supplementary notes) and also in Fuhrmann: see p. 232 below.

LIST OF WORKS CITED IN ABBREVIATED FORM

AfD	*Archiv für Diplomatik.*
AUF	*Archiv für Urkundenforschung.*
Bl. dt. LG	*Blätter für deutsche Landesgeschichte.*
DA	*Deutsches Archiv für Erforschung* [till 1944: *für Geschichte*] *des Mittelalters.*
HZ	*Historische Zeitschrift.*
JB(b)	*Jahrbuch, -bücher.*
LG	*Landesgeschichte.*
MGH	*Monumenta Germaniae Historica.*
Separate series:	
Const.	*Constitutiones.*
DD	*Diplomata* (*D* with ruler's name: *DF*(rederick) I, *DCo*(nrad) III, etc.).
SS	*Scriptores.*
SS rer. Germ.	*Scriptores rerum Germanicarum in usum scholarum.*
UHdL	*Die Urkunden Heinrichs des Löwen.*
MIÖG	*Mitteilungen des Instituts für Österreichische Geschichtsforschung.*
Nds. Jb.	*Niedersächsisches Jahrbuch für Landesgeschichte.*
UB	*Urkundenbuch.*

ZRG Germ. Abt.   Zeitschrift der Savigny-Stiftung für Rechtsgeschichte,
                  Germanistische Abteilung.
Zs.   Zeitschrift.

Am Ende, B., *Studien zur Verfassungsgeschichte Lübecks im 12. und 13.
Jahrhundert* (Veröffentl. zur Geschichte der Hansestadt Lübeck, Reihe B
2, 1975).

Bärmann, J., *Die Städtegründungen Heinrichs des Löwen und die Stadtver-
fassung des 12. Jahrhunderts* (Forschungen zur deutschen Rechtsgeschichte, 1, 1961).

Bradler, G., *Heinrich der Löwe in Oberschwaben*, Beiträge zur Landeskunde, Beilage zum Staatsanzeiger für Baden-Württemberg 1978, no. 2,
pp. 1 ff.

Büttner, H., 'Staufer und Welfen im politischen Kräftespiel zwischen
Bodensee und Iller während des 12. Jahrhunderts', *Zs. für württemb. LG*
20 (1961), 17 ff.; repr. in id., *Schwaben und Schweiz im frühen und hohen
Mittelalter*, Gesammelte Aufsätze (Vorträge und Forschungen, Konstanzer Arbeitskreis für mittelalterliche Geschichte, 15, 1972), pp. 337 ff.

Cartellieri, A., *Das Zeitalter Friedrich Barbarossas* (Weltgeschichte als
Machtgeschichte, 5, 1972).

Classen, P., 'Das Wormser Konkordat in der deutschen Verfassungsgeschichte', in *Investiturstreit und Reichsverfassung* (Vorträge und Forschungen, Konstanzer Arbeitskreis für mittelalterliche Geschichte, 17,
1973), pp. 411 ff.

Diestelkamp, B., 'Welfische Stadtgründungen und Stadtrechte des 12.
Jahrhunderts', *ZRG Germ. Abt.* 81 (1964), 164 ff.

Eggert, O., 'Die Wendenzüge Waldemars I. und Knuts VI. nach Pommern
und Mecklenburg', *Baltische Studien*, NF 29 (1927), 1 ff.

—— 'Dänisch-wendische Kämpfe in Pommern und Mecklenburg (1157–
1200)', ibid. 30. 2 (1928), 1 ff.

Feldmann, K., *Herzog Welf VI. und sein Sohn* (diss. Tübingen, 1971).

Giesebrecht, W. von, *Geschichte der deutschen Kaiserzeit*, vol. v (1880), vol.
vi, ed. B. von Simson (1895).

Glaeske, G., *Die Erzbischöfe von Hamburg–Bremen als Reichsfürsten (937–
1258)* (Quellen und Darstellungen zur Geschichte Niedersachsens, 60,
1962).

Hamann, M., *Mecklenburgische Geschichte* (Mitteldeutsche Forschungen,
51, 1968).

Hasenritter, F., *Beiträge zum Urkunden- und Kanzleiwesen Heinrichs des
Löwen* (Greifswalder Abhandlungen zur Geschichte des Mittelalters, 6,
1936).

Heilig, K. J., 'Ostrom und das Deutsche Reich um die Mitte des 12.
Jahrhunderts', in *Kaisertum und Herzogsgewalt im Zeitalter Friedrichs I.*

(Schriften des Reichsinstituts für ältere deutsche Geschichtskunde [*MGH*] 9, 1944), pp. 1 ff.

Hein, L., 'Anfang und Fortgang der Slavenmission', in *Schleswig-Holsteinische Kirchengeschichte*, vol. i (1977), pp. 105 ff.

Heinemann, W., *Das Bistum Hildesheim im Kräftespiel der Reichs- und Territorialpolitik, vornehmlich des 12. Jahrhunderts* (Quellen und Darstellungen zur Geschichte Niedersachsens, 72, 1968).

Heydel, J., 'Das Itinerar Heinrichs des Löwen, *Nds. Jb.* 6 (1929), 1 ff.

Hildebrand, R., *Der sächsische 'Staat' Heinrichs des Löwen (Historische Studien* 302, 1937).

Hoffmann, E., 'Vicelin und die Neubegründung des Bistums Oldenburg/Lübeck', in *Lübeck 1226, Reichsfreiheit und frühe Stadt* (1976), pp. 115 ff.

Hoppe, W., 'Erzbischof Wichmann von Magdeburg', *Geschichtsbl. für Stadt und Land Magdeburg*, 43 (1908), 134 ff., and ibid. 44 (1909), 38 ff.; now in id., *Die Mark Brandenburg, Wettin und Magdeburg, Ausgewählte Aufsätze* (1965), pp. 1 ff.

Jesse, W., *Münz- und Geldgeschichte Niedersachsens* (Braunschweiger Werkstücke, 15, 1952).

Jordan, K., *Die Bistumsgründungen Heinrichs des Löwen* (Schriften des Reichsinstituts für ältere deutsche Geschichtskunde [*MGH*] 3, 1939).

—— 'Heinrich der Löwe und Dänemark', in *Geschichtliche Kräfte und Entscheidungen, Festschrift für Otto Becker* (1954), pp. 16 ff.

—— 'Herzogtum und Stamm in Sachsen während des hohen Mittelalters', *Nds. Jb.* 30 (1958), 1 ff.

—— 'Nordelbingen und Lübeck in der Politik Heinrichs des Löwen', *Zs. des Vereins für lübeck. Geschichte und Altertumskunde*, 39 (1959), 29 ff.

—— 'Die Städtepolitik Heinrichs des Löwen', *Hansische Geschichtsbl.* 78 (1960), 1 ff.

—— 'Goslar und das Reich im 12 Jahrhundert', *Nds. Jb.* 35 (1963), 49 ff.

—— '800 Jahre Braunschweiger Burglöwe, Gedanken zur Städtepolitik Heinrichs des Löwen', in K. Jordan and M. Gosebruch, *800 Jahre Braunschweiger Burglöwe* (Braunschweiger Werkstücke, 38, 1967), pp. 13 ff.

—— 'Heinrich der Löwe und das Schisma unter Alexander III.', *MIÖG* 78 (1970), 224 ff.

—— 'Sachsen und das deutsche Königtum im hohen Mittelalter', *HZ* 210 (1970), 529 ff.

—— 'Das politische Kräftespiel an Oberweser und Leine um die Mitte des 12. Jahrhunderts', in *Festschrift für Hermann Heimpel* 2 (Veröffentl. des Max-Planck-Instituts für Geschichte, 36. 2, 1972), pp. 1042 ff.

—— 'Lübeck unter Graf Adolf II. von Holstein und Heinrich dem Löwen', in *Lübeck 1226, Reichsfreiheit und frühe Stadt* (1976), pp. 143 ff.

—— 'Der Harzraum in der Geschichte der deutschen Kaiserzeit', in Festschrift für Helmut Beumann (1977), pp. 163 ff.

Keinast, W., Deutschland und Frankreich in der Kaiserzeit, 2nd edn. (Monographien zur Geschichte des Mittelalters, 9. 1–3, 1974–5).

Lamma, P., Comneni e Staufer, 2 vols. (Istituto storico italiano per il medio evo, Studi storici 14–18, 22–5, 1955 and 1957).

Lange, K.-H., Der Herrschaftsbereich der Grafen von Northeim 950 bis 1144 (Studien und Vorarbeiten zum historischen Atlas Niedersachsens, 24, 1969).

Läwen, G., Die herzogliche Stellung Heinrichs des Löwen in Sachsen (diss. Königsberg, 1937).

Lechner, K., Die Babenberger (Veröffentl. des Instituts für österreichische Geschichtsforschung, 23, 2nd edn., 1976).

Mitteis, H., Politische Prozesse des früheren Mittelalters in Deutschland und Frankreich (Sitzungsberichte der Heidelberger Akademie der Wissenschaften, phil.-hist. Klasse 1926–7. 3, 1927).

Opll, F., Das Itinerar Kaiser Friedrichs I. (Forschungen zur Kaiser- und Papstgeschichte des Mittelalters, suppl. to F. J. Böhmer, Regesta Imperii, vol. i, 1978).

Patze, H., 'Kaiser Friedrich Barbarossa und der Osten', in Probleme des 12. Jahrhunderts (Vorträge und Forschungen, Konstanzer Arbeitskreis für mittelalterliche Geschichte, 12, 1968), pp. 337 ff.

Petke, W., Die Grafen von Wöltingerode-Wohldenberg (Veröffentl. des Instituts für historische Landesforschung der Universität Göttingen, 4, 1971).

Prinz, F., 'Bayern vom Zeitalter der Karolinger bis zum Ende der Welfenherrschaft. Die innere Entwicklung', in Handbuch der bayerischen Geschichte, ed. M. Spindler, vol. i (1967), pp. 268 ff.

Rassow, P., Honor Imperii. Die neue Politik Friedrich Barbarossas 1152–1159 (2nd edn., 1961).

Reindel, K., 'Bayern vom Zeitalter der Karolinger bis zum Ende der Welfenherrschaft. Die politische Entwicklung', in Handbuch der bayerischen Geschichte, vol. i (1967), pp. 183 ff.

Reinecke, K., Studien zur Vogtei- und Territorialentwicklung im Erzbistum Bremen (937–1184) (Einzelschriften des Stader Geschichts- und Heimatvereins, 23, 1971).

Riezler, S. von, Geschichte Baierns, vol. i, pt. 2 (2nd edn., 1927, repr. 1964).

Schmid, K., Graf Rudolf von Pfullendorf und Kaiser Friedrich I. (Forschungen zur oberrheinischen LG, 1, 1954).

Schulze, H. K., Adelsherrschaft und Landesherrschaft (Mitteldeutsche Forschungen, 29, 1963).

Simonsfeld, H., Jahrbücher des Deutschen Reiches unter Friedrich I., vol. i (1908, repr. 1967).

*Starke, H.-D., 'Die Pfalzgrafen von Sommerschenburg (1088–1179)', Jb.
für die Geschichte Mittel- und Ostdeutschlands*, 4 (1955), 1 ff.
(Quellen und Darstellungen zur Geschichte Niedersachsens, 57, 1959).
Wadle, E., *Reichsgut und Königsherrschaft unter Lothar III. (1125–1137)*
(Schriften zur Verfassungsgeschichte, 12, 1969).

SURVEY OF PRINCIPAL SOURCES AND LITERATURE

Chronicles and Annals. A critical survey is now available in W. Wattenbach
and F. J. Schmale, *Deutschlands Geschichtsquellen im Mittelalter vom Tode
Heinrichs V. bis zum Ende des Interregnums*, vol. i (1976). The main
contemporary sources for the history of Henry the Lion, dating from
between 1163 and 1172, are the *Cronica Slavorum* by Helmold of Bosau, ed.
B. Schmeidler, *MGH SS rer. Germ.* (3rd edn., 1937)—also published, with a
German translation, by H. Stoob, *Ausgewählte Quellen zur deutschen
Geschichte des Mittelalters*, 19 (2nd edn., 1973), and its continuation, dating
from about 1210, the *Cronica Slavorum* by Arnold of Lübeck, ed. M.
Lappenberg, *MGH SS rer. Germ.* (1868).

Among contemporary North German annals, important information on
the duke's history is furnished by the *Annales Palidenses* (Pöhlde in the Harz
district), *Pegavienses* (Pegau near Merseburg), *Magdeburgenses*, and *Stederburgenses* (Steterburg near Wolfenbüttel), also the *Annales Stadenses* compiled in the mid-thirteenth century by Albert of Stade (all in *MGH SS* 16).
The main source for imperial history in the first years of Frederick I's reign,
down to 1160, is the *Gesta Friderici imperatoris* by Otto of Freising and his
continuator Rahewin, ed. G. Waitz and B. von Simsor, *MG SS rer. Germ.*
(3rd edn., 1912) and, with a German translation by A. Schmidt, ed. F. J.
Schmale in *Ausgewählte Quellen . . .*, 17 (2nd edn., 1974). The basic source
for the early Welfs and the history of the dynasty in South Germany is
Historia Welforum, ed. E. König, Schwäbische Chroniken der Stauferzeit,
vol. i (1938, repr. 1977).

[*Translator's note.* For English translations of Helmold and Otto/Rahewin
see respectively *The Chronicle of the Slavs by Helmold, priest of Bosau*, trans.
and ed. F. J. Tschan, New York, 1935, and *The Deeds of Frederick
Barbarossa*, trans. and ed. C. C. Mierow, New York, 1953.]

*Charters and Diplomata. Die Urkunden Heinrichs des Löwen, Herzogs von
Sachsen und Bayern*, ed. K. Jordan, *MGH* (1941–9), repr. 1957–60 =
UHdL). Of the imperial and royal charters of the Hohenstaufen we have so
far only Conrad III's diplomata, ed. F. Hausmann, *MGH DD* 9 (1969), and
the first volume, extending to 1158, of the diplomata of Frederick I, ed. H.
Appelt, *MGH DD* 10. 1 (1975). Important material on the history of Saxony

is to be found in *Regesten der Erzbischöfe von Bremen*, vol. i, ed. O. H. May (1937) (= May, *Reg.*); *Regesten der Erzbischöfe von Köln im Mittelalter*, vol. ii, ed. R. Knipping (1901) (= Knipping, *Reg.*); and *Regesten der Markgrafen von Brandenburg aus askanischem Haus*, ed. H. Krabbo (1910–) (= Krabbo, *Reg.*).

Narrative accounts. For the annals of the Empire under Frederick I we have only the first volume, ed. Simonsfeld (*Jahrbücher des Deutschen Reiches . . .*, 1908), extending to 1158; hence Giesebrecht's *Deutsche Kaiserzeit* (see bibliography above) is still important for the imperial history of the time. The account of Frederick I's reign by Cartellieri, published in 1972, was completed shortly after 1945. Still valuable are K. Hampe, *Deutsche Kaisergeschichte in der Zeit der Salier und Staufer*, ed. F. Baethgen (12th edn., 1968), and id., *Das Hochmittelalter* (6th edn., 1977). For a shorter survey: O. Engels, *Die Staufer* (2nd edn., 1977). The most recent account of the period, important for the new questions it raises, is H. Fuhrmann, *Deutsche Geschichte im hohen Mittelalter* (Deutsche Geschichte, ed. J. Leuschner, vol. ii, 1978).

Important new collections of essays. Probleme des 12. Jahrhunderts (Vorträge und Forschungen, Konstanzer Arbeitskreis für mittelalterliche Geschichte, 12, 1968); *Friedrich Barbarossa*, ed. G. Wolf (Wege der Forschung 390, 1975); *Die Zeit der Staufer* (catalogue of Stuttgart exhibition, 1977), vol. iii, *Aufsätze* (essays), vol. iv, *Karten und Stammtafeln* (maps and genealogies).

Recent biographies of Frederick I. K. Jordan, *Friedrich Barbarossa* (2nd edn., 1967); M. Pacaut, *Frédéric Barberousse* (1967, German trans. 1969, English trans. 1970); P. Munz, *Frederick Barbarossa* (1969; see, however, *HZ* 211, pp. 120 ff.).

Henry the Lion. The older biographies—those by H. Prutz, *Heinrich der Löwe, Herzog von Baiern und Sachsen* (1865), and M. Philippson, *Geschichte Heinrichs des Löwen, Herzogs von Bayern und Sachsen und der staufisch-welfischen Politik seiner Zeit*, 2 vols. (1867, 2nd edn. in 1 vol. entitled *Heinrich der Löwe und seine Zeit*, 1918)—are out of date and only have a certain value for the material they contain. A briefer account in A. L. Poole, *Henry the Lion* (The Lothian Historical Essay for 1912), 1912. An erroneous view in E. Gronen, *Die Machtpolitik Heinrichs des Löwen und sein Gegensatz gegen das Kaisertum* (Historische Studien, 139, 1919). A useful conspectus of the source material in chronological order in J. Heydel, *Das Itinerar Heinrichs des Löwen* (see bibliography). More recent, briefer assessments: K. Hampe, 'Heinrich der Löwe', in id., *Herrschergestalten des deutschen Mittelalters* (7th edn., 1967), pp. 194 ff.; H. H. Jacobs, *Heinrich der Löwe* (Colemans kleine Biographien, 24, 1933); H. Mau, *Heinrich der*

Löwe (1943); Th. Mayer, 'Friedrich I. und Heinrich der Löwe', in *Kaisertum und Herzogsgewalt im Zeitalter Friedrichs I.* (Schriften des Reichsinstituts für ältere deutsche Geschichtskunde, 9, 1944), pp. 365 ff., also published separately in 1958; K. Jordan, 'Heinrich der Löwe', in *Neue deutsche Biographie*, vol. viii (1969), pp. 388 ff. More literary in style are P. Barz, *Heinrich der Löwe* (1977) and H. Hiller, *Heinrich der Löwe* (1978).

REFERENCES TO PARTICULAR CHAPTERS

Chapter 1

Welf historiography in the 12th century: K. Schmid, 'Welfisches Selbstverständnis', in *Adel und Kirche. Festschrift für G. Tellenbach* (1968), 389 ff.; O. G. Oexle, 'Die "sächsische Welfenquelle" als Zeugnis der welfischen Hausüberlieferung', *DA* 24 (1968), 435 ff.; id., 'Bischof Konrad von Konstanz in der Erinnerung der Welfen und der welfischen Hausüberlieferung während des 12. Jahrhunderts', *Freiburger Diöz.-Archiv*, 95 (1975), 7 ff.— The Frankish origin of the Welfs has been clarified by J. Fleckenstein, 'Über die Herkunft der Welfen und ihre Anfänge in Süddeutschland', in *Studien und Vorarbeiten zur Geschichte des grossfränkischen und frühdeutschen Adels*, ed. by G. Tellenbach (Forschungen zur oberrhein. LG 4, 1957), pp. 71 ff.; cf. also G. Tellenbach, 'Über die ältesten Welfen im West- und Ostfrankenreich', ibid., pp. 335 ff., and G. Schnath, 'Neue Forschungen zur ältesten Geschichte des Welfenhauses', *Nds. Jb.* 31 (1959), 255 ff., with new genealogical tree.—On 'Henry of the golden wain' see W. Metz in *Bl. dt. LG* 107 (1971), 136 ff.

Genealogy of the later Welfs: still important is F. Curschmann, *Zwei Ahnentafeln. Ahnentafeln Kaiser Friedrichs I. und Heinrichs des Löwen* (Mitteil. der Zentralstelle für deutsche Personen- und Familiengeschichte, 27, 1921).—History of the Welf estates: R. Goes, 'Die Hausmacht der Welfen in Süddeutschland' (diss. Tübingen, 1960, typescript); H. Schwarzmaier, 'Hochadelsbesitz im 12. Jh. (Zähringer-Welfen)', map V 3 with explanations, in *Historischer Atlas von Baden-Württemberg* (1974).— Foundation of monasteries: E. König, *Die süddeutschen Welfen als Klostergründer* (1934); C. Buhl, 'Weingarten-Altdorf, die Anfänge', in *Weingarten 1056–1956, Festschrift zur 900–Jahrfeier des Klosters* (1956), pp. 12 ff.—Welf beginnings in Bavaria: Riezler, *Geschichte* vol. 1. pt. 2, pp. 116 ff., and Reindel in *Handbuch der bayer. Geschichte* vol. i, pp. 246 ff.

Lothair III. Still important as a collection of material is W. Bernhardi, *Lothar von Supplinburg* (Jbb. der deutschen Geschichte, 1879, repr. 1975); individual works cited by Jordan in Gebhardt-Grundmann vol. i, pp. 369 ff. (paperback edn., pp. 90 ff.). On the royal election H. Stoob, 'Die Königswahl Lothars von Sachsen', in *Historische Forschungen für W. Schlesinger* (1974), pp. 438 ff.

Changing conditions around 1100: K. Jordan, 'Das Zeitalter des Investiturstreites als politische und geistige Wende des abendländischen Hochmittelalters', *Geschichte in Wissenschaft und Unterricht*, 23 (1972), 513 ff.; Classen, pp. 411 ff., and especially Fuhrmann, *Deutsche Geschichte*, pp. 39 ff.

Duchy of Bavaria: Prinz in *Handbuch der bayer. Geschichte*, vol. i, pp. 302 ff.—Duchy of Saxony: Jordan, 'Herzogtum und Stamm', pp. 1 ff.; id., 'Sachsen und das deutsche Königtum', pp. 529 ff. On particular questions: H.-J. Freytag, *Die Herrschaft der Billunger in Sachsen* (Studien und Vorarbeiten zum historischen Atlas Niedersachsens, 20, 1951); R. G. Hucke, *Die Grafen von Stade 900–1144* (Einzelschriften des Stader Geschichts- und Heimatvereins, 8, 1956); Lange, *Herrschaftsbereich*.

Lothair as duke: Vogt, esp. pp. 4 ff. and regests, pp. 148 ff.; H. Stoob, 'Die sächsische Herzogswahl im Jahre 1106', in *Landschaft und Geschichte, Festschrift für F. Petri* (1970), pp. 499 ff. On Lothair's dynastic policy during his period as duke see also Wadle, pp. 141 ff.

Northern and eastern parts of the Empire under Lothair: Jordan, 'Heinrich der Löwe und Dänemark', pp. 16 ff.; Hoffmann, pp. 115 ff.; Hein, pp. 127 ff.; H. Stoob, 'Gedanken zur Ostseepolitik Lothars III.', in *Festschrift für F. Hausmann* (1978), pp. 531 ff. For a general assessment: F. J. Schmale, 'Lothar und Friedrich I. als Könige und Kaiser', in *Probleme des 12. Jahrhunderts*, pp. 33 ff., repr. in the collection of essays *Friedrich Barbarossa*, pp. 121 ff.

Conrad III. Still important for its material is W. Bernhardi, *Konrad III.* (Jbb. der deutschen Geschichte, 1883, repr. 1975); individual works cited by Jordan in Gebhardt-Grundmann vol. i, pp. 377 ff. (paperback edn., pp. 104 ff.). A recent survey of his reign by F. Hausmann: 'Die Anfänge des staufischen Zeitalters unter Konrad III.' in *Probleme des 12. Jahrhunderts*, pp. 53 ff.

Henry the Proud. A biography is still lacking. For his trial: Mitteis, pp. 42 ff.—The surname 'Leo' used for him: Helmold, chs. 35 and 56; cf. the lost Paderborn Annals for 1138: 'similis factus leoni in operibus suis', P. Scheffer-Boichorst, *Annales Patherbrunnenses* (1870), p. 167, also the *Chronica Regia Coloniensis* (Cologne), ed. by G. Waitz, *MGH SS rer. Germ.* (1880), p. 76.— On the coinage of Henry the Proud and Welf VI see Jesse, p. 26, and G. Braun von Stumm, 'Der Münzfund von Merzig', in *Bericht VI. der staatlichen Denkmalspflege im Saarland* (1953), 83 ff., esp. 112 f.

Chapter 2

Date of Henry the Lion's birth: indication of his age at death, *Annales Stederburgenses*, *MGH SS* 16, 231. The *Annales Welfici Weingartenses*, ed. König, *Historia Welforum*, p. 88, give 1135 as the year of his baptism; but, as they record that Henry the Proud went to Italy in the same year, 1136 is also a possibility: König, p. 123 n. 156. For 1134–5 as the date of birth see esp. A. Hofmeister, 'Puer, Iuvenis, Senex', in *Papsttum und Kaisertum, Festschrift für P. Kehr* (1926), pp. 287 ff., esp. pp. 309 f.; Heydel, p. 2; König p. 123 n. 156 and, with further arguments, K. Feldmann, 'Welf VI., Schwaben und das Reich', *Zs. für württemb. LG, 30 (1971), 317 ff.*—1129–30 as the date of birth is maintained by K. Hampe, 'Zu Heinrichs des Löwen 800. Geburtstag', *Braunschweigisches Magazin* 1929, cols. 81 f., and H. Grundmann, *Der Cappenberger Barbarossakopf* (Münsterische Forschungen, 12, 1959), p. 29.

Fighting after the death of Henry the Proud: Bernhardi, p. 128 ff.; Büttner, 'Staufer und Welfen', pp. 36 ff. (repr., pp. 355 ff.); Feldmann, 'Welf IV und sein Sohn', pp. 13 ff.—Weinsberg: K. Weller, 'Die neuere Forschung über die Geschichte von den treuen Weinsberger Weibern', *Zs. für württemb. LG* 4 (1940), 1 ff.

Nordalbingia from 1137 onwards: Jordan, 'Nordelbingen', pp. 33 ff.—Foundation of Lübeck: Helmold, ch. 57, also Am Ende, pp. 92 ff.; Jordan, 'Lübeck', pp. 143 ff.; G. Fehring, 'Neue archäologische Erkenntnisse und Entdeckungen zur frühen Geschichte der Hansestadt Lübeck', *Der Wagen, ein lübeck. Jb.* (1978), 165 ff. The view that a German trading settlement existed from the time of Lothair III onwards on the river island of Bucu near Alt-Lübeck was put forward by H. Stoob in a paper entitled 'Schleswig-Lübeck-Wisby' and delivered to a Baltic colloquium at Lübeck in 1977; thanks to his kindness I have been able to see this in MS.

Stade inheritance: besides the Stade Annals, *MGH SS* 16, p. 324, the principal source consists in the diplomata of Conrad III, *DCo* 122, 123, and 125, supplemented by Helmold, ch. 102; also Glaeske, pp. 143 ff., Patze, pp. 342 ff., and esp. M. Hohmann, 'Das Erzstift Bremen und die Grafschaft Stade im 12. und frühen 13. Jahrhundert', *Stader Jb.* (1969), 64 ff.

Acquisition of the Boyneburg inheritance by the Winzenburgers: Lange, *Herrschaftsbereich*, pp. 125 ff.; Jordan, 'Das politische Kräftespiel', pp. 1048 ff.—Dispute over Fischbeck and Kemnade: K. Lübeck, 'Korveys Kampf um das Stift Kemnade', *Westfäl. Zs.*, 101–2 (1953), 401 ff.; H. W. Krumwiede, *Das Stift Fischbeck an der Weser* (Studien zur Kirchengeschichte Niedersachsens, 9, 1958), pp. 98 ff., and F. Stephan-Kühn, *Wibald als Abt von Stablo und Corvey und im Dienst Konrads III.* (diss., Cologne, 1973), pp. 96 ff.

Diet of Frankfurt, 1147: Bernhardi, pp. 545 ff.—Wendish crusade: besides Helmold, chs. 62 ff., the main sources are the Magdeburg Annals, *MGH SS* 16, p. 188. For an assessment see esp. H. D. Kahl, 'Zum Ergebnis des Wendenkreuzzuges von 1147', *Wichmann-Jb.*, 11–12 (1957/8), pp. 99 ff., repr. in *Heidenmission und Kreuzzugsgedanke in der deutschen Ostpolitik des Mittelalters*, ed. H. Beumann (1963), pp. 275 ff. Also F. Lotter, 'Bemerkungen zur Christianisierung der Abodriten', in *Festschrift für W. Schlesinger*, 2 (Mitteldeutsche Forschungen 74. 2, 1972), pp. 395 ff., and id.,

Die Konzeption des Wendenkreuzzugs (Vorträge und Forschungen, Konstanzer Arbeitskreis für mittellterliche Geschichte, Sonderband 23, 1977). Expedition against Ditmarsh: *UHdL* 12, also H. Stoob, 'Meldorf als Landesvorort Dithmarschens in staufischer Zeit', in *700 Jahre Meldorf* (1965), pp. 41 ff.—Dispute over the Danish crown: Jordan, 'Heinrich der Löwe und Dänemark', pp. 19 ff.

Dispute with Hartwig of Bremen: Helmold, ch. 69, and Jordan, *Bistumsgründungen*, pp. 81 ff.; Glaeske, pp. 155 ff.; Hoffmann, pp. 131 ff.

Conrad's policy during and after the Second Crusade: Rassow, pp. 26 ff.; Heilig, pp. 146 ff.; W. Ohnsorge, *Das Zweikaiserproblem im früheren Mittelalter* (1947), pp. 91 ff.; Lamma, vol. i, pp. 56 ff.

Henry's marriage to Clementia: Helmold, ch. 68.—Fighting in South Germany: Feldmann, pp. 27 ff.—Conrad's advance into Saxony: Helmold, ch. 72.

Chapter 3

For the first years of Frederick I's reign: Simonsfeld and now Cartellieri, pp. 3 ff.—Frederick's election: O. Engels, Beiträge zur Geschichte der Staufer im 12. Jh. (I), *DA* 27 (1971), 373 ff., esp. 399 ff., expressing the view that Henry the Lion may originally have been a candidate, and H. Appelt, 'Heinrich der Löwe und die Wahl Friedrich Barbarossas', in *Festschrift für H. Wiesflecker* (1973), pp. 39 ff., with evidence of a meeting between Frederick and Henry before the election.

The question of the advocacy for Goslar is still in dispute owing to the inadequacy of sources. The view argued by Jordan, 'Goslar und das Reich', pp. 62 ff., S. Wilke, *Das Goslarer Reichsgebiet und seine Beziehungen zu den territorialen Nachbargewalten* (Veröffentl. des Max-Planck-Instituts für Geschichte, 32, 1970, pp. 100 ff.), and H. Lubenow, 'Heinrich der Löwe und die Reichsvogtei Goslar', *Nds. Jb.* 45 (1973), 337 ff., is that Frederick I granted the advocacy as a fief to Henry the Lion, who in turn granted it to his *ministerialis* Anno. On the other hand Heinemann, pp. 237 ff., Petke, *Wöltingerode*, pp. 303 ff., and id., 'Pfalzstadt und Reichsministerialität, *Bl. dt. LG* (1973), 270 ff. (somewhat less categorically in this case) maintain that Frederick granted the fief directly to Anno. On the whole question cf. Jordan, 'Harzraum', pp. 177 ff.

Arbitration of the dispute over the Danish crown: E. Hoffmann, *Königserhebung und Thronfolgeordnung in Dänemark bis zum Ausgang des Mittelalters* (Beiträge zur Geschichte und Quellenkunde des Mittelalters, 5, 1976), pp. 88 ff.

Privilege for Weissenau: *UHdL* 15, also Büttner, 'Staufer und Welfen', pp. 42 f. (repr. pp. 362 f.) and Bradler, p. 3.

Lawsuit and negotiations for Bavaria down to 1156: most recently H. Fichtenau, *Von der Mark zum Herzogtum* (2nd edn., 1965), pp. 30 ff.:

H. Appelt, *Privilegium minus* (1973), pp. 32 ff., and Lechner, pp. 142 ff. The investiture privilege granted to Henry: *DF* I 80, also Jordan, *Bistumsgründungen*, pp. 85 f., and Classen, p. 435.
Treaty of Constance: *DF* I 51 and 52; for its interpretation esp. Rassow, pp. 45 ff.
First Italian expedition: Simonsfeld, pp. 233 ff.; on Frederick's itinerary also Opll, pp. 13 ff.—Henry's agreement with the margraves of Este: *UHdL* 30.—Events at the imperial coronation: critical review of sources in Simonsfeld, *Exkurs* vol. v, pp. 689 ff.
Diet of Regensburg, 1156: Otto of Freising, *Gesta* vol. ii, ch. 55, ed. Waitz, p. 160, and, with German trans., in Appelt, *Privilegium minus*, pp. 100 ff. The *Privilegium* most recently printed in *DF* I 151, with a discussion of problems of source-criticism; German trans. in Appelt, *Privilegium*, pp. 97 f. The view most recently put forward by Heilig, pp. 48 ff., that a second copy of the diploma, no longer extant, was made for Henry the Lion is untenable: cf. H. Fichtenau, 'Zur Überlieferung des Privilegium minus', *MIÖG* 73 (1965), 1 ff. The literature on these events is voluminous: I will cite only H. Büttner, 'Das politische Handeln Friedrich Barbarossas im Jahre 1156', *Bl. dt. LG* 106 (1970), 54 ff., and the above-mentioned works by Fichtenau, pp. 36 ff.; Appelt, pp. 49 ff.; and Lechner, pp. 154 ff.—On the much debated question as to which were the three counties that, according to Otto of Freising, had always belonged to the March, see now Lechner, pp. 159 ff., and M. Weltin, 'Die "tres comitatus" Ottos von Freising und die Grafschaften der Mark Österreich', *MIÖG* 84 (1976), 31 ff.

Reinald of Dassel: R. M. Herkenrath, 'Rainald von Dassel, Reichskanzler und Erzbischof von Köln' (diss. Graz, 1962, typescript); W. Grebe, 'Studien zur geistigen Welt Rainalds von Dassel', *Ann. des hist. Vereins für den Niederrhein*, 171 (1969), 5 ff., repr. in the collection of essays *Friedrich Barbarossa*, pp. 245 ff. For his background also W. Föhl, 'Studien zu Reinald von Dassel', *Jb. Köln. Gesch.-Verein*, 17 (1935), 234 ff., and 20 (1938), 238 ff. In 1156 he is mentioned as witness to a document of Henry the Lion's: *UHdL* 34.

End of the contest for the Danish throne: Jordan, 'Heinrich der Löwe und Dänemark', pp. 21 ff.

Barbarossa's Polish campaign: Simonsfeld, pp. 545 ff.

Diet of Besançon: W. Heinemeyer, ' "beneficium—non feudum, sed bonumfactum". Der Streit auf dem Reichstag zu Besançon 1157', *AfD* 15 (1969), 155 ff. Henry as mediator: Jordan, 'Heinrich der Löwe und das Schisma', pp. 226 ff. The date of the punitive expedition against the counts of Eppen is uncertain: it has sometimes been put in 1158, but according to the itinerary 1159 is more probable: Heydel, p. 46.

Frederick I's arbitration between Henry and Otto of Freising: *DF* I 218. For the foundation of Munich see under Chapter 7 below.

Settlement with Bremen: Frederick I's documents of March–April 1158 relating to the Bremen church, now in *DF* I 208–10, 213 and 214; that of June 1158, *DF* I 219; cf. Glaeske, pp. 162 f., and Patze, pp. 363 f.

Frederick I's second Italian expedition: Giesebrecht vol. v, pp. 141 ff., and vol. vi, pp. 359 ff.; Cartellieri, pp. 78 ff.—On the diet of Roncaglia V. Colorni, 'Le tre leggi perdute di Roncaglia (1158), ritrovate in un manuscritto parigiano', in *Scritti in memoria di A. Giuffrè* (1967), pp. 111 ff.; German trans. by G. Dolazelek (Untersuch. zur deutschen Staats- und Rechtsgeschichte, NF 12, 1969).—For Henry's part in the campaign in 1159–60 and 1161 see Heydel, p. 46, with detailed itinerary.

Disputed papal election: J. Haller, *Das Papsttum* vol. iii (2nd edn. 1952, repr. 1962), pp. 145 ff. Henry's position: Jordan, 'Heinrich der Löwe und das Schisma', pp. 227 ff.

Diet of the princes at Erfurt: sources in Heydal, p. 48.

Siege of Milan. The detailed account in Giesebrecht vol. v, pp. 278 ff., and vol. vi, pp. 400 ff., is still valuable. The statement that Frederick I designated as his successor, in the event of his death, his nephew Duke Frederick of Swabia and, as second choice, Henry the Lion can be found in Sigebert of Gembloux, *Auctarium Affligemense*, *MGH SS* 6, p. 408, now ed. P. Gorissen (Verhandel. van de Koninkl. Vlaamse Acad. voor Wetenschappen . . . Klassen der Letteren Nr. 15, 1952), p. 143.

Events on the Saône: W. Heinemeyer, 'Die Verhandlungen an der Saône im Jahre 1162', *DA* 20 (1964), 155 ff.; F. J. Schmale, 'Friedrich I. und Ludwig VII. im Sommer des Jahres 1162', *Zs. für bayer. LG* 31 (1968), 315 ff., and Kienast, pp. 204 ff., with reproduction of sources pp. 669 ff.

Divorce of Clementia: *Annales Welfici Weingartenses* for 1162, ed. König, *Historia Welforum*, p. 90. According to Giselbert of Mons in his chronicle of Hainault (ed. L. Vanderkindere, 1904, p. 65), the Emperor pressed for the divorce as he was afraid of too strong a combination between Welfs and Zähringer.—The sources do not agree as to whether Henry and Clementia had one or two daughters. The latter is more probable: cf. Eggert, 'Wendenzüge', pp. 67 ff., and Jordan, 'Heinrich der Löwe und Dänemark', p. 25 n. 55.

Chapter 4

For Henry's actions in Nordalbingia down to the beginning of the 1170s the most important sources, besides Helmold, are the duke's charters (partly forged, however) concerning the bishoprics of Oldenburg-Lübeck, Ratzeburg, and Schwerin, and some charters of Archbishop Hartwig of Bremen and Frederick I. For a critique of the documents cf. Jordan, *Bistumsgründungen*, pp. 13 ff.; for the actual events ibid., pp. 85 ff., and M. Hamann, pp. 68 ff.

Founding and endowment of the see of Ratzeburg: Helmold, ch. 77, and the duke's charter of 1158 (falsified in the 13th century), *UHdL* 41; also W. Prange, *Siedlungsgeschichte des Landes Lauenburg im Mittelalter* (Quellen und Forschungen zur Geschichte Schleswig-Holsteins 41, 1960), pp. 88 ff. Refoundation of Lübeck and code of laws for the citizens: Helmold, ch. 86. For the chronology: A. von Brandt, 'Zur Einführung und Begründung', *Zs. des Vereins für lübeck. Geschichte und Altertumskunde*, 39 (1959), pp. 1 ff.—The history of the foundation was for a long time a subject of lively controversy, aroused by the publication in 1921 of F. Rörig's study 'Der Markt von Lübeck' (repr. with his other works on the origins of Lübeck in his *Wirtschaftskräfte im Mittelalter*, 2nd edn., 1971), which advanced the view that a consortium of merchant entrepreneurs was the real basis of the civic foundation. This theory was afterwards considerably modified by Rörig himself, and the controversy has been overtaken by the results of more recent urban history. For the state of research at the end of the 1950s see Jordan, 'Städtepolitik', pp. 8 ff. More recent works are: Bärmann, *Städtegründungen, passim* (but the theory of a foundation based on mere right of lordship is not tenable); Diestelkamp, pp. 164 ff., esp. pp. 185 ff.; W. Schlesinger, 'Zur Frühgeschichte des norddeutschen Städtewesens', *Lüneburger Bl.* 17 (1966), pp. 5 ff.; W. Ebel, *Lübisches Recht* vol. i (1971), pp. 10 ff. and 128 ff.; B. Scheper, *Frühe bürgerliche Institutionen norddeutscher Hansestädte* (Quellen und Darstellungen zur hansischen Geschichte, NF 20, 1975), pp. 99 ff.; Am Ende, pp. 89 ff.; Jordan, 'Lübeck unter Graf Adolf I und Heinrich dem Löwen', pp. 148 ff.—On the question as to which provisions of the privilege granted to Lübeck by Frederick I in 1188 and forged in about 1225 (*UB der Stadt Lübeck* vol. i (1843), p. 8, no. 7; the operative clauses last printed in *Elenchus fontium historiae urbanae* vol. i (1967), p. 156, no. 95) were based on Henry the Lion's lost charter for the city, and on the probable date of that charter, see Am Ende, pp. 27 ff., and Jordan, 'Lübeck', pp. 153 ff. The Low German text of the alleged ordinance of Henry the Lion concerning the election of the Lübeck town council (*UHdL* 63) is an out-and-out forgery dating from the end of the thirteenth century. B. Scheper, in 'Über Ratsgewalt und Gemeinde in nordwestdeutschen Hansestädten des Mittelalters', *Nds. Jb.* 49 (1977), 87 ff., has considerably modified his original view (*Bürgerliche Institutionen*, pp. 115 ff. and 170 ff.) that the Lübeck municipal council was instituted by the duke in 1163.—As regards the *Vogt* (city governor), see G. W. von Brandt, 'Vogtei und Rektorat in Lübeck während des 13. Jahrhunderts', *Bl. dt. LG* (1971), 162 ff.

For the lost commercial treaties, known only from their subsequent confirmation, with Sweden and the principality of Novgorod: *UHdL* *115 and *116; also W. Rennkamp, *Studien zum deutsch-russischen Handel bis zum Ende des 13. Jahrhunderts. Nowgorod und Dünagebiet* (Bochumer historische Studien, mittelalterliche Geschichte, 2, 1977), pp. 29 ff. and 49 ff.

The most important sources for Valdemar I's expeditions to Mecklenburg and Hither Pomerania are Saxo, Gesta Danorum, lib. xix, chs. 25 ff., ed. J. Olrik and H. Raeder, vol. i (1931), pp. 427 ff., and the *Knytlinga Saga,* chs. 120 ff., ed. C. af Petersens and E. Olson (1919–23), pp. 264 ff. Their chronology has been established by Eggert, 'Wendenzüge', pp. 32 ff. On these expeditions and Valdemar's relations with Henry the Lion see id., 'Dänisch-wendische Kämpfe', pp. 1 ff.; Jordan, 'Heinrich der Löwe und Dänemark', pp. 23 ff.; Hamann, pp. 76 ff.

The fighting and settlement of 1160: Helmold, ch. 88.—City status of Schwerin: *UHdL* *46 and Jordan, 'Städtepolitik', pp. 16 f.; Bärmann, *Städtegründungen, passim.*—Transfer of the bishopric of Oldenburg to Lübeck: Helmold, ch. 90.

Charter for the Gotlanders: *UHdL* 48, also Rennkamp, op. cit.; Odelrich's advocacy, *UHdL* 49. The view often expressed by Scandinavian scholars—most recently A. E. Christensen, 'Das Artlenburg-Privileg und der Ostseehandel Gotlands und Lübecks im 12. und 13. Jahrhundert', *Nerthus,* 2 (1969), pp. 219 ff.—that Odelrich was not an advocate of the duke's in Gotland but one of his officials in Nordalbingia, is untenable. So is Christensen's theory of a later forgery of the privilege: cf. K. Jordan, 'Zu den Gotland-Urkunden Heinrichs des Löwen', *Hansische Geschichtsbl.* 91 (1973), pp. 24 ff., with earlier literature.

Endowment of the sees of Ratzeburg and Lübeck, and settlement of the question of tithes: Helmold, chs. 84 and 90; *UHdL* 52 for Ratzeburg, 59 and 60 for Lübeck; W. Prange, 'Die 300 Hufen des Bischofs von Lübeck', in *Aus Reichsgeschichte und Nordischer Geschichte* (Kieler Historische Studien, 16, 1972), pp. 244 ff. Archbishop Hartwig's charter: May, no. 549.

Tithe dispute in the see of Lübeck: Helmold, ch. 92.

Fighting in Mecklenburg: Hamann, pp. 85 ff.—Settlement of 1167: Helmold, ch. 103.

Settlement concerning the Ratzeburg and Lübeck dioceses: *UHdL* 81 and 82, also Jordan, *Bistumsgründungen,* pp. 110 ff.—Endowment of the see of Schwerin: *UHdL* 89.

Installation of Bishop Henry in Lübeck; laying of foundation stone of the cathedral: Arnold, lib. i, ch. 13 (p. 35).

Chapter 5

For Henry's possessions and lordships in Saxony the basic work is still L. Hüttebräuker, *Das Erbe Heinrichs des Löwen* (Studien und Vorarbeiten zum historischen Atlas von Niedersachsen, 9, 1927); also the two maps in *Geschichtlicher Handatlas von Niedersachsen* (1939): no. 29, Eigengüter Heinrichs des Löwen, and nos. 30–1, Der Machtbereich Heinrichs des Löwen.

Henry and his opponents: Hildebrand, pp. 209 ff., supplemented and corrected by later research.—Particular territories: Bremen: Reinecke, pp. 136 ff.; Hildesheim: Heinemann, pp. 225 ff.; K. Bogumil, *Das Bistum Halberstadt im 12. Jahrhundert* (Mitteldeutsche Forschungen, 69, 1972), pp. 235 ff.; D. Claude, *Geschichte des Erzbistums Magdeburg bis ins 12. Jahrhundert* vol. ii (Mitteldeutsche Forschungen, 67 II, 1975), pp. 71 ff.; the Ascanian dominions: H. K. Schulze, pp. 105 ff.; Sommerschenburg: Starke, pp. 1 ff., esp. 52 ff.; southern Saxony: K. A. Eckhardt, *Heinrich der Löwe an Werra und Oberweser* (Beiträge zur Geschichte der Werralandschaft 6, 2nd edn., 1958); H. Patze, *Die Entstehung der Landesherrschaft in Thüringen* vol. i (Mitteldeutsche Forschungen, 22, 1962), pp. 221 ff.; W. Schöntag, *Untersuchungen zur Geschichte des Erzbistums Mainz unter den Erzbischöfen Arnold und Christian I.* (Quellen und Forschungen zur hessischen Geschichte, 22, 1973), pp. 150 ff.

Henry's policy in the Harz district: Jordan, 'Harzraum', pp. 179 ff. The Riechenberg charter of 1154: *UHdL* 27. Frederick I's two charters of 1 Jan. 1158: *DF* I 199 and 200, also Patze, *Friedrich Barbarossa*, pp. 359 ff.

Westphalia: Hildebrand, pp. 275 ff., and A. K. Hömberg, *Westfalen und das sächsische Herzogtum* (Schriften der historischen Kommission Westfalens, 5, 1963), pp. 32 ff. However, the latter's view that ducal rule extended primarily to the districts of Engern and Westphalia is untenable: cf. G. Schnath's review in *Nds. Jb.* 35 (1963), 227 ff.—The words ascribed to Henry 'terminum ducatus sui Westphalie se extendere in quantum eques lanceam a littore Reni apud Tuicium in Renum sagittare posset' occur in a letter from Archbishop Philip of Cologne, recorded at a very late date: Knipping, *Reg.* 2, no. 1106; cf. Hömberg, p. 46 and n. 142.

Disputes with the counts of Schwalenberg: Läwen, pp. 14 ff.; F. Forwik, *Die staatsrechtiche Stellung der ehemaligen Grafen von Schwalenberg* (Geschichtliche Arbeiten zur westfälischen Landesforschung, 5, 1963), pp. 32 ff.; Hömberg, pp. 49 f.; Jordan, 'Das politische Kräftespiel', pp. 1058 ff. On Henry's proceedings, his two letters in *UHdL* 35, 36.—Measures against Count Henry of Arnsberg: Knipping, no. 809, and Hömberg, p. 47.

Fighting in Saxony. In the absence of a modern account, Giesebrecht vol. v (pp. 512 ff. and 606 ff.) and vol. vi (pp. 456 f. and 482 f.) are still important. The principal sources, including Helmold, chs. 103 f. and the various Saxon annals, esp. the *Pöhlder Annalen*, are collected in Krabbo *Reg.*, nos. 354 ff., and Knipping *Reg.*, nos. 854 and 896 f. On the chronology: Heydel, pp. 61 ff.—The letter from Bishop Albert of Freising on the planned conspiracy of 1163 is in H. Sudendorf, *Registrum oder merkwürdige Urkunden* vol. i (1849), p. 66, no. 24.—Defeat of Adalbert of Sommerschenburg: Starke, pp. 43 f.—On the fighting in eastern Saxony see also Hoppe, pp. 197 ff. (repr. pp. 54 ff.); D. Claude, *Geschichte des Erzbistums Magdeburg* vol. ii (1975), pp. 148 ff.—Agreement between the church of Cologne and the east Saxon princes: *UB des Erzstifts Magdeburg* vol. i (Geschichtsquellen der Provinz

Sachsen und des Freistaates Anhalt, NF 18, 1937), p. 421, no. 324.—Rumour of a grave defeat of Henry in a letter by John of Salisbury: J. C. O. Robertson, *Materials for the History of Thomas Becket* 6 (Rer. Brit. medii aevi SS. 67. 6, 1882), p. 415, no. 410; cf. Krabbo, *Reg.*, no. 366. Frederick I's attempts to make peace: Giesebrecht vol. v, pp. 613, 635 f. and 654 f.; vol. vi, pp. 484, 489, and 493; Cartellieri, pp. 247 ff.

Events in Bremen after Hartwig's death: Glaeske, pp. 165 ff.—The charter for Frederick of Mackenstedt: *UHdL* no. 88.

The acquisition of the inheritance of Otto of Assel is mentioned only quite briefly by Helmold, ch. 102. The Sommerschenburg inheritance: Starke, pp. 48 f.

Chapter 6

County administration under Lothair III and Henry the Lion: Hildebrand, pp. 359 ff.; Vogt, pp. 124 ff.; K. Mascher, *Reichsgut und Komitat am Südharz im Hochmittelalter* (Mitteldeutsche Forschungen, 9, 1957); Wadle, pp. 142 ff. and 209 ff.; Petke, pp. 261 ff.; Schulze, pp. 79 ff. on Lüchow and 90 ff. on Dannenberg.

Ministeriales: O. Haendle, *Die Dienstmannen Heinrichs des Löwen* (Arbeiten zur deutschen Rechts- und Verfassungsgeschichte, 8, 1930); H. Lubenow, 'Die welfischen Ministerialen in Sachsen' (diss. Kiel, 1964, typescript); on Lothair's *ministeriales*, also Wadle, pp. 161 ff.

Policy towards cities: a summary of earlier research in Jordan, 'Städtepolitik', pp. 1 ff.; brief survey in id., 'Burglöwe', pp. 13 ff.; also Bärmann, *Städtegründungen* (though dubious in many respects); Diestelkamp, 'Stadtgründungen', pp. 164 ff.—Recent literature on particular towns: Brunswick: M. Garzmann, *Stadtherr und Gemeinde in Braunschweig im 13. und 14. Jahrhundert* (Braunschweiger Werkstücke, 53, 1976), also important for the earlier period; on Henry the Lion, esp. pp. 126 ff.—Stade and Bremen: Reinecke, pp. 149 ff.; Jordan, 'Heinrich der Löwe und Bremen', in *Stadt und Land in der Geschichte des Ostseeraums. Festschrift für W. Koppe* (1973), pp. 11 ff.—Bardowick and Lüneburg: U. Reinhardt, 'Bardowick–Lüneburg–Lübeck', in *Lübeck 1226, Reichsfreiheit und frühe Stadt* (1976), pp. 207 ff.—Hanover: H. Plath, 'Die Anfänge der Stadt Hannover', *Hannov. Geschichtsbl.*, NF 15 (1961), pp. 167 ff.—(Hannoversch.-)Münden: K. Heinemeyer, 'Die Gründung der Stadt Münden', *Hess Jb. für LG* 23 (1973), 141 ff., with full bibliography; quite inadequate is R. Grenz, *Die Anfänge der Stadt Münden nach den Ausgrabungen in der St. Blasius-Kirche* (1973).—Göttingen: O. Fahlbusch, *Die Topographie der Stadt Göttingen* (Studien und Vorarbeiten zum historischen Atlas von Niedersachsen, 21, 1952), pp. 14 ff.—Haldensleben: B. Schwineköper, in *Die Kunstdenkmale des Kreises Haldensleben* (Die Kunstdenkmale im Bezirk Magdeburg, 1, 1961), pp. 316 ff.; id., 'Haldensleben', in *Provinz Sachsen, Anhalt*

(Handbuch der historischen Stätten Deutschlands, 11, 1975), pp. 174 ff.
Coinage: W. Jesse, 'Die Brakteaten Heinrichs des Löwen', *Braunschw. Jb.*
30 (1949), 10 ff.; id., *Münz- und Geldgeschichte*, pp. 26 ff.; id., *Der zweite Braktetenfund von Mödesse und die Kunst der Brakteaten zur Zeit Heinrichs des Löwen* (Braunschweiger Werkstücke 21, 1957); G. Welter, *Die Münzen der Welfen seit Heinrich dem Löwen*, 2 vols. (1971–3), esp. vol. i, 1 ff. and corresponding reproductions in vol. ii, tables 1 ff.—For Bremen in particular, G. A. Löning, *Das Münzrecht im Erzbistum Bremen* (Quellen und Studien zur Verfassungsgeschichte des Deutschen Reiches in Mittelalter und Neuzeit, 7. 3, 1937), pp. 74 ff.

Policy towards churches and monasteries: Hildebrand, pp. 393 ff., and Vogt, pp. 115 ff. On particular questions, esp. the legal situation of the monasteries of Bursfelde, Homburg, Northeim, and Reinhausen, which are sometimes obscure owing to forgery or distortion of ducal and other charters, see also Jordan, 'Studien zur Klosterpolitik Heinrichs des Löwen', *AUF* 17 (1941), 1 ff.

Administrative clergy: Hildebrand, pp. 417 ff.—Chapel and chancery: Hasenritter, esp. pp. 144 ff.; Jordan, introduction to edition of documents, pp. xx ff.

Nature of ducal power: Hildebrand, pp. 11 ff., rightly rejects the earlier view that Henry's aim was to revive the old 'stem' duchy; but her own theory that his rule was only a conglomeration of margraviate and county rights, advocacies, and lordships, is itself too one-sided. Cf., besides reviews of her book, Läwen, pp. 45 ff.; Jordan, 'Herzogtum und Stamm', pp. 24 ff., and esp. the balanced discussion in G. Schnath, *Vom Sachsenstamm zum Lande Niedersachsen* (1966), pp. 26 ff.—The expression 'stammesbezogenes Herzogtum' is from K. G. Hugelmann, *Stämme, Nation und Nationalstaat im deutschen Mittelalter*, vol. i (1955), p. 179.

Chapter 7

Henry's power base and policy in Bavaria: still important is Riezler, vol. i, pt. 2, pp. 297 ff. and 369 ff.; also R. Hildebrand, *Studien über die Monarchie Heinrichs des Löwen* (diss. Berlin, 1931), though this interprets Henry's policy too exclusively in economic terms. For the present state of research see Reindel in *Handbuch der bayer. Geschichte* vol. i, pp. 263 ff., and Prinz, ibid., pp. 270 ff.

Imperial property enfeoffed to the duke: H. C. Faussner, 'Herzog und Reichsgut im bairisch-österreichischen Rechtsgebiet im 12. Jahrhundert', *ZRG Germ. Abt.* 85 (1968), 1 ff.—On possessions and lordships in Swabia and on the Lech see also G. Bradler, *Studien zur Geschichte der Ministerialität im Allgäu und in Oberschwaben* (Göppinger Akademische Beiträge, 50, 1973), pp. 331 ff., and id., *Heinrich der Löwe in Oberschwaben*, pp. 2 ff.—On the controversial question whether the TTraungau belonged to Bavaria up to 1180 see Reindel, p. 263, with earlier literature, and Lechner, pp. 161 f. Foundation of Munich: extensive bibliography s.v. 'München' in *Bayerisches Städtebuch* pt. 2 (Deutsches Städtebuch 5. 2, 1974), pp. 394 ff. A summary of earlier research in Jordan, 'Städtepolitik', pp. 5 ff. Later studies in Bärmann, pp. 26 ff. and elsewhere, disputable in some details, and E. Pitzer, 'Der Föhringer Streit im Lichte des Rechtes und der Politik', *Sammelbl. des historischen Vereins Freising*, 25 (1965), 17 ff. Also M. Schattenhofer, 'Die Anfänge Münchens', in *Abensberger Vorträge*, 1977 (*Zs. für bayer. LG*, Beiheft 9, Reihe B, 1978), pp. 7 ff., with a critical review of the problems involved.

Landsberg: H. J. Rieckenberg, 'Landsberg-Phetine, ein Beitrag zur Geschichte der freiherrlichen Familie von Pfetten', *Bl. des bayer. Landesvereins für Familienkunde*, 27 (1964), 465 ff.; P. Fried, 'Die Stadt Landsberg am Lech in der Städtelandschaft des frühen bayerischen Territorialstaats', *Zs. für bayer. LG* 32 (1969), 68 ff.

Reichenhall: H. Vogel, 'Geschichte von Reichenhall', *Oberbayer. Archiv*, 94 (1971), 1 ff., esp. 21 ff.

Burghausen: Hildebrand, pp. 28 ff.

Regensburg: P. Schmid, *Regensburg, Stadt der Könige und Herzöge im Mittelalter* (Regensburger historische Forschungen, 6, 1977), pp. 180 ff. and *passim*.

Monasteries: Hildebrand, pp. 58 ff.—The Münsteuer dispute: P. Classen, 'Der Prozess um Münsteuer (1154–1176) und die Regalienlehre Gerhochs von Reichersberg', *ZRG Germ. Abt.* 77 (1960), pp. 324 ff.

Effects of the schism in Bavaria: Riezler, vol. i, pt. 2, pp. 316 ff.; R. Bauerreiss, *Kirchengeschichte Bayerns*, vol. iii (1951), pp. 64 ff.; Jordan, 'Heinrich der Löwe und das Schisma', pp. 227 ff. G. Hödl, 'Das Erzstift Salzburg und das Reich unter Kaiser Friedrich Barbarossa', *Mitteil. der Gesellschaft für Salzburger Landeskunde* 114 (1975), 37 ff.

Chapter 8

On Frederick I's policy from 1163 onwards see Giesebrecht, vol. v, pp. 382 ff., and vol. vi, pp. 422 ff.; Cartellieri, pp. 143 ff.

Manuel I's policy of alliances: Ohnsorge, *Zweikaiserproblem*, pp. 109 ff.; Lamma, vol. ii, pp. 88 ff. and 123 ff.; P. Classen, 'La politica di Manuele Comneno tra Federico Barbarossa e le città italiane', in *Popolo e stato in Italia nell'età di Federico Barbarossa* (Relazioni e communicazioni al XXXIII congresso storico subalpino, 1970), pp. 263 ff.; id., 'Die Komnenen und die Kaiserkrone des Westens', *Journal of Medieval History* 3 (1977), 207 ff.— Greek embassy to Brunswick: Helmold, ch. 101.

Reinald's embassy to England: sources collected in Knipping, *Reg.*, no. 816.

Diet of Würzburg, 1165: *MGH Const.* vol. i, pp. 314 ff., nos. 223–6;

Knipping, *Reg.*, no. 818; G. Rill, 'Zur Geschichte der Würzburger Eide von 1165', *Würzburger Diözesangeschichtsbl.* 22 (1960), 7 ff.

Frederick I's fourth expedition to Italy: Giesebrecht, vol. v, pp. 522 ff., and vol. vi, pp. 458 ff.; Cartellieri, pp. 196 ff. The Lombard League: G. Fasoli, 'Federico Barbarossa e le città lombarde', in *Probleme des 12. Jahrhunderts*, pp. 121 ff. (German trans. in the collective volume *Friedrich Barbarossa*, pp. 149 ff.); also her 'La Lega Lombarda—Antecedenti, formazione, struttura', in *Probleme*, op. cit., pp. 143 ff.; on particular questions also the contributions to *Popolo e stato . . .*, op. cit.

Henry's marriage to Matilda: esp. Helmold, ch. 106. The precise date appears from Henry's charter for the church at Minden, *UHdL* 77. Also H. Lubenow, 'Die politischen Hintergründe der Trauung Heinrichs des Löwen 1168 in Mindener Dom', *Mindener Heimatbl.* 40 (1968), 35 ff.

Embassy to Henry II and Louis VII. For the sources, which in part vary considerably, see Knipping, *Reg.*, nos. 915–17; also Kienast, pp. 222 f. The latter, referring to the account by Stephan of Rouen, even thinks it possible that Frederick I, as successor to Charlemagne, claimed the French throne for himself and offered to confer it as a fief on Henry II's eldest son, the 'young king' Henry; but this is unlikely.

German–Byzantine negotiations from 1170 onwards: Lamma, pp. 227 ff. Meeting at Vaucouleurs: *MGH Const.* vol. i, p. 331, no. 237, and Kienast, p. 224.

Henry's pilgrimage: Arnold of Lübeck, lib. i, chs. 1–12; also E. Joranson, 'The Palestine Pilgrimage of Henry the Lion', in *Medieval and Historical Essays in Honor of J. W. Thompson* (1938), pp. 146 ff.—Henry's grant to the church of the Holy Sepulchre: *UHdL* 94. While Joranson emphasizes the religious character of the journey, W. Ohnsorge contends that it also had a strong political aspect: see his 'Die Byzanzpolitik Friedrich Barbarossas und der "Landesverrat" Heinrichs des Löwen', *DA* 6 (1943), 118 ff. (repr. in his *Abendland und Byzanz, Gesammelte Aufsätze*, 1958, pp. 456 ff.). However, the sources supply no evidence for Ohnsorge's belief that Henry held out to Manuel the prospect of territorial concessions by Frederick I in Italy: on this cf. also Lamma vol. ii, pp. 230 ff.

The story of Frederick I's alleged agreement with the duke's Saxon vassals is recorded in the *Cosmodromius* of Gobelinus Person, ed. H. Meibom, *Rerum Germanicarum*, vol. i (1688), p. 271. It deserves little credence, as was pointed out by K. Hampe ('Heinrichs des Löwen Sturz in historisch-politischer Beurteilung', *HZ* 109 (1912), 49 ff.) in reply to J. Haller, 'Der Sturz Heinrichs des Löwen', *AUF* 3 (1911), 326 ff.

Frederick I's territorial policy in Swabia: K. Schmid, esp. pp. 169 ff.; Büttner, 'Staufer und Welfen', pp. 54 f. (repr., pp. 375 f.); id., 'Staufische Territorialpolitik im 12. Jahrhundert', *Württemb.-Franken* 47 (1963), 5 ff.

The inheritance of Welf VI; the chief source is the *Continuatio*

Staingadensis to the *Historia Welforum*, ed. E. König, *Historia Welforum*, pp. 68 ff. On the dates of Welf's agreements with Henry and Frederick I: König, pp. 134 f.; Feldmann, 'Welf VI', pp. 73 ff.; on the importance of the inheritance see also H. Schwarzmaier, *Die Heimat der Staufer* (2nd edn., 1977), pp. 48 ff., and Bradler, *Heinrich der Löwe*, pp. 4 f.

Building activities in Brunswick: E. Döll, *Die Kollegiatstifte St. Blasius und St. Cyriacus zu Braunschweig* (Braunschweiger Werkstücke, 36, 1967), p. 34. For the specialized literature see below, p. 250, also as regards the Gmunden Evangeliarium. For the interpretation of the coronation picture see esp. J. Fried, 'Königsgedanken Heinrichs des Löwen', *Archiv für Kulturgesch.* 55 (1973), 312 ff., esp. 325 ff.

Henry's royal ambitions. The view expressed by H. Mau (*Heinrich der Löwe*, pp. 47 ff.) that Henry wished to set up a kingdom of his own in North Germany is developed in Fried, 'Königsgedanken', pp. 312 ff., and O. Engels, 'Neue Aspekte zur Geschichte Friedrich Barbarossas und Heinrichs des Löwen' in *Selbstbewusstsein und Politik der Staufer* (Schriften zur staufischen Geschichte und Kunst, 3, 1977), pp. 28 ff.

Chapter 9

Frederick I's fifth expedition to Italy: Giesebrecht, vol. v, p. 733, and vol. vi, p. 511; Cartellieri, pp. 319 ff.—Peace of Montebello: W. Heinemeyer, 'Der Friede von Montebello', *DA* 11 (1954–5), 101 ff.

Chiavenna: The theory that no meeting took place between the Emperor and the duke has in more recent times been chiefly advanced by F. Güterbock in *Der Prozess Heinrichs des Löwen* (1909), pp. 5 ff., and *Die Gelnhäuser Urkunde und der Prozess Heinrichs des Löwen* (Quellen und Darstellungen zur Geschichte Niedersachsens, 32, 1920), pp. 157 ff. However, this author subsequently conceded that there might have been a meeting: see his 'Über Otto von St. Blasien, Burchard von Ursberg und eine unbekannte Welfenquelle mit Ausblick auf die Chiavennafrage', in *Kritische Beiträge zur Geschichte des Mittelalters, Festschrift für R. Holtzmann* (Historische Studien, 238, 1933), pp. 191 ff. Güterbock's view was challenged by J. Haller, 'Der Sturz Heinrichs des Löwen', *AUF* 3 (1911), 297 ff., and K. Hampe, 'Heinrich der Löwe in politisch-historischer Beurteilung', *HZ* 109 (1912), 57 ff.—The demand for Goslar: Jordan, 'Goslar und das Reich', pp. 64 ff., with sources and earlier literature. The view of P. Munz—'Frederick Barbarossa and Henry the Lion in 1176', *Historical Studies, Australia and New Zealand*, 12 (1965), 1 ff., and *Frederick Barbarossa*, p. 310—that Henry made this demand in order to test Frederick's broader political aims does not seem to me to be tenable.

Preliminary peace of Anagni: *MGH Const.* vol. i, 349 ff., nos. 249 and 250.—Documents on the peace of Venice, ibid., pp. 360 ff., nos. 259–73; cf. Cartellieri, pp. 340 ff.

Fighting in Saxony from 1177 onwards: W. Biereye, 'Die Kämpfe gegen Heinrich den Löwen in den Jahren 1177–1181', in *Forschungen und Versuche zur Geschichte des Mittelalters und der Neuzeit, Festschrift für D. Schäfer* (1915), pp. 149 ff.; Hoppe, pp. 232 ff. (repr., pp. 85 ff.). On the chronology, which is not always certain, see Knipping, *Reg.*, nos. 1105 and 1137, and Heydel, pp. 87 ff.; for details also H. Grundmann, 'Rotten und Brabanzonen', *DA* 5 (1942), 419 ff.

Trial of Henry the Lion. The best edn. of the Gelnhausen diploma, the interpretation of which has been a subject of lively debate, is in Güterbock, *Gelnhäuser Urkunde*, pp. 23 ff. For the extensive later literature see Jordan in Gebhardt-Grundmann, p. 408 n. 3 (paperback edn., p. 154 n. 3). Important works, in addition to those by Güterbock and Haller already mentioned, are Mitteis, *Prozesse*, pp. 48 ff., and C. Erdmann, 'Der Prozess Heinrichs des Löwen', in *Kaisertum und Herzogsgewalt im Zeitalter Friedrichs I.* (Schriften des Reichsinstituts für ältere deutsche Geschichtskunde, 9, 1944), pp. 273 ff. However, Erdmann's theses are partly untenable: cf. H. Mitteis, 'Zur staufischen Verfassungsgeschichte', *ZRG Germ. Abt.* 65 (1947), 325 ff., repr. in id., *Die Rechtsidee in der Geschichte* (1957), pp. 490 ff. That the trials under customary law and under feudal law took place successively is clear from the Gelnhausen diploma. The date of the sentence of simple outlawry (*Acht*)—possibly 29 June 1179—follows from that of the *Oberacht* pronounced at the diet of Regensburg at the end of June 1180. It is impossible to accept Erdmann's view that the proceedings under customary law were stayed at the diet of Magdeburg in June 1179 and that the *Acht* was first pronounced together with the feudal judgement at Würzburg in January 1180; however, he is right in holding that a declaratory judgment concerning possible later outlawry (*Acht*) was pronounced at Worms in January 1179. Again, it is not possible to hold with Erdmann that a second trial under customary law took place following the first such trial—which was supposedly not brought to a conclusion—based on the charge of high treason brought by the Margrave Dietrich of Landsberg. When the Gelnhausen diploma speaks of 'evidens reatus maiestatis' (evident *lèse-majesté*) it clearly refers not to any kind of treason but to failure to appear before the king's court.

'Plot' by the Swabian magnates: Erdmann, pp. 315 ff.; K. Schmid, pp. 194 ff.; Bradler, pp. 3 ff.

Attitude of Henry II to the fall of Henry the Lion: F. Trautz, *Die Könige von England und das Reich 1272–1377. Mit einem Rückblick auf ihr Verhältnis zu den Staufern* (1961), pp. 73 f., with earlier literature.— Attitude of Philip II of France and Philip of Flanders: A. Cartellieri, *Philipp II. August*, vol. i (1900), pp. 71 ff., and appendices, pp. 45 ff.; Kienast, pp. 25 f.

On the fighting in 1180–1: Biereye, pp. 174 ff., and Hoppe, pp. 239 ff.

(repr., pp. 100 ff.). For the chronology see also Knipping, *Reg.* no. 1167, and Heydel, pp. 92 ff.

Diet of Altenburg: Riezler vol. i, pt. 2, pp. 360 ff.; M. Spindler in *Handbuch der bayer. Geschichte*, vol. ii (1969), pp. 15 ff.

Events at Lübeck: F. Curschmann, 'Die Belehnung Herzog Bogislavs I. im Lager vor Lübeck 1181', *Pommersche Jbb.* 31 (1937), 5 ff.; Jordan, 'Heinrich der Löwe und Dänemark', p. 28.

Diet of Erfurt: Giesebrecht, vol. v, pp. 943 ff., and vol. vi, pp. 578 ff.; Cartellieri, p. 391.

Effects of Henry's fall. Among more recent works on this often-discussed problem I would mention in particular Th. Mayer, 'Friedrich I. und Heinrich der Löwe', in *Kaisertum und Herzogsgewalt*, pp. 401 ff. (repr., pp. 56 ff.). Development of the estate of imperial princes: esp. E. E. Stengel, 'Land- und lehnrechtliche Grundlagen des Reichsfürstenstandes', *ZRG Germ. Abt.* 66 (1948), 294 ff., repr. in id., *Abhandlungen und Untersuchungen zur mittelalterlichen Geschichte* (1960), pp. 133 ff. On the Cologne duchy: G. Kallen, 'Das Erzstift Köln und der ducatus Westfalie et Angarie', *Jb. Köln. Geschichtsverein*, 31–2 (1957), 78 ff.

Leihezwang: W. Goez, *Der Leihezwang* (1962), pp. 226 ff., takes issue with the view, expressed in particular by H. Mitteis (*Lehnrecht und Staatsgewalt*, 1933, repr. 1958, pp. 690 ff., and *Der Staat des hohen Mittelalters*, 8th edn., 1968, pp. 264 ff.), that the principle of *Leihezwang* was enacted as a matter of imperial law in 1180. On the whole problem cf. H. G. Krause, 'Der Sachsenspiegel und das Problem des sogenannten Leihezwangs', *ZRG Germ.* 93 (1976), 21 ff.

Chapter 10

The period of exile: A. L. Poole, 'Die Welfen in der Verbannung', *DA* 2 (1938), pp. 129 ff.; R. Moderhack, Heinrich der Löwe und England', in *Braunschweiger Kalender* 1948, pp. 29 ff.—The two poems by Bertran: *Bertran de Born*, ed. A. Stimming (2nd edn., 1913), pp. 129 ff., nos. 34 and 35, also Introduction, pp. 16 f.; *Die Lieder Bertrans de Born*, ed. C. Appel (1932), pp. 18 ff., nos. 7 and 8. German trans. of no. 35 (Stimming) in F. Wellner, *Die Trobadors*, ed. H. G. Tuchel (1966), p. 129.

The court at Mainz, 1184: J. Fleckenstein, 'Friedrich Barbarossa und das Rittertum', in *Festschrift für H. Heimpel*, vol. ii (Veröffentl. des Max-Planck-Instituts für Geschichte, 36. 2, 1972), pp. 1023 ff.; Henry's presence there: Poole, 'Die Welfen', pp. 133 f.; Cartellieri, p. 408.—Philip of Cologne's journey to England: Knipping, *Reg.*, no. 1232, and Poole, p. 135.—Marriage plans for young Matilda: Poole, pp. 139 ff.

Nordalbingia after 1180: H.-J. Freytag, 'Der Nordosten des Reiches nach dem Sturz Heinrichs des Löwen', *DA* 25 (1969), 471 ff.

The letters in which Henry petitions the Emperor for the restoration of his honour and possessions and for help against his enemies (*UHdL*, nos. 137–9) are stylistic exercises, like most other letters in the later Hildesheim collection dating from the end of the 12th century, but may be based on actual requests by Henry. On the value of this collection as a source for the period *c.*1185–90 see B. Scheper, 'Beiträge zum Quellenwert der Hildesheimer Formelsammlung', *Nds. Jb.* 33 (1961), 223 ff., and F. Opll, 'Beiträge zur historischen Auswertung der jüngeren Hildesheimer Briefsammlung', *DA* 33 (1977), 473 ff., with earlier literature.

On the duke's seals see *UHdL*, pp. xlvi f.; reproductions of all seals in Hasenritter, *Siegeltafel*; on particular seals also the exhibition catalogue *Die Zeit der Staufer*, vol. i (1977), p. 44, nos. 65 and 66, with reproductions, vol. ii, nos. 13 and 14.

The court at Mainz, 1188: F. W. Wentzlaff-Eggebert, *Der Hoftag Jesu Christi 1188 in Mainz* (Vorträge des Instituts für europäische Geschichte Mainz, 32, 1962), and Fleckenstein, op. cit.

Diet of Goslar and Frederick I's proposals: Arnold, lib. iv, ch. 7; but see critical remarks in Giesebrecht, vol. vi, pp. 190 f., and Poole, 'Die Welfen', p. 141.

The Third Crusade: H. E. Mayer, *Geschichte der Kreuzzüge* (1965), pp. 129 ff.; trans. *The Crusades* (1972), pp. 134 ff.; E. Eickhoff, *Friedrich Barbarossa im Orient* (Deutsches Archäologisches Institut Istanbul, Mitteilungen, Beiheft 17, 1977).

Henry's return to Germany and fighting in Saxony: Arnold, lib. v, chs. 1 ff., and Freytag, pp. 494 ff.

Foundation of the Hamburg *Neustadt*: H. Reincke, 'Das städtebauliche Wesen und Werden Hamburgs bis zum Ausgang der Hansezeit', in id., *Forschungen und Skizzen zur Geschichte Hamburgs* (Veröffentl. aus dem Staatsarchiv der Hansestadt Hamburg, 3, 1951), pp. 7 ff., esp. 33 ff.; id., 'Die ältesten Urkunden der Hansestadt Hamburg', ibid., pp. 93 ff. For the lost charter issued by Henry see *UHdL* no. 123, and Reincke, pp. 158 ff. On pp. 161 ff. Reincke expresses the view that Henry granted a second charter to the town, also lost; but see review by the present author in *Hansische Geschichtsbl.* 71 (1952), pp. 93 f.

Peace of Fulda: Arnold, lib. v, ch. 3.

Henry VI's expedition to Italy, and desertion by Henry of Brunswick: most recently K. Jordan, 'Papst Cölestin III. und die Welfen zu Beginn seines Pontifikats', *AfD* 23 (1978), 242 ff.; the Pope's *privilegium*, *JL* 16376.

Further fighting in Germany: Freytag, pp. 497 ff.; Jordan, 'Papst Cölestin III.', p. 255.

Capture of Richard I and the negotiations for his release: all source material now in *UB zur Geschichte der Babenberger*, 4. 1 (1968), pp. 218 ff.; there also the most recent printing of the treaty between Henry VI and Richard, pp. 223 ff., no. 926. On the subject itself see Lechner, pp. 186 f.

Marriage of Henry of Brunswick: *Annales Stederburgenses, MGH SS* 16, p. 227; Arnold, lib. v, ch. 20 (p. 183).

Meeting at Tilleda: *Annales Stederburgenses*, p. 227.

Henry's last years and death: *Annales Stederburgenses*, p. 230; Arnold, lib. v, ch. 24 (p. 193).

Burial in Brunswick cathedral. Of the many works on the disputed question whether the duke's remains were those found in the excavations of 1935, I would mention only: E. Fischer, 'Heinrichs des Löwen sterbliche Überreste', *Welt als Geschichte* 12 (1952), 233 ff., with anthropological evidence; on the other hand, M. Hackenbroch and W. Holtzmann, 'Die angeblichen Überreste Heinrichs des Löwen', *DA* 10 (1954), 488 ff. The view that the remains are those of Henry is upheld by F. Bock, 'Um das Grab Heinrichs des Löwen in S. Blasien in Braunschweig', *Nds. Jb.* 31 (1959), 271 ff., with extract from report of the excavations. Most recently, with citation of all the literature, T. Schmidt, 'Die Grablege Heinrichs des Löwen im Dom zu Braunschweig', *Braunschweiger Jb.* 55 (1974), 250 ff., arguing that the remains found in the stone sarcophagus are those of the Duchess Matilda.

Chapter 11

Henry and the fine arts: the basic work is still G. Swarzenski, 'Aus dem Kunstkreis Heinrichs des Löwen', *Städel-Jb.* 7–8 (1932), 241 ff.

Brunswick cathedral: H. Meyer-Bruck, 'Die Stellung des Braunschweiger Domes in der sächsischen Baukunst des 12. Jahrhunderts' (diss. Göttingen, typescript, 1952); J. C. Klamt, *Die mittelalterlichen Monumentalmalereien im Dom zu Braunschweig* (diss., Berlin FU, 1968); a brief survey in A. Quast, *Der Sankt-Blasius-Dom zu Braunschweig, seine Geschichte und seine Kunstwerke*, 2nd edn., 1975.—Our Lady's altar: H.-H. Möller, 'Zur Geschichte des Marienaltars im Braunschweiger Dom', *Deutsche Kunst und Denkmalpflege*, 25 (1967), 107 ff.—The seven-branched candelabrum: P. Bloch, 'Siebenarmige Leuchter in christlichen Kirchen', *Wallraf-Richartz-Jb.* 23 (1961), 55 ff.—The Imervard cross: R. Haussherr, 'Das Imervardkreuz und der Volto-Santo-Typ', *Zs. für Kunstwissenschaft*, 16 (1962), 129 ff., and W. S(auerländer) in *Die Zeit der Staufer*, exhibition catalogue of 1977, vol. i, p. 343, no. 462, with earlier literature.—Processional cross: A. Fink, 'Das Imervardkreuz und das Triumpfkreuz Heinrichs des Löwen für den Braunschweiger Dom', *Braunschweigisches Magazin*, 31 (1925), cols. 65 ff.

Earliest wall-paintings. On the controversy between W. Berges and H. J. Rieckenberg, 'Eilbertus und Johannes Gallicus' (*Nachrichten der Akademie der Wissenschaften in Göttingen*, 1951, phil.-hist. Klasse Nr. 2) and R. Drögereit, 'Eilbertus und Johannes Gallicus', *Nds. Jb.* 24 (1952), 144 ff., as to whether the 'Johannes Gallicus' mentioned in an inscription is identical with

Henry the Lion's notary Johannes (cf. the two rejoinders in *Nds. Jb.* 25 (1953), 132 ff. and 142 ff.) see now Klamt, op. cit., pp. 181 ff. Dankwarderode castle: an up-to-date architectural account is lacking. Lübeck and Ratzeburg cathedrals: A. Kamphausen, *Die Baudenkmäler der deutschen Kolonisation in Ostholstein* (Studien zur schleswig-holsteinischen Kunstgeschichte, 3, 1938), pp. 68 ff. and 80 ff.; M. Venzmer, 'Der Dom zu Lübeck' (diss. Hamburg, 1957, typescript), and id., 'Der Lübecker Dom als Zeugnis bürgerlicher Kolonisationskunst', *Zs. des Vereins für lüb. Geschichte und Altertumskunde*, 39 (1959), 49 ff.; A. Kamphausen, *Der Ratzeburger Dom*, 1954.—Mandelsloh: H. J. Rieckenberg, 'Mandelsloh— ein Kirchenbau Heinrichs des Löwen?', *Nds. Jb.* 49 (1977), 303 ff.

Book illumination: F. Jansen, *Die Helmarshausener Buchmalerei zur Zeit Heinrichs des Löwen*, 1933; K.-H. Usener, 'Buchmalerei bis 1200', in *Kunst und Kultur im Weserraum 800–1600*, Ausstellung des Landes Nordrhein-Westfalen, Corvey, 1966, catalogue vol. ii, pp. 464 ff.; E. Krüger, *Die Schreib- und Malwerkstatt der Abtei Helmarshausen bis in die Zeit Heinrichs des Löwen* (Quellen und Forschungen zur hessischen Geschichte, 21. 1–3, 1972); on the London Psalter, also R. H(aussherr) in *Die Zeit der Staufer*, exhibition catalogue, vol. i, p. 584, no. 755, with reproductions, vol. ii, nos. 547 and 548.

The Welf treasury: O. von Falke, R. Schmidt, and G. Swarzenski, *Der Welfenschatz*, 1930; G. Swarzenski, 'Der Welfenschatz', *Jb. der Stiftung Preussischer Kulturbesitz*, 2 (1963), 91 ff.; several exhibition catalogues, most recently D. Kötzsche, *Der Welfenschatz im Berliner Kunstgewerbemuseum* (Bilderhefte der Staatlichen Museen Preussischer Kulturbesitz, 20–1, 1973). As regards the Apostle's arm, see also catalogue of the Staufen exhibition, vol. i, p. 448, no. 578, and reproduction, vol. ii, no. 387. Reliquary of Henry II; ibid., vol. i, p. 444, no. 577, with reproduction, vol. ii, no. 384.

Literary activity: L. Wolff, 'Welfisch-Braunschweigische Dichtung der Ritterzeit', *Jb. des Vereins für niederdeutsche Sprachforschung* 71–3 (1948– 50), 68 ff.; R. Lejeune, 'Rôle littéraire de la famille d'Aliénor d'Aquitaine', *Cahiers de la civilisation médiévale*, vol. i (1958), 319 ff.; K. Bertau, *Deutsche Literatur im europäischen Mittelalter*, vol. i (1972), pp. 456 ff. and *passim*.

Rolandslied. The standard edition is by C. Wesle, *Das Rolandslied des Pfaffen Konrad*, revised by P. Wapneski (Altdeutsche Textbibliothek, 69, 1967). In addition: *Das Rolandslied des Pfaffen Konrad*: Middle High German text, translation, and afterword by D. Kartschoke (Fischer-Bücherei, 1970), with earlier literature. For the date (*c.* 1170 onwards) and interpretation see D. Kartschoke, *Die Datierung des deutschen Rolandsliedes* (Germanistische Abhandlungen, 9, 1965); also K. Bertau 'Das Rolandslied und die Repräsentationskunst Heinrichs des Löwen', *Der Deutschunterricht*, 20 (1968), 4 ff., and T. Urbanek, 'The Rolandslied by Pfaffe Conrad.

Some Chronological Aspects and its Historical and Literary Background', *Euphorion*, 65 (1971), 219. The view, which I do not believe to be tenable, that the work originated as late as 1193–5 is expressed in H. E. Keller, 'Der Pfaffe Konrad am Hofe von Braunschweig', in *Wege der Worte, Festschrift für W. Fleischhauer*; I am indebted to the author for letting me see this work when it was still in the press.

Tristant. New edition: *Eilhart von Oberg, Tristant. Édition diplomatique des manuscrits et traduction en français par D. Buschinger* (Göppinger Arbeiten zur Germanistik, 202, 1967). The latter's 'Le Tristant d'Eilhart von Oberg' (thesis, Université de Paris IV, 1974) does not go into the question of the date or the poet's identity. The state of research on these two questions is given by M. Last, 'Eilhart von Oberg', in *Niedersächsische Lebensbilder*, 8 (1973), 19 ff., with full bibliography. On Eilhart's relation to Heinrich von Veldeke: L. Wolff, 'Heinrich von Veldeke und Eilhart von Oberg', in *Kritische Bewahrung, Festschrift für Werner Schröder* (1974), pp. 241 ff., emphasizing the individual manner in which Eilhart made use of the *Eneide*.—I do not find convincing the view expressed by J. Goossens ('Tristam von Hoberge', in *'Sagen mit Sinne', Festschrift für M.-L. Dittrich*, Göppinger Arbeiten zur Germanistik, 180, 1976, pp. 63 ff.) that Eilhart may have been a member of the Brabant family of 'von Hobergen' which later resided near Malines.

The *Lucidarius*. The rhyming preface of the older version should not be used in the inadequate edition of the work by F. Heidlauf (Deutsche Texte des Mittelalters, 28, 1915), but after E. Schröder, 'Die Reimvorreden des deutschen Lucidarius', *Nachrichten der Gesellschaft der Wissenschaften zu Göttingen*, phil.-hist. Klasse 1917, pp. 153 ff. The state of research is given in K. Stackmann, 'Lucidarius', in *Die deutsche Literatur des Mittelalters*, Verfasserlexikon, vol. v (1955), cols. 621 ff., and in H. D. Kreuder's afterword to the facsimile edition of the *Volksbuch* of 1479 in *Apollonius von Tyrus, Griseldis, Lucidarius* (Deutsche Volksbücher in Faksimiledrucken, Reihe A, vol. ii, 1975). On the *Elucidarium* of Honorius see Y. Lefèvre, *L'Elucidarium et les lucidaires* (Bibliothèque des écoles françaises d'Athènes et de Rome, 180, 1954), but this does not mention the German *Lucidarius*.

Chapter 12

Henry's personal appearance: H. Reincke, 'Gestalt, Ahnenerbe und Bildnis Heinrichs des Löwen', *Zs. des Vereins für lüb. Geschichte und Altertumskunde* 28 (1936), 203 ff.

Monument: F. N. Steigerwald, *Das Grabmal Heinrichs des Löwen und Mathildes im Dom zu Braunschweig* (Braunschweiger Werkstücke, 47, 1972), but very contestable in detail. A better account of the state of research by W. S(auerländer) in *Die Zeit der Staufer*, catalogue, vol. i, p. 325 and no. 447.

Portraits in the London Psalter and the Gmunden Evangeliarium: see literature cited on p. 251 above. The view of Steigerwald (p. 48 n. 37) and Schmidt (*Braunschw. Jb.* 55, p. 32) that the coronation picture in the *Evangeliarium* shows Matilda in a standing position seems to me untenable if this picture is closely compared with the dedicatory picture in the Evangeliarium: the fall of the duchess's robe is quite different in the two cases.

Description by Acerbus Morena: *Das Geschichtswerk des Otto Morena und seiner Fortsetzer . . . neu hg. von F. Güterbock, MGH SS rer. Germ* NS 7 (1930), p. 169; Rahewin's description, *Gesta Friderici* lib. iv, ch. 46, ed. Mierow, p. 279.

Different views of historians: U. Jentzsch, *Heinrich der Löwe im Urteil der deutschen Geschichtsschreibung von den Zeitgenossen bis zur Aufklärung* (Beiträge zur mittelalterlichen und neueren Geschichte, 11, 2nd edn., 1942); W. Rasche, 'Die Gestalt Heinrichs des Löwen im Spiegel mittelalterlicher Quellen' (diss. Kiel, 1949, typescript), extract printed as 'Heinrich der Löwe im Siegel ausländischer Quellen des Mittelalters', *Braunschw. Jb.* 32 (1951), 70 ff. References to sources are given in the above works and are therefore not repeated here. Most recently K. Jordan, 'Die Gestalt Heinrichs des Löwen im Wandel des Geschichtsbildes', *Geschichte in Wissenschaft und Unterricht*, 26 (1975), 226 ff. On particular questions F. Graus, 'Heinrich der Löwe als Gegenspieler Barbarossas und Organisators der Ostkolonisation', in id., *Lebendige Vergangenheit, Überlieferung im Mittelalter und in den Vorstellungen vom Mittelalter* (1975), pp. 354 ff.

The legend: K. Hoppe, *Die Sage von Heinrich dem Löwen* (Schriften des niedersächsischen Heimatbundes, 22, 1952); J. Ruland, 'Die Sage von Heinrich dem Löwen am Mittelrhein', *Rhein.-Westfälische Zs. für Volkskunde*, 1 (1954), 112 ff.; P. Paulsen, *Drachenkämpfer, Löwenritter und Heinrichsage*, 1966, esp. pp. 175 ff.; W. Baumann, *Die Sage von Heinrich dem Löwen bei den Slaven* (Slavistische Beiträge, 73, 1975); R. Moderhack, 'Spätmittelalterliche Wandmalereien zur Heinrichsage in Karden a.d. Mosel', *Braunschweig. Heimat*, 64 (1978), 52 ff.

Welf historiography in the 17th and 18th centuries: A. Reese, *Die Rolle der Historie beim Aufstieg des Welfenhauses 1680–1714* (Quellen und Darstellungen zur Geschichte Niedersachsens, 71, 1967).

Sybel–Ficker controversy: the relevant writings have been republished by Fr. Schneider in *Universalstaat oder Nationalstaat*, 1941. See also H. Ritter von Srbik, *Geist und Geschichte vom deutschen Humanismus bis zur Gegenwart*, vol. ii (1951), pp. 33 ff., and H. Gollwitzer, 'Zur Auffassung der mittelalterlichen Kaiserpolitik im 19. Jahrhundert', in *Dauer und Wandel der Geschichte, Festgabe für K. von Raumer* (1966), pp. 483 ff.

Bismarck's comment: 'Erinnerung und Gedanke', in *Die gesammelten Werke*, vol. xv (1932), p. 202; trans. *Bismarck, the Man and the Statesman*, ed. A. J. Butler, 1898, vol. i, 321.—Ranke's judgement: *Neun Bücher Preussischer Geschichte* vol. i (1847), p. 3; a slightly modified version in Zwölf Bücher Preussischer Geschichte, last ed. G. Küntzel in the complete edition of Ranke's works by the Deutsche Akademie, vol. i (1930), p. 14, and in *Weltgeschichte* vol. viii (1887), p. 195.

Principal Dates

Genealogical Tables

Versions of the Welf dynastic tradition differ so widely that a genealogical table of the earlier Welfs is hard to establish and must remain conjectural at several points. The succession of generations is known with certainty only from the beginning of the eleventh century onwards: cf. the works, cited on p. 233 above, by Fleckenstein, Tellenback, Schnath, and Oexle. I am particularly obliged to Professor Oexle for further information.

There is also considerable uncertainty as regards the later Welfs. The indications in W. K. Prinz zu Isenburg, *Stammtafeln zur Geschichte europäischer Staaten* vol. i (2nd edn., 1953), table 11, are partly subject to correction. The order of the children of Henry the Black is uncertain. Among descendants of the marriage between Frederick II of Swabia and the Welf Judith, only those are shown here who are mentioned in the present work. A full genealogy of the Hohenstaufen can be found in H. Decker-Hauff, 'Das staufische Haus', in *Die Zeit der Staufer*, vol. iii, pp. 339 ff., and the two synoptic tables in vol. iv, nos. XV and XVI; see also E. Assmann, 'Friedrich Barbarossas Kinder', *DA* 33 (1977), 435 ff.

The order of the children of Henry the Lion by his first marriage to Clementia of Zähringen, by whom he almost certainly had two daughters (cf. p. 64 above), is doubtful. The name of Henry's concubine is unknown. It is given as 'Ida' in recent literature—e.g. E. Brandenburg, *Die Nachkommen Karls des Grossen* (1935, repr. 1964), p. 44, no. XII 188c—but this is an error deriving from *Origines Guelficae* vol. iii, pp. 181 f. and note *k*. In that passage, listing the children of Count Godfrey of Blieskastel, the word *illam*, which occurs in the Chronicle of Alberich von Trois-Fontaines (*MGH SS* 23, p. 851, lines 11 ff.), is mistakenly altered to 'Idam'. Cf. A. Hofmeister, 'Genealogische Untersuchungen zur Geschichte des pommerschen Herzogshauses', *Pomm. Jbb.* 32 (1938), 18 f. and note 111.

The Earlier Welfs

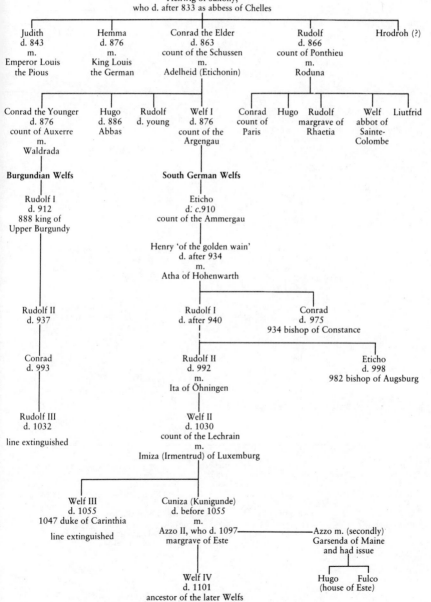

Ruthard
d. before 790
count of the Argengau

Welf
d. before 825
count of Schussen and Argengau
m.
Heilwig of Saxony,
who d. after 833 as abbess of Chelles

Judith	Hemma	Conrad the Elder	Rudolf	Hrodroh (?)
d. 843	d. 876	d. 863	d. 866	
m.	m.	count of the Schussen	count of Ponthieu	
Emperor Louis	King Louis	m.	m.	
the Pious	the German	Adelheid (Etichonin)	Roduna	

Conrad the Younger — Hugo — Rudolf — Welf I — Conrad — Hugo — Rudolf — Welf — Liutfrid
d. 876 — d. 886 — d. young — d. 876 — count of — margrave of — abbot of
count of Auxerre — Abbas — — count of the — Paris — Rhaetia — Sainte-
m. — — — Argengau — — — Colombe
Waldrada

Burgundian Welfs

Rudolf I
d. 912
888 king of
Upper Burgundy

South German Welfs

Eticho
d. c.910
count of the Ammergau

Henry 'of the golden wain'
d. after 934
m.
Atha of Hohenwarth

Rudolf II
d. 937

Rudolf I
d. after 940

Conrad
d. 975
934 bishop of Constance

Conrad
d. 993

Rudolf II
d. 992
m.
Ita of Öhningen

Eticho
d. 998
982 bishop of Augsburg

Rudolf III
d. 1032

line extinguished

Welf II
d. 1030
count of the Lechrain
m.
Imiza (Irmentrud) of Luxemburg

Welf III
d. 1055
1047 duke of Carinthia

line extinguished

Cuniza (Kunigunde)
d. before 1055
m.
Azzo II, who d. 1097 —————— Azzo m. (secondly)
margrave of Este — — Garsenda of Maine
— — and had issue

Welf IV
d. 1101
ancestor of the later Welfs

Hugo — Fulco
(house of Este)

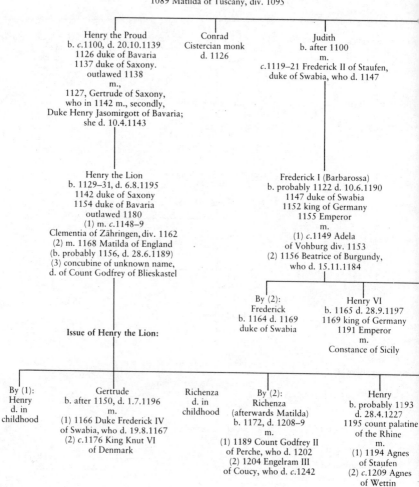

Issue of (3):
Welf V
b. c.1073, d. 24.9.1120
1101 duke of Bavaria
m.
1089 Matilda of Tuscany, div. 1095

Henry the Proud
b. c.1100, d. 20.10.1139
1126 duke of Bavaria
1137 duke of Saxony.
outlawed 1138
m.,
1127, Gertrude of Saxony,
who in 1142 m., secondly,
Duke Henry Jasomirgott of Bavaria;
she d. 10.4.1143

Conrad
Cistercian monk
d. 1126

Judith
b. after 1100
m.
c.1119–21 Frederick II of Staufen,
duke of Swabia, who d. 1147

Henry the Lion
b. 1129–31, d. 6.8.1195
1142 duke of Saxony
1154 duke of Bavaria
outlawed 1180
(1) m. c.1148–9
Clementia of Zähringen, div. 1162
(2) m. 1168 Matilda of England
(b. probably 1156, d. 28.6.1189)
(3) concubine of unknown name,
d. of Count Godfrey of Blieskastel

Frederick I (Barbarossa)
b. probably 1122 d. 10.6.1190
1147 duke of Swabia
1152 king of Germany
1155 Emperor
m.
(1) c.1149 Adela
of Vohburg div. 1153
(2) 1156 Beatrice of Burgundy,
who d. 15.11.1184

By (2):
Frederick
b. 1164 d. 1169
duke of Swabia

Henry VI
b. 1165 d. 28.9.1197
1169 king of Germany
1191 Emperor
m.
Constance of Sicily

Issue of Henry the Lion:

By (1):
Henry
d. in
childhood

Gertrude
b. after 1150, d. 1.7.1196
m.
(1) 1166 Duke Frederick IV
of Swabia, who d. 19.8.1167
(2) c.1176 King Knut VI
of Denmark

Richenza
d. in
childhood

By (2):
Richenza
(afterwards Matilda)
b. 1172, d. 1208–9
m.
(1) 1189 Count Godfrey II
of Perche, who d. 1202
(2) 1204 Engelram III
of Coucy, who d. c.1242

Henry
b. probably 1193
d. 28.4.1227
1195 count palatine
of the Rhine
m.
(1) 1194 Agnes
of Staufen
(2) c.1209 Agnes
of Wettin

The Later Welfs

Welf IV
b. *c.*1030–40, d. 9.11.1101
1070 duke of Bavaria
m.
(1) unknown Italian
(2) Ethelinde of Northeim,
repudiated 1070
3) Judith of Flanders, d. 1094

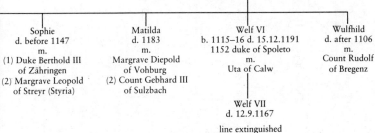

Issue of (3):
Henry the Black
b. *c.*1074, d. 13.12.1126
1120 duke of Bavaria
m.
1095–1100 Wulfhild of Saxony, who d. 29.12.1126

Sophie	Matilda	Welf VI	Wulfhild
d. before 1147	d. 1183	b. 1115–16 d. 15.12.1191	d. after 1106
m.	m.	1152 duke of Spoleto	m.
(1) Duke Berthold III	Margrave Diepold	m.	Count Rudolf
of Zähringen	of Vohburg	Uta of Calw	of Bregenz
(2) Margrave Leopold	(2) Count Gebhard III		
of Streyr (Styria)	of Sulzbach		

Welf VII
d. 12.9.1167

line extinguished

Conrad
(afterwards Frederick)
b. 1167 d. 1191
duke of Swabia

eight other
legitimate children

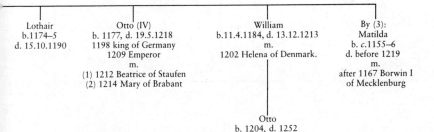

Lothair	Otto (IV)	William	By (3):
b.1174–5	b. 1177, d. 19.5.1218	b.11.4.1184, d. 13.12.1213	Matilda
d. 15.10.1190	1198 king of Germany	m.	b. *c.*1155–6
	1209 Emperor	1202 Helena of Denmark.	d. before 1219
	m.		m.
	(1) 1212 Beatrice of Staufen		after 1167 Borwin I
	(2) 1214 Mary of Brabant		of Mecklenburg

Otto
b. 1204, d. 1252
first duke of Brunswick-Lüneburg

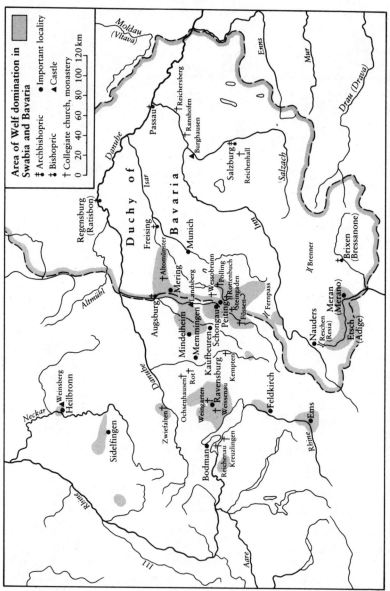

Based on the map by H. Schwarzmaier, 'Hochadelsbesitz im 12. Jahrhundert. Welfenbesitz' in *Historischer Atlas von Baden-Württemberg*, Beiwort zu Karte V 3 (1974). The information has been supplemented, especially for Bavaria.

The Duchy of Saxony under
the Lion (down to 1180)

Henry the Lion's claim to authority
over the western part of the Saxon
tribal area

Countships and allodial lands:
area of special density

Dominion east of the Elbe

‡ Archbishopric ‡ Bishopric
† Collegiate church, monastery ▲ Castle
● Important locality
■ Imperial residence

0 20 40 60 80 km

Based on the corresponding map by G.Schnath in *Grosser Historischer Weltatlas* (Bayerischer Schulbuch-
Verlag), 2. Teil: Mittelalter (1970), Karte 111b, supplemented in a few points.

Index